PENGUIN BOOKS
MISGOVERNANCE

Edmund Terence Gomez is former professor of Political Economy at the Faculty of Economics and Administration, Universiti Malaya, Malaysia. He specializes in state–market relations and the linkages between politics, policies, and business development. He has also held appointments at the University of Leeds (England) and Murdoch University (Australia) and served as Visiting Professor at Kobe University (Japan) and at the Universities of Michigan (Ann Arbor) and California (San Diego, United States). Between 2005 and 2008, he served as a research coordinator at the United Nations Research Institute for Social Development (UNRISD), in Geneva, Switzerland. Other academic appointments include visiting fellowships at the Australian National University, Canberra, and at the Nordic Institute of Asian Studies, Denmark.

His publications include *Malaysia's Political Economy: Politics, Patronage and Profits* (Cambridge University Press, 1997), *Chinese Business in Malaysia: Accumulation, Ascendance, Accommodation* (University of Hawaii Press, 1999), *Political Business in East Asia* (Routledge, 2002), *The State of Malaysia: Ethnicity, Equity and Reform* (Routledge, 2004), *The State, Development and Identity in Multi-ethnic Countries: Ethnicity, Equity and the Nation* (Routledge, 2008), *The Politics of Resource Extraction: Indigenous Peoples, Multinational Corporations and the State* (Palgrave Macmillan, 2012), *Affirmative Action, Ethnicity and Conflict* (Routledge, 2013), *Government-Linked Companies and Sustainable, Equitable Development* (Routledge, 2014), *Minister of Finance Incorporated: Ownership and Control of Corporate Malaysia* (Palgrave Macmillan, 2017), *Malaysia's 14th General Election and UMNO's Fall: Intra-Elite Feuding and the Pursuit of Power* (Routledge, 2019), and *China in Malaysia: State-Business Relations and the New Order of Investment Flows* (Palgrave Macmillan, 2020).

MIS GOVER NANCE

GRAND CORRUPTION IN MALAYSIA

Edmund Terence Gomez

PENGUIN BOOKS
An imprint of Penguin Random House

PENGUIN BOOKS

Penguin Books is an imprint of the Penguin Random House group of companies whose addresses can be found at global.penguinrandomhouse.com

Published by Penguin Random House SEA Pte Ltd
40 Penjuru Lane, #03-12, Block 2
Singapore 609216

First published in Penguin Books by Penguin Random House SEA 2024

Copyright © Edmund Terence Gomez 2024

All rights reserved

10 9 8 7 6 5 4 3 2 1

The views and opinions expressed in this book are the author's own and the facts are as reported by him which have been verified to the extent possible, and the publishers are not in any way liable for the same.

Please note that no part of this book may be used or reproduced in any manner for the purpose of training artificial intelligence technologies or systems.

ISBN 9789815233919

Typeset in Garamond by MAP Systems, Bengaluru, India

This book is sold subject to the condition that it shall not, by way of trade or otherwise, be lent, resold, hired out, or otherwise circulated without the publisher's prior consent in any form of binding or cover other than that in which it is published and without a similar condition including this condition being imposed on the subsequent purchaser.

www.penguin.sg

Contents

List of Figures	vii
List of Tables	vii
Foreword	ix
Preface	xiii
List of Abbreviations	xvii
Chapter 1: Corruption, the Law, and the Political–GLC Complex	1
Chapter 2: Grand Corruption and the Political–GLC Complex	39
Chapter 3: Case Studies	81
Chapter 4: The Lessons Learned	129
Chapter 5: Conclusion: The Reforms Malaysia Needs	153
Acknowledgements	177
Appendix 1	179
Appendix 2	221

List of Figures

2.1: Power structure of the GLC ecosystem—five levels
2.2: Corporate networks of four ministries: PMD, MoF, MRRD, and Mindef
2.3: Executive control over regulatory institutions
2.4: Control over the banking sector
3.1: Charting the award of Jana Wibawa Projects
3.2: Mapping of Muhyiddin–Zafrul family ties
3.3: History of the LCS scandal
3.4: FELCRA: Before and after corporatization
3.5: MRRD's control over FELCRA Bhd
3.6: Menara FELCRA controversy
3.7: MARA's control over companies
3.8: MARA's foreign enterprises in Australia and the British Virgin Islands
3.9: MARA's chain of command

List of Tables

1.1: Varieties of corruption: Its complex forms
2.1: Public institutions collectively classified as GLCs
2.2: Politicians appointed as GLC directors by Muhyiddin
2.3: Politicians appointed as GLC directors by Anwar
3.1: List of chairpersons of FELCRA
4.1: Lessons from case studies

Foreword

In 2015, a report entitled *Reforms for Transparent and Accountable Political Funding in Malaysia* was published by the Center to Combat Corruption and Cronyism (C4 Center). It revealed that a colossal volume of unregulated money was flowing into the political system. When preparing this report, we, at C4 Center, realized that much of this money, a major source of funding for political and electoral activities, had been obtained through the extensive abuse of government projects and public institutions, collectively termed as government-linked companies (GLCs). This abuse of GLCs and the public procurement system had contributed to an appalling number of major corporate scandals linked to governing politicians.

Grand corruption, defined as the abuse of high-level power that benefits the few at the expense of the many,[1] had become endemic. There was, undoubtedly, a pressing need to examine how these scandals had occurred and explain why, even with the relevant legislation in place, it was difficult to hold governing politicians accountable for their abuse of power. It was essential to comprehensibly describe what was contributing to endemic corruption, including why so few of those implicated in these scandals had been convicted. Indeed, a number of politicians who had faced serious allegations of corruption or had cases pending

---

[1] *Transparency International*: https://www.transparency.org/en/our-priorities/grand-corruption

in court continued to run as candidates in federal elections, with some returning to hold a position in the cabinet.

Given this dire situation, we realized there was an urgent need to tackle the definition of corruption within the Malaysian context, since we were aware that the United Nations Convention Against Corruption (UNCAC) had not done so. Our central concern was that discourses about corruption—and most public campaigns about it—revolved around the issue of bribery, which is primarily a petty form of corruption occurring in society. We feared this focus on bribery was distracting attention from—and analysis of—grand corruption occurring with much regularity because of public misgovernance. There was a need to educate the public of the ways and means through which the government apparatus could be covertly abused, leading to huge wastage of public funds.

Our principal objective was to identify how Malaysia's political, economic, and legislative structures allow the abuse of a public governance system where grand corruption thrives. A key enabler of grand corruption is, unquestionably, Malaysia's vast GLC ecosystem, which comprises a multitude of different government-linked institutions. These institutions include statutory bodies, development financial institutions (DFIs), special purpose vehicles (SPVs), foundations, holding companies, publicly-listed and unquoted firms, and the seven enormous, financially well-endowed government-linked investment companies (GLICs), which comprise a sovereign wealth fund, pension funds, and investment agencies. The mismanagement of these enterprises by governing politicians who controlled them led to unscrupulous government intrusion in the world of business.

The nexus between politics and business in this ecosystem is complicated, intricate, and covert, making these different GLCs ideal vehicles for abuse, profiteering, and corrupt practices. We were aware that the complexity of this vast byzantine GLC ecosystem inhibited public interest in exploring and deciphering how government ownership and control of public and private institutions served as a core tool for the conduct of corruption.

Studies identify, map, and analyse this GLC ecosystem to determine the extent of its influence over the economy, corporate sector, and society.[2] Studies have traced how GLCs have been employed to pursue the government's socio-economic and development objectives.[3] However, this body of literature focuses insufficiently on the abuse of this GLC ecosystem, even though the recurring themes emerging from an assessment of these enterprises are selective patronage, cronyism, and nepotism.

This book introduces a novel concept, the 'Political–GLC complex', to frame the nexus between politics, GLCs, and grand corruption. Much attention is devoted to cabinet control of regulatory institutions, a fundamental factor that explains why so few governing politicians who have abused their public office have been convicted. This concept is employed to offer deeper insights into the close ties between the political system and the GLC world and how this nexus aids misgovernance.

The foremost scandals that have occurred in Malaysia over the past four decades—which have deeply impaired the economy, the financial sector, and public services—are the Bumiputra Malaysia Finance (BMF) controversy of the 1980s, the numerous defence-related debacles between the 1990s and 2018, and the current and highly embarrassing 1MDB catastrophe, which led to Malaysia being called a kleptocracy. Just these three major controversies, which garnered worldwide attention, indicated serious abuse of GLCs, public policies, and the procurement process by governing politicians.

This book offers a thoughtful view of what 'grand corruption' means. The study expands the understanding of corruption by focusing on how it has been conducted through GLCs. Even

---

[2] See, for example, Edmund Terence Gomez, Francois Bafoil and Cheong Kee Cheok (eds). 2016. *Government-Linked Companies and Sustainable, Equitable Development*. London: Routledge. Edmund Terence Gomez, et al. 2018. *Governments in Business: Diverse Forms of Intervention*. Kuala Lumpur: Institute for Democracy & Economic Affairs (IDEAS).

[3] Ibid.

though politicians who have called for GLC reforms have come to power, there have been no attempts by them to restructure this ecosystem, specifically to curb abuse of power. There is, evidently, no political will to reform this GLC ecosystem, even as politicians lament debilitating grand corruption.

I thank Dr Terence Gomez and C4 Center's research team for their dedication and commitment to this project. They have achieved our aim of producing a narrative of a complex issue—the nexus between GLCs, politics, and corruption—that the readers will find easy to understand. This book also provides an insightful view on the different types of grand corruption in Malaysia and of the strategic roles that GLCs play as conduits in their perpetration and perpetuation. Governing elites have spent decades developing ways and means to optimize their abuse of this GLC ecosystem for their own benefit.

It is our hope that this book will encourage more thoughtful discussions about the causes of corruption and of the reforms required to dismantle and realign Malaysia's important GLC ecosystem. After all, GLCs were created to foster just development, equitably redistribute wealth, and aid the eradication of poverty. The GLC ecosystem should be reformed to allow the institutions in it to return to pursuing their original purpose, not serve the personal interests of governing elites.

—Pushpan Murugiah,
chief executive officer, C4 Center

Preface

During Malaysia's epochal general elections of 2018, the nation overwhelmingly voted against an authoritarian government that was deeply mired in serious allegations of kleptocracy and the use of slush funds. Although this incumbent regime had bent most rules of fair play in its bid to win this election, it was so soundly beaten that it shocked not only the governing elites but also the opposition. Four years later, following another controversial general election ridden with allegations of abuse of money to court support, newly-minted Prime Minister Anwar Ibrahim acknowledged that because little had been done to address corruption, his primary objective would be to rid Malaysia of this malaise, which he saw as entrenched and systemic.

However, persistent allegations of diverse forms of misgovernance have drawn attention to the need for us to rethink corruption. Moreover, since corruption is seen as a 'word with many meanings',[4] it has, inevitably, been viewed from different perspectives. A micro-level perspective—the most widely-held one—focuses primarily on short-term, usually one-off decisions made by individuals, with debates centred on bribery as well as reforms based on curbing unethical acts by instilling ethics. A macro approach pays attention to the structural features of a government that enable corruption. Another perspective

---

[4] Richard Rose and Caryn Peiffer. 2019. Understanding Corruption in Different Contexts. In Heike M. Grimm (ed.), *Public Policy Research in the Global South: A Cross Country Perspective*. Berlin: Springer: 27–41.

assesses interactions and networks created by corrupt actors in the public and private sectors that can be long-term.[5] In the world of business, with its interactions and interlocking networks encompassing government-based economic institutions and private sector enterprises, corruption is viewed through the lens of corporate governance in spite of concerns that governing elites have abused public office.

This study adopts a state–business relations perspective, with an understanding of corruption as a phenomenon that goes beyond bribery. An analysis of the maladministration of Malaysia's vast state–business nexuses most plainly reveals it exists in an entwined web of government-linked companies (GLCs) that has evolved into a huge shadow economy. This veiled economy is controlled by politicians in a governance system where power is concentrated with the office of the prime minister. An intricate and covert 'Political–GLC complex' has been created by governing elites, which has contributed to grand corruption in the country.

Exacerbating this problem are similar state-business relations prevailing in all thirteen states in the Malaysian federation. Moreover, in Malaysia's now extremely fragmented political system, at least six different political parties control one or more of the thirteen states in the federation. These parties also have seats in parliament as part of the governing or opposition coalitions. The Malaysian dilemma is that no governing party, in the federal and state governments, has any desire to reform the extremely corrupt and intricate Political–GLC complex. Appallingly, too, a common feature in analyses of corporate scandals is the political abuse of state–business ties that were conceived to address poverty, ensure sustainable development, and equitably redistribute wealth and land.

---

[5] David Jancsics. 2014. Interdisciplinary Perspectives on Corruption. *Sociology Compass*, 8 (4): 358–372.

There is scant understanding of Malaysia's complex web of state–business interactions through its knotty GLC ecosystem and how it can be—and has been—deployed to consolidate power. There is also a need to appreciate Malaysia's long history of networks between politics and business to understand how the Political–GLC complex emerged. Following epochal moments in history, especially during economic crises and debilitating feuds between political elites, monumental shifts have occurred in relationships between politics and business.

This book examines the Political–GLC complex through the inner workings of the multi-faceted interactions between government and business. Specific attention has been devoted to understanding how the government's vast GLC ecosystem has been severely corrupted. The state–business relations perspective adopted here serves as a means to understand how a system employing GLCs to rectify social and economic inequities has been captured by governing elites and extensively abused by them to accumulate personal wealth and enhance political power. This book focuses on grand corruption, with case studies that offer insights into the intimate and illicit connections between governing politicians and the businesses they control, shedding light on the exploitation of the public delivery system and the mismanagement of GLCs.

Rather than overwhelm the reader with information about alleged corporate crimes by politicians through the enterprises they control, the outcomes of a lengthy list of misgoverned state–business relations have been placed in Appendix 1, with a brief description of these controversies that occurred between 1980 and 2023. Although case studies have been provided, they do not offer intricate details about corporate malfeasance—this has already been done by journalists in Malaysia and abroad. These case studies aim to explain how various types of corruption can occur when public assets vested in the GLC ecosystem are mishandled. A review of the way corruption happened through these case studies offers insights into the Political–GLC complex, which this book reveals as a well-constructed, multi-layered infrastructure deeply entrenched in public procurement and the delivery of policies.

While governing elites have deeply undermined a state–business ecosystem fashioned to rectify socio-economic injustices to pursue their vested political and business interests, few politicians who have abused public office have been successfully prosecuted. To provide insights into this puzzle, an assessment of the legislation on the statutes has been provided. Legislative reforms have been proposed to deal with the different types of corruption that occur during the implementation of policies through Malaysia's vast GLC ecosystem. To not burden the reader with legal jargon, Appendix 2 provides a review of these laws and the proposed reforms.

Based on this review of this Political–GLC complex, reforms have been proposed to curb corruption, primarily by dismantling and restructuring the GLC ecosystem, a core component of the government's institutional infrastructure. These reforms would ensure effective implementation of policies and efficient, accountable, and transparent delivery of public goods and services.

—Terence Gomez, March 2024

List of Abbreviations

1MDB	1Malaysia Development Bhd
AES	Automated enforcement system
AFC	Asian Financial Crisis
AGC	Attorney General's Chambers
Amanah	Parti Amanah Negara (National Trust Party)
AMLATFPUA	Anti-Money Laundering, Anti-Terrorism Financing and Proceeds of Unlawful Activities
APs	Approved Permits
ASB	Amanah Saham Bumiputera (Bumiputera Unit Trust Scheme)
ASN	Amanah Saham Nasional (National Unit Trust Scheme)
ASNB	Amanah Saham Nasional Bhd
BCIC	Bumiputera Commercial & Industrial Community
BEEP	Bumiputera Economic Empowerment Plan
Bersatu	Parti Pribumi Bersatu Malaysia (Malaysian Indigenous Unity Party)
BHIC	Boustead Heavy Industries Corporation Sdn Bhd
BMF	Bumiputra Malaysia Finance Bhd
BN	Barisan Nasional (National Front)
BNS	Boustead Naval Shipyard Sdn Bhd

BOO	Build, operate, and own
BOT	Build, operate, and transfer
BPA	Biro Pengaduan Awam (Public Complaints Bureau)
BVI	British Virgin Islands
CAD	Contraves Advanced Devices Sdn Bhd
CBT	Criminal breach of trust
CCB	Cooperative Central Bank
CCCC	China Communications Construction Company
CCM	Companies Commission of Malaysia
CED	Contraves Electrodynamics Sdn Bhd
CEO	Chief executive officer
CIDB	Construction Industry Development Board
CIMB	CIMB Group Holdings Bhd
CMI	Chief Minister Incorporated
CMS	Cahya Mata Sarawak
CMS	Combat Management System
CULS	Convertible unsecured loan stocks
DAP	Democratic Action Party
DCNS	Direction des Constructions Navales
DFIs	Development Financial Institutions
DID	Department of Irrigation and Drainage
DNAA	Discharge not amounting to an acquittal
EAIC	Enforcement Agency Integrity Commission
EC	Economic Council
ECRL	East Coast Rail Link

E&E	Electronics and Electrical sector
EPF	Employees Provident Fund
EPU	Economic Planning Unit
ETP	Economic Transformation Programme
EXIM Bank	Export-Import Bank of Malaysia Bhd
FAMA	Federal Agricultural Marketing Agency
FATF	Financial Action Task Force
FELCRA	Federal Land Consolidation and Rehabilitation Authority
FELDA	Federal Land Development Authority
FDI	Foreign direct investment
FGV	FELDA Global Ventures Holdings Bhd
FIC	FELDA Investment Corporation Sdn Bhd
FLC	Federal Lands Commissioner
FPI	Foreign portfolio investment
GLCs	Government-Linked Companies
GLCT	Government-Linked Companies Transformation Plan
GLICs	Government-Linked Investment Companies
GPS	Gabungan Parti Sarawak (Sarawak Parties Alliance)
GSP	Global Supplier Programme
GTP	Government Transformation Programme
HICOM	Heavy Industries Corporation of Malaysia Bhd
HRD Corp	Human Resources Development Corporation
IDEAS	Institute for Democracy and Economic Affairs

IPO	Initial public offering
IPCC	Independent Police Conduct Commission
IPP	Independent Power Producer
IRDA	Iskandar Regional Development Authority
ITMB	Institut Terjemahan and Buku Malaysia (Malaysian Institute of Translation and Books)
IWK	Indah Water Konsortium
JPA	Jabatan Perkhidmatan Awam (Public Service Department)
KADA	Lembaga Kemajuan Pertanian Kemubu (Kemubu Agricultural Development Board)
KAJD	KAJ Development Sdn Bhd
KEDA	Kedah Regional Development Authority
KEJORA	Johor Tenggara Development Authority
KESEDAR	South Kelantan Development Authority
KETENGAH	Terengganu Tengah Development Authority
Khazanah Nasional	Khazanah Nasional Bhd
KLK	Kuala Lumpur-Kepong Bhd
KLSE	Kuala Lumpur Stock Exchange
KPB	Konsortium Perkapalan Bhd
KPRJ	Kumpulan Prasarana Rakyat Johor Sdn Bhd
KUB	Koperasi Usaha Bersama
KVSB	Kelana Ventures Sdn Bhd
KWAP	Kumpulan Wang Persaraan Diperbadankan (Retirement Fund Incorporated)
LCS	Littoral Combat Ship
LGM	Lembaga Getah Malaysia (Malaysia Rubber Board)

LKIM	Lembaga Kemajuan Ikan Malaysia (Fisheries Development Authority of Malaysia)
LKTN	Lembaga Kenaf dan Tembakau Negara (National Kenaf and Tobacco Board)
LPKMN	Lembaga Pelabuhan Kemaman (Kemaman Port Authority)
LPP	Lembaga Pertubuhan Peladang (Farmers' Organisation Authority)
LPPKN	Lembaga Penduduk dan Pembangunan Keluarga Negara (National Population and Family Development Board)
LTAT	Lembaga Tabung Angkatan Tentera (Armed Forces Savings Fund)
LTH	Lembaga Tabung Haji (Pilgrims Savings Fund)
MACC	Malaysian Anti-Corruption Commission
MADA	Lembaga Kemajuan Pertanian Muda (Muda Agricultural Development Authority)
MAHB	Malaysia Airports Holdings Bhd
MAIWP	Majlis Agama Islam Wilayah Persekutuan
MARA	Majlis Amanah Rakyat (Council of Trust for Indigenous People)
MAS	Malaysia Airlines
MATRADE	Malaysia External Trade Development Corporation
Maybank	Malayan Banking Bhd
MBI	Menteri Besar Incorporated
MBSB	Malaysian Building Society Bhd

MCA	Malaysian Chinese Association
MCB	Malaysian Cocoa Board
MDV	Malaysia Debt Ventures Bhd
MDeC	Multimedia Development Corporation Bhd
MIC	Malaysian Indian Congress
MICT	Melaka International Cruise Terminal
MIDF	Malaysian Industrial Development Finance Bhd
Mindef	Ministry of Defence
MISC	Malaysian International Shipping Corporation Bhd
MITI	Ministry of International Trade & Industry
MMEA	Malaysian Maritime Enforcement Agency
MMHE	Malaysia Marine and Heavy Engineering Holdings Bhd
MNCs	Multi-national companies
MoF	Ministry of Finance
MoF Inc.	Minister of Finance (Incorporated)
MP	Member of Parliament
MPA	Malacca Port Authority
MPHB	Multi-Purpose Holdings Bhd
MPOB	Malaysian Palm Oil Board
MPOC	Malaysian Palm Oil Council
MPOCC	Malaysian Palm Oil Certification Council
MRCB	Malaysian Resources Corporation Bhd
MRL	Malaysian Rail Link Sdn Bhd
MRRD	Ministry of Rural and Regional Development
MTCC	Malaysian Timber Certification Council
MTIB	Malaysian Timber Industry Board
MyHSR Corp	MyHSR Corporation Sdn Bhd

MyIPO	Malaysia Intellectual Property Corporation
NEM	New Economic Model
NEP	New Economic Policy
NFA	No Further Action
NFC	National Feedlot Corporation
NGOs	Non-governmental organisations
NIOSH	National Institute of Occupational Safety and Health
OECD	Organisation for Economic Cooperation and Development
OPVs	Offshore patrol vessels
PAC	Public Accounts Committee
PAS	Parti Islam Se-Malaysia (Malaysian Islamic Party)
PBB	Parti Pesaka Bumiputera Bersatu
PBM	Parti Bangsa Malaysia (Malaysian National Party)
PDP	Parti Demokratik Progresif (Progressive Democratic Party)
PDRM	Royal Malaysia Police
Petronas	Petroliam Nasional Bhd (National Petroleum Corporation)
PEPs	Politically Exposed Persons
PFI	Private finance initiative
PHREC	Perak Hydro Renewable Energy Corporation Sdn Bhd
PKA	Port Klang Authority
PKBM	Persatuan Kontraktor Bumiputera Malaysia (Bumiputera Contractors Association of Malaysia)
PKFZ	Port Klang Free Zone

PKR	Parti Keadilan Rakyat (People's Justice Party)
PMD	Prime Minister's Department
PMO	Prime Minister's Office
PNB	Permodalan Nasional Bhd (National Equity Corporation)
PNS	Perbadanan Nasional Bhd
PNSB	Permodalan Negeri Selangor Bhd
PPB	Putrajaya Perdana Bhd
PPC	Penang Port Commission
PPPs	Public–private partnerships
PRS	Parti Rakyat Sarawak (Sarawak Peoples' Party)
PSC	Penang Shipbuilding Corporation Bhd
PTPK	Perbadanan Tabung Pembangunan Kemahiran (Skills Development Fund Corporation)
PUNB	Perbadanan Usahawan Nasional Bhd
PUTRA	Projek Usahasama Transit Ringan Automatik
PWD	Public Works Department
R&D	research and development
RIDA	Rural and Industrial Development Authority
RISDA	Rubber Industry Smallholders Development Authority
ROS	Registrar of Societies
RMN	Royal Malaysian Navy
SC	Securities Commission
Sdn Bhd	Sendirian Berhad (Private Limited)
SEDA	Sustainable Energy Development Authority

SEDC	State Economic Development Corporation
SMEs	Small- and medium scale enterprises
SME Bank	Small Medium Enterprise Development Bank (M) Bhd
SMIDEC	Small and Medium Industries Development Corporation
SOCSO	Social Security Organisation
SOEs	State-owned enterprises
SPAN	Suruhanjaya Perkhidmatan Air Negara (National Water Services Commission)
SPNB	Syarikat Perumahan Negara Bhd
SPVs	Special Purpose Vehicles
SPV	Shared Prosperity Vision
STAR	Sistem Transit Aliran Ringan Sdn Bhd
STM	Syarikat Telekom Malaysia
SWF	Sovereign wealth fund
TEKUN	Tekun National Foundation
THHE	TH Heavy Engineering Bhd
THSB	Tadmansori Holdings Sdn Bhd
TLDM	Tentera Laut Diraja Malaysia (Royal Malaysian Navy)
TNB	Tenaga Nasional Bhd
UDA	Urban Development Authority
UEM	United Engineers Malaysia Bhd
UKSB	Ultra Kirana Sdn Bhd
UMBC	United Malayan Banking Corporation
UMNO	United Malays National Organisation
UNCAC	United Nations Convention against Corruption
VDP	Vendor Development Programme

VLN	Foreign visa system
YPB	Yayasan Pelaburan Bumiputera (Bumiputera Investment Foundation)
YWP	Yayasan Wilayah Persekutuan

Chapter 1

Corruption, the Law, and the Political–GLC Complex

Misgoverning State–Business Relations

Before Muhyiddin Yassin, Malaysia's former prime minister, was charged in court in 2023 on multiple counts of abuse of power, he asserted two specific things. Muhyiddin first declared: 'I did not commit any wrongdoing in the eyes of the law.'[6] He then emphasized that 'there's no law yet that has been enacted in parliament, as far as the people's donation (to a party) is concerned.'[7] Later that year, a high court judge acquitted Muhyiddin of four of these charges, as they were found to be 'vague, flawed and unfounded because they did not specify the details of the offences committed.'[8] When the prosecution took this matter to the Court of Appeal, a bench of three judges found that there were 'appealable

---

[6] *The Edge Markets* (10 March 2023): https://ceomorningbrief.theedgemalaysia.com/article/2023/0536/Home/4/658541

[7] *New Straits Times* (21 February 2023): https://www.nst.com.my/news/nation/2023/02/882064/muhyiddin-says-he-upheld-truth-jana-wibawa

[8] *Bernama* (15 August 2023): https://www.astroawani.com/berita-malaysia/high-court-freed-muhyiddin-four-power-abuse-charges-432908?

errors' in the high court judge's decision and that, in their view, the 'four charges are clear and unambiguous.'[9]

As for another former prime minister, Mahathir Mohamad, during his long tenure in government from 1981 to 2003, serious allegations of cronyism, collusion, and nepotism were persistently levelled against him. Mahathir's critics subsequently included his former protégé, Najib Razak, who took office as prime minister in 2009 and served for nearly a decade. When Mahathir accused Najib of rampant corruption, the latter hit back by releasing a list of public concessions that Mahathir's three sons had secured during his two decades-long administration. Mahathir's retort to such criticisms has been that these were 'political accusations'.[10]

In the case of Najib, the unexpected loss of political power that he encountered during the 2018 general election was attributed to widespread corruption. At the heart of these criticisms of extensive corruption was a government enterprise he controlled, 1Malaysia Development Bhd (1MDB), whose massive financial mismanagement had dire economic and business repercussions.[11] When Najib was questioned during an interview about the problems accruing to him personally from the 1MDB scandal, his response was telling. He said: 'The system failed me.'[12]

---

[9] *The Edge* (28 February 2024): https://theedgemalaysia.com/node/702721

[10] See, for example, Mahathir's interview with Al Jazeera on 7 July 2019: https://www.youtube.com/watch?v=Jz1p33HMREA&ab_channel=AlJazeeraEnglish. In this interview, Mahathir made this point about his twenty-two years as prime minister: 'There was no accusation of stealing money against me, and all the other accusations were just political accusations with no proof as to what they say being true.'

[11] Prime Minister Najib was then concurrently serving as minister of finance. In this capacity, Najib controlled 1MDB, through the government's main equity holding company, Minister of Finance Incorporated (MoF Inc.).

[12] This interview, where Najib made this point when discussing 1MDB, was in the documentary, *Man on the Run*, released in 2023. For a review of this documentary, which described the 1MDB controversy as one that featured 'stark corruption' and 'shameless grift', see *The Guardian* (5 September 2023): https://www.theguardian.com/film/2023/sep/05/man-on-the-run-review-the-malaysian-scandal-that-rocked-wall-street-and-hollywood

Remarkably, too, five of Malaysia's six prime ministers since 2003 have admitted that the country is enmeshed in endemic corruption that is embedded in public governance.[13] Over the past four decades, from 1980 till 2023, as outlined in Appendix 1, a colossal number of alarming, even reprehensible, state–business-related controversies have occurred, suggesting horrendous exploitation of government-based institutions by governing politicians. The long—but still partial—catalogue of controversies listed in Appendix 1, indicating different forms of state–business relations, draws attention to what can be classified as grand corruption. Yet, in spite of this litany of disconcerting controversies over these forty-odd years, there has only been one conviction of a governing politician for corruption entailing abuse of a government-owned enterprise—Najib.[14]

---

[13] The exception was Ismail Sabri Yaakob (2021–2022), Najib's close associate. The other prime ministers since 2003 were Abdullah Ahmad Badawi (2003–2009), Najib Razak (2009–2018), Mahathir Mohamad (2018–2020), and Muhyiddin Yassin (2020–2021). Anwar Ibrahim was appointed prime minister after the 2022 general election.

[14] Tan Koon Swan, a well-known politician-cum-businessman, served jail time in Singapore in the late 1980s for criminal breach of trust of a publicly-listed company he controlled, Pan-Electric Industries, then mired in huge debts that resulted in the country's largest corporate collapse. Tan was a prominent corporate figure when he entered politics. He rapidly secured the post of president of the Malaysian Chinese Association (MCA), though only for a short period (November 1985 to September 1986). After serving time in Singapore, Tan was sentenced to jail in Malaysia and was declared bankrupt. Though the leader of the second largest component party in the Barisan Nasional (BN or National Front) coalition that was then governing Malaysia, Tan did not serve in cabinet. For a brief history of Tan's political and business career, see *The Edge* (11 September 2012): https://theedgemalaysia.com/article/rise-and-fall-tan-koon-swan. For a comprehensive analysis of this corporate scandal and Tan's role in it, see: Monetary Authority of Singapore. 2004. *Case Study on Pan-Electric Crisis*. MAS Staff Paper No. 32.

In August 2022, Najib received a twelve-year imprisonment term for seven counts of abuse of power, money laundering, and criminal breach of trust of funds belonging to SCR International, an obscure 1MDB subsidiary.[15] Najib's incarceration was a defining moment in Malaysian history. Significantly, too, the court noted that Najib 'did not dispute that RM42 million entered his personal bank accounts'.[16] This money was purportedly used during the campaign of the intensely contested general election in 2013.[17]

A few years prior to 1980, Harun Idris—a prominent leader of the United Malays National Organisation (UMNO), which led the BN, and then the chief minister of the state of Selangor—was given a six-year sentence for abuse of funds belonging to Bank Rakyat, a government-controlled development financial institution of which he was the chairman. After serving three years of his sentence, Harun was given a royal pardon (*The Star*, 31 August 2016): https://www.thestar.com.my/news/nation/2016/08/31/several-top-brass-engulfed-in-scandals-in-the-past

In November 2023, Syed Saddiq Abdul Rahman, who served as Minister of Youth and Sports between 2018 and 2020, was convicted of abetting a criminal breach of trust, misappropriating assets, and money laundering. He was given a seven-year sentence and fined a hefty amount. His conviction was not for the abuse of funds of a government enterprise. However, his conviction raised serious concerns about how political funds are handled by politicians. The court charges against Syed Saddiq pertained to funds belonging to the youth wing of Parti Pribumi Bersatu Malaysia (Bersatu) of which he was then the president. One charge for which he was convicted was the embezzlement of RM1 million from Bersatu's youth wing when he left the party, after it crossed over to another coalition, leading to the fall of the government, an event described as the 'Sheraton Move'. Syed Saddiq filed an appeal over this jail sentence. For reports on Syed Saddiq's conviction, see *The Edge* (9 November 2023): https://theedgemalaysia.com/node/689410 and *The Star* (9 November 2023): https://www.thestar.com.my/news/nation/2023/11/09/i-will-clear-my-name-says-syed-saddiq-after-guilty-verdict

[15] *Channel News Asia* (23 August 2022): https://www.channelnewsasia.com/asia/najib-1mdb-jail-sentence-fail-appeal-overturn-guilty-verdict-2894851

[16] *Malaysiakini* (23 August 2022): https://www.malaysiakini.com/news/633133

[17] For an in-depth assessment of this general election in 2013, see: Meredith L. Weiss (ed.). 2013. *Electoral Dynamics in Malaysia: Findings from the Grassroots*. Singapore / Petaling Jaya: Institute of Southeast Asian Studies / Strategic Information and Research Development Centre.

Political–GLC Complex and Dark Money

A unique feature of Malaysia's political economy is the government's ownership and control of a considerable number of well-interlocked business-based institutions, commonly classified as government-linked companies or GLCs. The immense presence of these GLCs in the economy and the corporate sector serves as a crucial tool for governing elites to practice patronage to muster electoral support, within their parties and during federal and state elections. The government's control over a diverse range of public institutions in this multi-dimensional GLC ecosystem has resulted in a confluence of political and economic power, in what can be termed as the Political–GLC complex. In it, members of the cabinet play an active, though covert and indirect, role in the corporate sector.

The origins of this GLC ecosystem can be traced back to the early 1950s, though the government's intervention in the economy escalated appreciably in the 1970s. Following riots in 1969, attributed to gross socio-economic inequities that had not been adequately tackled twelve years after Independence, the government heavily intervened in the economy through public enterprises and statutory bodies to implement remedial-type public policies. These policies aimed to tackle hardcore poverty, address wealth inequities, and craft compacts with private companies to nurture domestic enterprise, cultivate pioneering industries, and promote rapid industrialization. As for statutory bodies, institutions established under a specific law, jurisdiction over each of them was assigned to a particular minister, depending on its function. Under such laws, ministers had the power to independently appoint the directors of the statutory bodies under their control, as well as their subsidiaries.

This ecosystem subsequently evolved to incorporate a grand assemblage of enterprises, including holding companies, asset management institutions, and a sovereign wealth fund, all of which are dominant players in the corporate sector. This huge infrastructure comprised multiple tiers of partially-owned, publicly-listed GLCs that, in turn, fully-owned a multitude of unlisted private firms. These big and small enterprises are all, ultimately, controlled by the executive arm of the government.

A core feature of this GLC ecosystem is its opacity. When this huge ecosystem came to be captured by politicians, its opacity allowed governing elites to create public concessions and move them around without any transparency and accountability. With the hijacking of this vast ecosystem by powerful elites and the advent of the Political-GLC complex, state–business relations fashioned to institute socio-economic reforms became a core tool for conducting corruption.

The list of a variety of state–business controversies since 1980 in Appendix 1 reveals how an array of GLC-type institutions controlled by politicians in power have been misused.[18] The most deplorable of these incidents occurred in the early 1980s when Bumiputra Malaysia Finance (BMF), a foreign subsidiary of a government institution, Bank Bumiputra, was mired in property speculation in Hong Kong.[19] In spite of this globally embarrassing financial scandal, featuring transnational crime, the murder of an auditor, and substantial mishandling of public funds by a government-owned bank, most of these themes subsequently figured in other state-business ties, including the now equally infamous 1MDB scandal.

---

[18] In most of the controversies listed in Appendix 1, the quantum of loss or wastage listed in news articles was substantial. However, after scrutinizing each of these controversies in depth, it was clear that the reported figures were not necessarily accurate. Moreover, tabulating an accurate figure for the volume of loss or wastage incurred in these state–business controversies proved difficult because there was little or no transparency in the award of most of these projects. For these reasons, the reported cost for each controversy was not included in Appendix 1.

[19] Teh Yik Koon. 2018. *From BMF to 1MDB: A Criminological and Sociological Discussion*. Petaling Jaya: Strategic Information & Research Development Centre (SIRD).

Bank-related controversies have persisted over these four decades since the BMF scandal broke. One major bank whose ownership was controversially circulated between government institutions and well-connected businesspeople was the United Malayan Banking Corporation (UMBC), later renamed RHB Bank.[20] Meanwhile, the lessons from the BMF controversy—the danger of speculating, or gambling, with public funds—were not learned. The Maminco–Makuwasa scandal was a disastrous failed attempt to corner the world tin market in 1981;[21] ten years later, covert foreign exchange trading similarly resulted in a huge loss.[22]

Policies were misused when interventionist programmes were actively employed from 1970 and when corporate development strategies, such as privatization, were aggressively pursued during the 1980s and early 1990s. Both types of policies entailed selective patronage, ostensibly to rapidly create large business groups, or conglomerates, owned by Bumiputeras.[23] However, well-connected non-Bumiputeras also benefited from these policies, indicating inconsistencies in government rhetoric, as well as the power vested in the cabinet to distribute contracts at will. Through privatization, the well-connected gained ownership of lucrative government bodies such as the gaming venture Sports

---

[20] For a detailed assessment of the shuffling of this bank's equity among companies owned or controlled by politicians and well-connected businesspeople, see Edmund Terence Gomez and Jomo K.S. 1997. *Malaysia's Political Economy: Politics, Patronage and Profits*. Cambridge: Cambridge University Press: 110–117. For a brief history of the shifting equity ownership of Malaysian banks once linked to the government, see Edmund Terence Gomez. 2005. The State, Governance and Corruption in Malaysia. In Nicholas Tarling (ed.), *Corruption and Good Governance in Asia*. London: Routledge: 214–244.

[21] Barry Wain. 2009. *Malaysian Maverick: Mahathir Mohamad in Turbulent Times*. Basingstoke: Palgrave Macmillan: 150–154.

[22] Ibid: 166–172.

[23] *Bumiputera* literally means 'sons of the soil', and refers to ethnic Malays, though it also includes indigenous groups in the Borneo states of Sabah and Sarawak.

Toto[24] as well as enterprises that were then monopolies, such as the national air-carrier, Malaysia Airlines (MAS)[25] and the telecommunications-based Celcom.[26] The now common alarm of unaccountable privatization of multi-million ringgit megaprojects commenced in 1987 when a company owned by the governing party was contracted to construct the North–South Highway.[27] Ownership of this company was later routed to private hands, reputedly business proxies of then governing politicians. Similar unaccountable selective patronage during policy implementation occurred during an endeavour to encourage domestic production of beef—referred to as the Cowgate scandal[28]—and the privatization of sewerage services.[29] A number of these projects were subsequently re-nationalized and offered bailouts during which there were allegations of nepotism when enterprises linked to family members of governing elites were rescued from bankruptcy.

Statutory bodies, including those that function as cooperatives and pension funds, have been consistently maladministered. Government-linked institutions once seen as success stories, such as the plantations-based Federal Land Development Authority (FELDA) and the Federal Land Consolidation and Rehabilitation Authority (FELCRA), have been mired in controversies while the members of these cooperatives have lost decision-making

---

[24] Edmund Terence Gomez. 1999. *Chinese Business in Malaysia: Accumulation, Ascendance, Accommodation.* Honolulu: University of Hawaii Pess: 112–127.

[25] Jeff Tan. 2008. *Privatisation in Malaysia: Regulation, Rent-Seeking and Policy Failure.* London: Routledge: 133–157.

[26] Gomez and Jomo. 1997: 148–152.

[27] Lim Kit Siang. 1987. *The RM62 Billion North-South Highway Scandal.* Kuala Lumpur: Democratic Action Party.

[28] *Reuters* (15 February 2012): https://www.reuters.com/article/idUSTRE81E041/

[29] Tan. 2007: 78–105.

control.³⁰ Savings- and pension-based statutory bodies, such as Tabung Haji (the pilgrims fund) and the Employees Provident Fund (EPF) respectively, were central actors in major corporate controversies. A more recent trend is the incorporation and abuse of foundations, another type of business-based institution now widely used by the government, political parties, and governing elites.³¹

Ministerial abuse of power has repeatedly occurred, though most evidently in the Ministry of Defence (Mindef). The first major controversy, the aid-for-arms affair that was linked to the construction of the Pergau Dam in the state of Kelantan, occurred in the late 1980s and involved the British government.³² In spite of the international furore that this incident generated, the Mindef remains at the heart of Malaysia's most controversial procurement-based scandals. These controversies have been linked to privatization, such as the contract to build offshore patrol vessels (OPVs) that was awarded to a politician-cum-businessman. Defence contracts were also allegedly corruptly awarded to a foreign enterprise to build and deliver two submarines.³³ A joint venture comprising a publicly-listed GLC and a German multinational enterprise was contracted to build six combat ships that were not constructed long after their delivery date.

---

³⁰ Center to Combat Corruption and Cronyism. 2018. *The FELDA Crisis*. Petaling Jaya: Center to Combat Corruption and Cronyism: https://c4center.org/wp-content/uploads/Felda-Crisis-Booklet-BI-WEB.pdf

³¹ For an in-depth discussion on the abuse of foundations, see Center to Combat Corruption and Cronyism. 2021. *Foundations and Donations: Political Financing, Corruption, and the Pursuit of Power*. https://c4center.org/wp-content/uploads/2021_c4_center_foundations_and_donations.pdf

³² Tim Lankester. 2013. *The Politics and Economics of Britain's Foreign Aid: The Pergau Dam Affair*. London: Routledge.

³³ *Reuters* (26 June 2012): https://www.reuters.com/article/idUSBRE85P08N/

Land matters figure prominently in debates about widespread misallocation of a public resource as a method to get rich quick. The large number of land parcels owned by the federal government are situated in a little-known but extremely important statutory body, the Federal Lands Commissioner (FLC), which has no board of directors and is under the jurisdiction of a ministry. The government, through the FLC, is endowed with the exclusive right to determine how this resource is used or distributed. The selective award of this resource, ostensibly for 'development' purposes, has led to allegations of environmental degradation, for example during the construction of dams, and the displacement of people.[34] As in major defence projects, a core feature of huge infrastructure projects is joint ventures comprising Malaysia's GLCs, private multinationals from Europe, and state-owned enterprises from China.

This array of state–business-related controversies suggests that at the heart of this Political–GLC complex is a monstrously large government infrastructure that is riddled with patronage and graft, as well as stupefying levels of elite impunity whereby even repeat offenders evade punishment. This Political–GLC complex comes across as a deeply rigged system that facilitates the rampant abuse of public resources and government assets.

Undoubtedly, a huge gulf exists between public governance and accountability. This disconnect has contributed to the proliferation of corporate-based corruption, along with the mounting presence of 'dark money' in electoral campaigns, including funds received by governing politicians from those securing public contracts.[35]

---

[34] For an analysis of the FLC, see: Pushpan Murugiah and Edmund Terence Gomez. 2023. The Private Finance Initiative (PFI): Another Shocking Scam Unravelled. In *State of Corruption: Power, Politics, and Policies in Malaysia*. Petaling Jaya: Center to Combat Corruption and Cronyism: 85-120.

[35] On the subject of 'dark money', see: Jane Mayer. 2016. *Dark Money: The Hidden History of the Billionaires Behind the Rise of the Radical Right*. New York: Double Day; Peter Geoghegan. 2020. *Democracy for Sale: Dark Money and Dirty Politics*. London: Head of Zeus.

However, as there is no law on political donations or the financing of politics, this has led to politicians charged with corruption being exonerated for receiving what appeared to be kickbacks. Although civil society groups have asked for the enactment of this law since 2009,[36] their repeated calls have been persistently ignored or delayed by governing politicians.

A core reason for the escalation of monetized politics and corruption was executive hegemony over public governance, which undermined institutions responsible for investigating and prosecuting corruption from acting impartially. The Malaysian Anti-Corruption Commission (MACC) and the Attorney General's Chamber fall under the jurisdiction of the prime minister. Institutions that oversee the economy and the corporate sector—Bank Negara, the central bank, and the Securities Commission, respectively—are controlled by the finance minister. The prime minister concurrently serves as finance minister, an unhealthy practice that began in 2001 and was only briefly halted between 2018 and 2022.

Of significance, too, is the difference between the rhetoric of change by governing elites and the real outcomes. In 2005, then Prime Minister Abdullah Badawi launched the Government-Linked Companies Transformation Plan (GLCT), a ten-year

---

[36] In 2010, Transparency International (Malaysia) published its study, *Reforming Political Financing in Malaysia*, which was endorsed by numerous non-governmental organizations. Then Prime Minister Najib did not act on this report, though he had called for this reform a year earlier when he took office. In 2015, Najib renewed his call for a law on political financing, his response to the astonishing exposé that a substantial amount of money—RM2.6 billion—had been deposited in his personal bank account. Najib claimed that these funds were a foreign donation for his political activities. Three years later, before Najib's fall, neither was this legislation enacted nor was one introduced by the three prime ministers who held office after him. In 2022, before an impending general election, another attempt was made by civil society to introduce a Political Financing Act, when a bill, drafted with the Bar Council, was submitted to the government to curb the deep monetization of politics.

programme to improve the governance of GLCs. When the GLCT plan ended in 2015, Najib called for measures to 'continue to institutionalize' its three principles of 'performance focus, nation building, and good governance and providing benefits to all stakeholders'.[37] That same year, the 1MBD scandal was exposed. One year later, Najib hailed the GLCT plan a success.[38]

The 1MDB scandal incriminated a then little-known unlisted GLC that had the trappings of proper governance, including a board of directors comprising prominent individuals. This controversy featured corruption of a global magnitude, with scarce checks and balances in public governance and poor corporate governance. Private institutions implicated in the 1MDB scandal comprised international financial institutions and consultancies.[39] It was alarming that major domestic— and foreign—private sector enterprises and banks were incriminated in the laundering of money in this scandal. After all, corporate governance reforms had been introduced after the Asian Financial Crisis (AFC) of 1997 to deal with corruption and cronyism ascribed as primary contributary factors to this economic debacle.[40] The OECD would later claim that Malaysia

---

[37] Quoted in the press release by Khazanah Nasional, the institution responsible for implementing the GLCT plan. See: *Khazanah Nasional* (15 May 2015): https://www.khazanah.com.my/news_press_releases/glcs-primed-to-successfully-graduate-from-10-year-transformation-programme/

[38] *Free Malaysia Today* (26 May 2016):
https://www.freemalaysiatoday.com/category/nation/2016/05/26/transformation-of-glcs-a-success-says-najib/

[39] A thorough appraisal of the 1MDB scandal is provided by: Tom Wright and Bradley Hope. 2018. *Billion Dollar Whale: The Man Who Fooled Wall Street, Hollywood, and the World*. New York: Hachette. See also: P. Gunasegaram and KINIBIZ. 2018. *1MDB: The Scandal that Brought Down a Government*. Petaling Jaya: Strategic Information & Research Development Centre (SIRD).

[40] In Indonesia, the popular catchphrase that emerged to capture the reason for the collapse of this country's economy in 1997 was 'KKN – Korupsi, Kolusi, Nepotisme' or 'Corruption, Collusion, Nepotism'. The following year, a similar cry, coupled with a call for 'Reformasi' (reformation), was taken up in Malaysia.

instituted one of the best corporate governance reforms seen globally.[41]

Defining Grand Corruption[42]

In spite of these major controversies, there is little awareness about how corruption has come to be entrenched, particularly through the abuse of institutions in this GLC ecosystem. To garner conceptual clarity on corruption,[43] insights into the forms it can take were obtained by analysing the state–business-based controversies listed in Appendix 1. These controversies feature abuse of public governance that allows for the:

1. accumulation of wealth, way beyond the salaries of elected representatives;
2. award of projects and contracts to family members and close associates—possibly business proxies—

---

[41] Vighneswaran Vithiatharan and Edmund Terence Gomez. 2014. Politics, Economic Crises and Corporate Governance Reforms: Regulatory Capture in Malaysia. *Journal of Contemporary Asia*, 44 (4): 599–615.

[42] For a useful discussion on the need for conceptual clarity when discussing corruption, see Edward L. Glaeser and Claudia Goldin (eds). *Corruption and Reform: Lessons from America's Economic History*. Chicago: Chicago University Press. See also: Ray Fisman and Miriam A. Golden. 2017. *Corruption: What Everyone Needs to Know*. New York: Oxford University Press.

[43] An important study on corruption in Southeast Asia was published in: Syed Hussein Alatas. 1986. *The Problem of Corruption*. Singapore: Times Book International. An earlier version of this book was published by Donald Moore Press, Singapore, in 1968, under the title *The Sociology of Corruption*. For Alatas, there are three types of corruption: bribery, extortion, and nepotism. Alatas noted, with great foresight, the three stages of corruption. In the first stage, corruption is fairly restricted. If left unchecked, corruption becomes widespread, leading to the third stage where it is self-destructive, deeply undermining economic development. Alatas asserts that the core factors that can curb corruption are an efficient public administration, inspiring leadership, and an educated public.

of governing politicians by abusing the public procurement system;
3. approval of overpayments when acquiring resources, products, and companies;
4. contribution of funds by private companies or businesspeople to politicians to sway a policy or public decision in their favour;
5. abuse of targeted policies where government concessions, including contracts and licences, are hijacked by those in power or their allies; and
6. use of insider information by politicians for strategic acquisitions or sales, such as publicly-listed corporate equity and land, to enrich themselves or their close allies.

These misgovernance practices are rife in the public delivery system and contribute to endemic corruption, thus necessitating appropriate reforms. These reforms are imperative. The serious allegations of corruption listed in Appendix 1 raise a probing question: Why is the conviction rate of political elites so low when corruption is systemic in government? This puzzle draws attention to two core issues that require rigorous analysis. First, what is the institutional architecture of this Political–GLC complex through which politicians can abuse the public resources they were entrusted to safeguard? Second, why is it that governing politicians can argue they have committed no crime when there is evidence that public concessions have been inappropriately channelled, under their watch, into the market?

To answer this puzzle and deal with the exploitation of the GLC ecosystem by political elites, there is a need to go beyond the commonplace definition of corruption as the abuse of public power for personal gain. Different types of 'corruption' occur through the misgovernance of this ecosystem. Equally important is the need to determine the adequacy of existing laws to deal with these forms of corruption.

The multifaceted and extremely complex political–GLC ties listed indicate diverse state–business relations.[44] Political–GLC links are shaped by policies with different orientations, such as the highly interventionist New Economic Policy (NEP) and the market-driven privatization and Private Finance Initiative (PFI). Both types of business-related policies have been misused to benefit political elites and their corporate allies. The NEP, introduced to aid the poor, was so exploited by power elites that one analyst lamented the rise of 'NEP-otism'.[45] Privatization was abused to the point that former Opposition Leader Lim Kit Siang referred to it as 'piratisation'.[46] Crucially, too, as studies have indicated, when a public enterprise is privatized, it does not mean this company is free of political interference.[47]

On the links between poor public governance and corruption, it is useful to quote Susan Ackerman:

> I use the common definition of corruption as the 'misuse of public power for private or political gain,' recognizing that 'misuse' must be defined in terms of some standard. Many corrupt activities under this definition are illegal in most countries—for example, paying and receiving bribes, fraud, embezzlement, self-dealing, conflicts-of-interest,

---

[44] Studies on the networks between political and business elites in Malaysian history include: James V. Jesudason. 1989. *Ethnicity and the Economy: The State, Chinese Business and Multinationals in Malaysia*. Singapore: Oxford University Press; Gomez and Jomo (1997); Peter Searle. 1999. *The Riddle of Malaysian Capitalism: Rent-Seekers or Real Capitalists*. Honolulu: University of Hawaii Press; Patricia Sloane. 1999. *Islam, Modernity and Entrepreneurship Among the Malays*. Basingstoke: Macmillan; Gomez (1999); and Wain (2009).

[45] James Clad. 1989. *Behind the Myth: Business, Money and Power in Southeast Asia*. London: Unwin Hyman: 54.

[46] *DAP Malaysia* (23 January 2005): https://dapmalaysia.org/all-archive/English/2005/jan05/lks/lks3345.htm

[47] See, for example, Jomo K.S. (ed.). 1995. *Privatizing Malaysia: Rents, Rhetoric, Realities*. Boulder: Westview Press; Tan. 2007.

and providing a quid-pro-quo in return for campaign gifts. However, part of the policy debate turns on where to draw the legal line and how to control borderline phenomena, such as conflicts-of-interest, which many political systems fail to regulate.[48]

The World Bank similarly adopts a broader definition of corruption, one that refers to a phenomenon caused by political systems that lack transparency, accountability, and what it refers to as 'good governance'.[49] Other relevant issues in the Malaysian context include how 'informal powers compete and interact with formal institutions'.[50]

Interestingly, the United Nations Convention against Corruption (UNCAC), the only legally binding international instrument for fighting corruption introduced in 2003, does not define corruption. The European Parliament's reasoning why the UNCAC does not provide one is there is 'no universally agreed definition of corruption'.[51] Ellen Gutterman and Mathis Lohaus

---

[48] Susan Rose-Ackerman. 2006. The Challenge of Poor Governance and Corruption. In Bjørn Lomborg (ed.), *How to Spend $50 Billion to Make the World a Better Place*. Cambridge: Cambridge University Press: 77–89.

[49] Rajni Bajpai and Bernard C. Myers. 2020. *Enhancing Government Effectiveness and Transparency: The Fight Against* Corruption. Washington, D.C.: World Bank Group.

[50] *CMI* (August 2021): https://www.cmi.no/publications/file/7849-corruption-definitions-and-their-implications-for-targeting-natural-resource-corruption.pdf

[51] European Parliament. 2021. *Fighting Corruption Globally: The Links With Human Rights*: https://www.europarl.europa.eu/RegData/etudes/ATAG/2021/690625/EPRS_ATA(2021)690625_EN.pdf
For a similar argument about the UNCAC 'purposely omitting a precise definition of corruption (because it) ensures itself a wider and longer applicability', see: Ophelie Brunelle-Quraishi. 2011. Assessing the Relevancy and Efficacy of the United Nations Convention against Corruption: A Comparative Analysis. *Notre Dame Journal of International & Comparative Law*, 2 (1): 164.

note that corruption is well-acknowledged as a concept that is 'notoriously difficult to define precisely, [as it] includes such varied and widespread aspects as nepotism, kleptocracy, cultural practices such as guanxi, black-marketeering, and the pursuit of advantage through both licit and illicit social networks [. . . while] anti-corruption norm is mainly identified with transactional bribery—that is, a focus on corruption as an illicit economic exchange between parties. This take on corruption ignores how corruption can be embedded in social and political networks, including elite institutions, patron-client relationships, and criminal networks.'[52]

The UNCAC does, however, expect all signatory states to 'ensure the existence of a body or bodies, as appropriate, that prevent corruption' and are independent, so that they can 'carry out its or their functions effectively and free from any undue influence'.[53] Apart from bribery, the UNCAC does discuss various types of corruption including money laundering, embezzlement, misappropriation of public property, trading in influence, illicit enrichment, concealment, and obstruction of justice.[54] On these issues, the UNCAC makes three vital points:

1. The role of the private sector in corruption should be noted.[55]
2. The growing transnational nature of these forms of corruption entails the involvement of foreign public officials.

---

[52] Ellen Gutterman and Mathis Lohaus. 2018. What is the 'Anti-corruption' Norm in Global Politics?: Norm Robustness and Contestation in the Transnational Governance of Corruption. In Ina Kubbe and Annika Engelbert (eds), *Corruption and Norms: Why Informal Rules Matter*. Basingstoke: Palgrave Macmillan: 241–268.

[53] UNCAC: Article 6 (1) and (2).

[54] UNCAC: Articles 14–25.

[55] UNCAC: Articles 21–22.

3. Governments should introduce necessary legislation to deal with different types of corruption to establish them as criminal offences, provided these laws are not on the statutes.[56]

Malaysia is a signatory to the UNCAC.

There is a need to distinguish grand and petty corruption. Richard Rose and Caryn Peiffer offer a useful insight to make this distinction:

> Corruption differs in impact between capital-intensive goods that cost many millions to produce, and public services that are retail in scale because they are relatively cheap to provide, such as birth certificates. Services also differ in who is involved. Capital-intensive activities such as building bridges or producing military aircraft involve a relatively small number of corporations that have the resources needed to produce such expensive high-tech goods. In countries where bureaucratic standards are weak, the prospect of big profits is an incentive for enterprises to offer big bribes for contracts and for groups of high-ranking politicians to accept them. Government negotiation of contracts for capital-intensive goods is handled over the heads of ordinary people.[57]

---

[56] There is no discussion of the role of GLCs or state-owned enterprises (SOEs) in the UNCAC, even though such companies have loomed large in major corruption scandals in numerous countries, including in Latin America and Africa. The UNCAC, in Article 2(a) does refer to such companies when defining the term 'public official' as one 'who performs a public function, including for a public agency or public enterprise'.

[57] Rose and Peiffer. 2019: 28.

While there is no universally agreed definition of grand corruption,[58] two issues that distinguish it from petty corruption are the presence of high-level public officials and the gross abuse of power leading to the appropriation of public resources to accumulate wealth.[59] Another core aspect of grand corruption is that it can have a transnational dimension, wherein it 'crosses borders',[60] with governing politicians engaging in well-constructed foreign fund-flow methods to transfer public resources to tax havens. Another form of grand corruption is when governing elites selectively allocate public resources to secure political support, a practice also known as 'clientelism'.[61] Malaysia's long list of controversial state–business relations features these trends.

A fundamental matter associated with the practice of grand corruption is 'state capture', as it facilitates the appropriation of public resources. In a standard definition of state capture, the focus is on the methods employed by companies to 'shape the laws, policies, and regulations of the state to their own advantage by providing illicit private gains to public officials'.[62] Another definition of state capture is that of a situation 'where legislation, formally developed and properly passed by the legislature or parliament, grants benefits in a corrupt manner'.[63]

---

[58] See Jorum Duri. 2020. *Definitions of Grand Corruption*. U4 Anti-Corruption Resource Centre: https://knowledgehub.transparency.org/assets/uploads/kproducts/Defining-grand-corruption_FINAL.pdf. This study defines petty corruption as 'small-scale and everyday corruption by public officials in their interactions with ordinary citizens, mostly during public service delivery'.

[59] Ben Bloom. 2014. Criminalizing Kleptocracy? The ICC as a Viable Tool in the Fight Against Grand Corruption. *American University International Law Review*, 29 (3): 634.

[60] Duri. 2020.

[61] An insightful review of the term clientelism is offered in: Allen Hicken. 2011. Clientelism. *Annual Review of Political Science*, 14 (1): 289–310.

[62] Joel Hellman and Daniel Kaufmann. 2001. Confronting the Challenge of State Capture in Transition Economies. *Journal of Finance & Development*, 38 (3): https://www.imf.org/external/pubs/ft/fandd/2001/09/hellman.htm

[63] Quoted in UNODC: https://www.unodc.org/e4j/en/anti-corruption/module-1/key-issues/corruption---baseline-definition.html

While these concerns prevail in Malaysia, another perspective of state capture must be considered in a context that features a Political–GLC complex, where the executive arm of government controls a vast volume of corporate stock as well as major financial institutions. In this context, state capture can occur when distinct predatory network structures comprising GLCs are created by governing politicians to allow them to pursue their political and economic objectives 'to the detriment of the public good'.[64]

Politicians—and businesspeople—seek public office to exercise control over the cabinet and open avenues to the government's vast corporate assets. Access to these corporate resources can be gained covertly through the GLC ecosystem, as a huge segment of the public and private institutions in this infrastructure function in an opaque manner. State capture allows cabinet members to also channel public funds to party members to develop their support base while practising selective patronage during the award of public concessions. These perspectives to state capture draw attention to the inadequacy of laws, particularly those that criminalize corruption or deal with misgovernance of public resources.

Varieties of Corruption and Legal Anomalies

Table 1.1 lists the forms of misgovernance occurring in state–business relations that constitute a key feature of Malaysia's Political–GLC complex. These forms of misgovernance, which constitute dimensions of grand corruption, are based on allegations levelled against governing politicians. Another feature of Table 1.1 is a catalogue of the laws in place to deal with these allegations of corruption in its different forms.

---

[64] Mihaly Fazekas and Istvan Janos Tóth. 2016. From Corruption to State Capture: A New Analytical Framework with Empirical Applications from Hungary. *Political Research Quarterly*, 69 (2): 320–334.

Table 1.1: Varieties of corruption: Its complex forms

Form of corruption	General definition	Relevant Malaysian laws/gaps therein
Patronage	The power of political actors, using their discretion, to create patron-client-based networks, manipulate the public delivery system, and appoint individuals to non-elective positions in the public sector, irrespective of the legality of the decision.[65]	Some baseline requirements for appointment to certain positions are statutorily stipulated, which limit the extent to which patronage / cronyism / nepotism can be conducted, e.g.: - Members of Election Commission must secure and enjoy public confidence per Article 114, Federal Constitution. - Local authority councillors should have wide experience in local government affairs, achieved distinction in profession, etc. per section 10, Local Government Act 1976.

---

[65] Francisco Panizza, Conrado Ricardo Ramos Larraburu, and Gerardo Scherlis. 2018. Unpacking Patronage: The Politics of Patronage Appointments in Argentina's and Uruguay's Central Public Administrations. *Journal of Politics in Latin America*, 10 (3): 59–98; Guillermo Toral. 2023. How Patronage Delivers: Political Appointments, Bureaucratic Accountability, and Service Delivery in Brazil. *American Journal of Political Science*. https://doi.org/10.7910/DVN/GHJ8JL

Form of corruption	General definition	Relevant Malaysian laws/gaps therein
Cronyism	When personal connections and political patronage, not entrepreneurial ability, determine who secures government concessions.[66] Also seen as a connection or a relationship between politicians and aligned actors involving implicit, unspecified, and reciprocal transactions in which favours are exchanged.[67]	As for the award of government contracts, there is no binding statutorily prescribed procurement regime (currently governed by non-binding treasury circulars). There is, thus, nothing to limit or prevent the granting of contracts to individuals or companies who are connected to the decision-makers. Regulation 4 of the Public Officers (Conduct and Discipline) Regulations 1993 prohibits public officers from subordinating their public duty to their private interests or from conducting themselves in a manner likely to bring their private interests into conflict with their public duties. However, these regulations do not apply to elected representatives and political leaders, as they are not deemed to be 'public officers'.

---

[66] Chang Ha-Joon. 2000. The Hazard of Moral Hazard: Untangling the Asian Crisis. *World Development*, 28 (4): 775–788.

[67] Sarbajit Chaudhuri, Krishnendu Ghosh Dastidar, and Sushobhan Mahata. 2021. Cronyism and Corruption in an Emerging Economy. *Journal of Economic Literature*. https://ssrn.com/abstract=3940811

Form of corruption	General definition	Relevant Malaysian laws/gaps therein
Nepotism	Favouritism towards relatives in public sector appointments and distribution of government concessions that go against public interest.[68]	
Collusion	Political–business collusion entails an arrangement between two or more parties designed to achieve an improper purpose, including improperly influencing the actions of another party,[69] typically	The Competition Act 2010 prohibits agreements that prevent, restrict, or distort competition in any market for goods or services, e.g., price fixing and bid-rigging (Section 4). However, these prohibitions do not apply to activities 'in the exercise of governmental authority' (Section 3). The Act, therefore, only covers collusion

[68] Rimvydas Ragauskas and Ieva Valeškaitė. 2020. Nepotism, Political Competition and Overemployment. *Political Research Exchange*, 2 (1): 10.1080/2474736X.2020.1781542

[69] World Bank, Guidelines. 2006. Procurement Under IBRD Loans and IDA Credits: Paragraph 1.14(a)(iii).

Form of corruption	General definition	Relevant Malaysian laws/gaps therein
	involving coordination to obtain an undue advantage or to avoid an obligation.[70]	within the private sector and not within the public sector, for example, collusion or cartels involved in public procurement exercises.
Rent-seeking	That part of the payment to an owner of resources over and above which those resources could command any alternative use.[71]	There are no laws to curb rent-seeking, probably because the term 'rent' is an economic concept that is not exclusively linked to corruption or misconduct in the public sector.
Embezzlement	Generally equivalent to criminal breach of trust (often used interchangeably in Malaysia); see below.	

---

[70] Transparency International and Equal Rights Trust. 2021. *Defying Exclusion: Stories and Insights on the Links Between Discrimination and Corruption*. Berlin and London: Transparency International and Equal Rights Trust: 10.

[71] James Buchanan. 1980. Rent Seeking and Profit Seeking. In James Buchanan, Robert Tollison, and Gordon Tullock (eds). *Towards a Theory of the Rent-Seeking Society*. College Station: Texas A&M University Press: 3.

Form of corruption	General definition	Relevant Malaysian laws/gaps therein
Slush funds	Off-budget, non-accountable, and discretionary revenues created discreetly by politicians. The fund is not bound by formal rules, procedures, and accountability. Slush funds serve to buy and maintain the loyalty of associates, rivals, and subordinates, both within the political system and among the populace at large. One method of holding such funds is through a foundation that ostensibly has a charitable or welfare function and whose financial account is seldom audited properly.[72]	Since there is no law on political financing, oversight of funds received by politicians or parties is extremely limited. Section 14(1) of the Societies Act 1966 does stipulate that every registered society (including registered political parties) must annually provide the registrar of societies the accounts of the last financial year, a balance sheet showing the financial position at the close of the last financial year, and descriptions of any money, property, or pecuniary benefit or advantage received from an entity located outside of the country. Section 14(2) goes on to state that the registrar may order any registered society to produce duly audited accounts as well.

---

[72] Howard Dick and Jeremy Mulholland. 2010. The State as Marketplace: Slush Funds and Intra-Elite Rivalry. In Edward Aspinall and Gerry van Klinken (eds). *The State and Illegality in Indonesia*. Leiden: Brill: 65–86.

Form of corruption	General definition	Relevant Malaysian laws/gaps therein
Bailouts	When a government makes payments (including loans, loan guarantees, cash, and other types of consideration) to a liquidity-constrained private agent to enable that agent to pay its creditors and counterparties, when the agent is not entitled to those payments under a statutory scheme.[73]	Previously, control and management of public finances was subject solely to the Financial Procedure Act 1957, which vested management of the Federal Consolidated Fund and supervision, control, and direction of all matters relating to the financial affairs of Malaysia in the minister of finance. There were no limits on the discretion afforded to the minister. The recently enacted Public Finance and Fiscal Responsibility Act 2023 aims to mitigate this by stipulating that public expenditure policy must be formulated based on certain objectives, for example, instilling fiscal discipline, ensuring transparency, and improving efficiency. This Act also places various duties and responsibilities on the finance minister

[73] Anthony J. Casey and Eric A. Posner. 2015. A Framework for Bailout Regulation. University of Chicago Coase-Sandor Institute for Law & Economics Research Paper No. 724, University of Chicago, Public Law Working Paper No. 530: https://ssrn.com/abstract=2564259 or http://dx.doi.org/10.2139/ssrn.2564259

Form of corruption	General definition	Relevant Malaysian laws/gaps therein
		with regards to the management of public finances. However, it is too soon to conclusively determine if this Act will prevent irresponsible bailouts.
Land abuse	A situation when people responsible for land governance become biased by vested interests or leverage their power for private gain.[74]	Sections 41 and 42 of the National Land Code grant the respective state authorities within Peninsular Malaysia general powers of disposal with respect to state land, reserved land, and mining land. Similar provisions are found under Sections 12 and 13 of the Sarawak Land Code and Sections 5 and 9 of the Sabah Land Ordinance for these states respectively.
Money muling	Engaging people who knowingly or, in certain cases, unknowingly, help criminal organizations launder their illicit money.	This falls within the ambit of the offence of money laundering under Section 4(b) or (c) of the Anti-Money Laundering, Anti-Terrorism Financing and Proceeds of Unlawful Activities Act 2001, i.e. 'any person who

[74] Rachael Knight. 2022. *Tackling Land Corruption by Political Elites: The Need For a Multi-Disciplinary, Participatory Approach*. FAO Legal Papers No. 111. Rome: Food & Agriculture Organization: 3.

Form of corruption	General definition	Relevant Malaysian laws/gaps therein
		acquires, receives, possesses, disguises, transfers, converts, exchanges, carries, disposes of or uses' or 'removes from or brings into Malaysia proceeds of an unlawful activity or instrumentalities of an offence'.
Conflict-of-interest	When officials conduct themselves in a manner likely to bring their private interests into conflict with their public duty or subordinate their public duty to their private interests.[75]	Regulation 4 of the Public Officers (Conduct & and Discipline) Regulations 1993, mentioned above under the section 'Cronyism', applies here too.

---

[75] Public Officers (Conduct and Discipline) Regulations 1993: Regulation 4.

Form of corruption	General definition	Relevant Malaysian laws/gaps therein
Price inflation (e.g. via variation orders, side payments)	Undue and unjustified exaggeration in costs of works, goods, or services, disproportionate to the quality and scope of works.	There is no binding legislative framework for the public procurement process (which is currently governed by non-binding treasury circulars) or a comprehensive progress monitoring system for public works projects. This allows for the continued occurrence of these forms of corruption.
Profiteering	Making undue profits not derived from one's actual productivity, siphoning funds.	
Abuse of power	The 'unauthorized or illegitimate exercise of power and decisions that are judged by accountability holders to be unwise or unjust [...] Those in power hold offices with specified duties so that power is not personal but, instead, is associated with the	The Malaysian Anti-Corruption Commission (MACC) Act, Section 23(1) prohibits officers of a public body from using their office or position for any gratification for themselves, their relatives, or associates. Within the context of the MACC Act, elected representatives are deemed to be officers of public bodies and, thus, are subsumed within the ambit of this particular offence.

Form of corruption	General definition	Relevant Malaysian laws/gaps therein
	authority of office [...] the standard for recognizing abuses of power will be violations of that trust: acting beyond the authority of the office or in violation of its purposes'.[76]	The definition of 'gratification' under the MACC Act is wide. Section 23(2) creates a presumption that an officer of a public body has used his office or position for gratification when he makes a decision or takes an action in relation to any matter in which he (or any relative or associate) has an interest, whether directly or indirectly.
Criminal breach of trust (CBT)	Committed by one entrusted with dominion over a resource, who dishonestly misappropriates or converts to their own use or dishonestly uses or disposes of that resource, in violation of any law or contract.	Sections 405 to 409 of the Penal Code set out various forms of criminal breach of trust. Section 405 is a general provision targeted at any individual entrusted with property or with any dominion over property. Section 406 states that the punishment is up to ten years' imprisonment, whipping, and a fine. Section 409 specifically covers breaches by public servants and

---

[76] Ruth W. Grant and Robert O. Keohane. 2005. Accountability and Abuses of Power in World Politics. *The American Political Science Review*, 99 (1): 29–43.

Form of corruption	General definition	Relevant Malaysian laws/gaps therein
		prescribes a higher punishment of two to twenty years' imprisonment, whipping, and a fine.
Money laundering	Involvement, in any manner, with a transaction of proceeds for an unlawful activity or instrumentalities of an offence.	Section 4 of the Anti-Money Laundering, Anti-Terrorism Financing and Proceeds of Unlawful Activities Act sets out the offence of money laundering, which essentially encompasses any person who deals in any manner with proceeds of an unlawful activity or instrumentalities of an offence.

Table 1.1 draws attention to a serious anomaly that indicates major fault lines within legislation. The primary laws in Malaysia that deal with corruption are the Malaysian Anti-Corruption Commission Act 2009, the Anti-Money Laundering, Anti-Terrorism Financing and Proceeds of Unlawful Activities Act 2001, and Sections 161 to 165 of the Penal Code. The MACC Act is the key anti-corruption legislation introduced in 2009 to replace the Anti-Corruption Act of 1997. However, there are inadequate laws in place to deal with a large number of issues that can be viewed as a form of corruption, more broadly defined.

This is most evident in the widespread practice of patronage, specifically selective patronage with concessions accruing to the well-connected. Table 1.1 further reveals that despite extensive allegations of cronyism and nepotism, no law deals with these forms of misgovernance. Other practices that have led to corruption are political–business-based collusion and rent-seeking, topics that have drawn comments from sitting prime ministers. For example, when Najib secured the premiership in 2009, he declared his resolve to deal with what he referred to as Malaysia's deep-seated problems of 'patronage' and 'rent-seeking' during the implementation of the country's long-standing affirmative action policy.[77] This was a laudable pronouncement. By 2009, office-holders were constantly channelling public concessions, such as licences, land, contracts, and approved permits, to themselves as well as their family members and close associates. Najib, however, did not heed his own call to deal with patronage and rent-seeking, though he was aware that these problems were deeply undermining the recovery of an economy in trouble following the

---

[77] This call was made by Najib when he presented his New Economic Model. For a discussion on this topic, see Edmund Terence Gomez. 2012. The Politics and Policies of Corporate Development: Race, Rents and Redistribution in Malaysia. In Hal Hill, Tham Siew Yean, and Ragayah Haji Mat Zin (eds), *Malaysia's Development Challenges: Graduating from the Middle*. London: Routledge: 63–82.

global financial crisis of 2008. These forms of misgovernance are seen as core reasons why Malaysia has been stuck in the 'middle-income trap' since the turn of the century.[78]

When affirmative action necessitating selective patronage was introduced in 1970, it was to serve as a short-term measure to rectify socio-economic injustices that had emerged during the country's long colonial rule of the British. Selective patronage has, however, become the norm. The government actively intervened in the economy through newly-created public enterprises to implement affirmative action, ostensibly a mechanism to nurture domestic enterprises. But it led to a close nexus between government and business. Governing politicians have persisted with affirmative action because concessions accruing from such policies, meant for the poor or to foster entrepreneurship, can be misused to serve their political or personal interests. Despite numerous allegations of malfeasance against politicians through this practice of selective patronage, it does not cross the line of legality. For this reason, governing politicians can claim that they have violated no law.

Another consequence of government intervention through public enterprises was the rise of 'bureaucrat capitalists',[79] though with positive outcomes, specifically a rapid decline in poverty and the emergence of a Bumiputera middle class.[80] If intervention in the economy was then through institutions led by bureaucrats, a distinctive change occurred after 1981. Since then, extensive political intervention in the distribution of concessions to well-connected individuals and companies

---

[78] Ibid.

[79] Jomo Kwame Sundaram. 1984. Malaysia's New Economic Policy: A Class Perspective. *Pacific Viewpoint*, 25 (2): 153–172: https://doi.org/10.1111/apv.252003

[80] An insightful study of the rise of this middle class is provided by Abdul Rahman Embong. 2001. *State-led Modernization and the New Middle Class in Malaysia*. Basingstoke: Palgrave.

through market-based policies, such as privatization, has become the trend. While governing politicians argued that they were moving to reduce government intervention in the economy and cut public expenditure, what they advanced was the politicization of the corporate sector. An alarming phenomenon that eventually emerged was a form of 'political capitalism',[81] heavily featuring cronyism and nepotism at the apex. Meanwhile, the growth of a government–business ecosystem has become a vital method to secure grassroots support, including through discourses on the importance of ethnic-based patronage.

Like patronage, difficulties arise when dealing with cronyism and nepotism from a legal perspective. Cronyism, as noted in Table 1.1, occurs when personal ties and political patronage, not entrepreneurial ability, determine who receives public concessions, bank credit, and other economic resources.[82] Nepotism entails similar preferential treatment of relatives. Cronyism and nepotism differ in the nature of the relationships of people privy to government concessions. However, both similarly encompass favouritism when deciding the distribution or award of public concessions. What complicates the matter is proving partisan favouritism.[83]

Rent-seeking, a term used liberally in Malaysia, requires careful assessment. Mushtaq Khan, the London-based professor of economics, notes that 'a person gets a rent if he or she earns an income higher than the minimum that person would have accepted, the minimum being usually defined as the income in

---

[81] Johan Saravanamuttu and Maznah Mohamad. 2020. The Monetisation of Consent and Its Limits: Explaining Political Dominance and Decline in Malaysia. *Journal of Contemporary Asia*, 50 (1): 56–73.

[82] Chang. 2000.

[83] Elizabeth Dávid-Barrett and Mihály Fazekas. 2020. Grand Corruption and Government Change: An Analysis of Partisan Favoritism in Public Procurement. *European Journal on Criminal Policy and Research*, 26: 411–430. A discussion about the problem of prosecuting acts of favouritism is provided in Appendix 2.

his or her next-best opportunity'.[84] As for rent-seeking, Anne Krueger, another economist, argues that government 'restrictions give rise to rents of a variety of forms and people often compete for the rents. Sometimes, such competition is perfectly legal. In other instances, rent-seeking takes other forms, such as bribery, corruption, smuggling, and black markets.'[85] Evidently, since rent-seeking is not necessarily illegal or even immoral, the issue at hand is one of accountability. However, Jagdish Bhagwati points out that rent-seeking activities can be 'directly unproductive' because they waste resources and can contribute to economic inefficiency.[86] Rents are unproductive when they are spent in resource reallocation rather than resource creation.

Other forms of corruption include conflict-of-interest, (inappropriate) bailouts, and the use of slush funds, all of which have occurred regularly and for which no charges have been filed and no governing politician has resigned when such incidents have been exposed. Land abuse—including large-scale property deals, even amid disputes over who owns the land—is well-recorded and is so extensive that it has led to the enrichment of the well-connected.[87]

'Influence peddling' has been defined as the intrusion of big business money into public life.[88] This type of intrusion into politics also occurs when prominent businesspeople or their family members run as candidates during a federal election. Indeed, a

---

[84] Mushtaq H. Khan. 2000. Rents, Efficiency and Growth. In Mushtaq H. Khan and Jomo K.S. (eds). *Rents, Rent-Seeking and Economic Development*. Cambridge: Cambridge University Press: 21. See also: Buchanan, Tollison, and Tullock. 1980.

[85] Anne O. Krueger. 1974. The Political Economy of the Rent-Seeking Society. *The American Economic Review*, 64 (3): 291–303.

[86] Jagdish N. Bhagwati. 1982. Directly Unproductive, Profit-Seeking (DUP) Activities. *The Journal of Political Economy*, 90 (5): 988–1002.

[87] Murugiah and Gomez. 2023.

[88] Fisman and Miriam. 2017: 44.

number of sitting members of parliament (MPs) and cabinet members in the Anwar Ibrahim administration own, or owned, a major business enterprise. This includes the sitting Minister of Tourism, Arts and Culture Tiong King Sing and Deputy Minister in the Prime Minister's Department (PMD) Hanifah Hajar Taib. Their presence in the cabinet draws attention to the 'revolving door' phenomenon, where businesspeople move in and out of politics.[89] Hanifah's brother, Sulaiman Abdul Rahman Taib, who is also well-entrenched in business, served one term as an MP and as deputy minister of tourism. Hanifah and Sulaiman are the children of Abdul Taib Mahmud, who became chief minister of Sarawak in 1981 and held this post for more than three decades.[90] Taib then served as governor of this state for another decade, from 2014 to 2024.[91] The most notable example of the revolving door trend is Daim Zainuddin, a well-known corporate figure who twice served as minister of finance.[92]

Legal anomalies can enable grand corruption. However, Appendix 1 and Table 1.1 clearly reveal the presence of a

---

[89] On the issue of businesspeople entering politics, see: Marika Carboni. 2017. *The Financial Impact of Political Connections: Industry-Level Regulation and the Revolving Door*. Cham: Palgrave Macmillan; Simon Weschle. 2021. Campaign Finance Legislation and the Supply-Side of the Revolving Door. *Political Science Research and Methods*, 9: 365–379: doi:10.1017/psrm.2019.46

[90] Between 1981 and 2014, Taib led the Parti Pesaka Bumiputera Bersatu (PBB), the longstanding single dominant party in Sarawak. A critical assessment of the business ventures of the Taib family is offered by: Bruno Manser Fund. 2012. *The Taib Timber Mafia: Facts and Figures on Politically Exposed Persons (PEPs) from Sarawak, Malaysia*. Basel: Bruno Manser Fund.

[91] Taib passed away at the age of eighty-seven in February 2024.

[92] A wide-ranging account of Daim Zainuddin's corporate and political ties was written by: Michael Backman. 2018. *Daim Zainuddin: Malaysia's Revolutionary and Trouble-Shooter*. Bangkok: River Books. For a critical assessment of how Daim functioned as minister of finance, UMNO Treasurer, and private businessman, see Edmund Terence Gomez. 1990. *Politics in Business: UMNO's Corporate Investments*. Kuala Lumpur: Forum.

perilous political–GLC nexus that enables disparate forms of misgovernance. Disheartingly, too, politicians who have been exposed for serious misgovernance, for which they have evaded punishment, repeatedly run for public office, get re-elected, and even get re-appointed to the cabinet. There is, thus, a need to reveal the inner workings of this Political–GLC complex where constraints on abuse of power have been discarded, public governance has been curbed, and governing elites have extensive control over a huge segment of the corporate sector, which allows for the considerable flow of dark money into electoral politics.

Chapter 2

Grand Corruption and the Political–GLC Complex

Emergence of the Political–GLC Complex

Since the GLC ecosystem can function as a major political resource, parties coming to power prefer that the shroud of secrecy over this structure remains in place. Moreover, as all four prime ministers since 2018 were once allies in the United Malays National Organisation (UMNO), they were well aware of how this Political–GLC complex could allow them covert access to public concessions and funds to consolidate their position in a deeply fractured political system. Inevitably, political abuse of the government's vast corporate base has continued unabated since UMNO's fall, including during the implementation of policies created in response to economic crises.

The story of how this Political–GLC complex came into being is a riveting account of a mix of activities in the worlds of politics and business. At the root of this story is the long rule of UMNO, the hegemonic force in the multi-party Barisan Nasional (BN, or United Front) coalition. This coalition was UMNO's political response to the party's disastrous performance in the 1969 general elections when it was nearly toppled from power. In the early 1970s, two epoch-making events occurred. First, the government's decision to intervene in the economy through public enterprises that were active in the corporate sector served as an avenue for UMNO to liberally distribute government concessions to its core electoral base—poor, rural-based Bumiputeras. The second pivotal event was the decision by UMNO's leaders that the party must venture actively in business to raise funds for its political activities. UMNO's access to funds would allow it to be more independent of the financial support provided by its BN partner—the Malaysian Chinese Association (MCA), a party founded by business tycoons. UMNO's holding company, Fleet Group, secured ownership of a bank and numerous businesses in diverse sectors of the economy, though its equity interests in Malaysia's leading media enterprises were its primary cash cows. The funds from Fleet Group gave UMNO a sound financial base.[93]

Politicians at the apex of UMNO's hierarchy channelled these funds down the pyramid to its division heads and branch leaders who, in turn, distributed the money to the party's grassroots base. Since UMNO reportedly had three million members by the early 1990s, the volume of money—and public concessions—swirling around in the party were stupendous.[94] Allegations abounded of large sums of money being used during party elections, a trend that started in 1981 and reached epic proportions in the 1993 UMNO electoral contest.[95]

As UMNO's presence in the economy grew, through its control of public enterprises and its burgeoning corporate base, the party's leading allies in the BN, the MCA and the Malaysian Indian Congress (MIC), moved to create holding companies and

---

[93] See, Edmund Terence Gomez. 1990. *Politics in Business: UMNO's Corporate Investments*. Kuala Lumpur: Forum, for a history of UMNO's business ventures between the 1970s and 1980s.

[94] Edmund Terence Gomez. 2012. Monetizing Politics: Financing Parties and Elections in Malaysia. *Modern Asian Studies*, 46 (5): 1370-1397.

[95] William Case. 1994. The UMNO Party Election in Malaysia: One for the Money. *Asian Survey, 34* (10): 916–930.

cooperatives to collect funds from the ethnic groups they claimed to represent. These funds were to be invested in the economy to boost Chinese and Indian ownership of corporate equity. The MCA's principal holding company, the highly-diversified Multi-Purpose Holdings Bhd group (MPHB), quickly emerged as a major corporate enterprise following a massive acquisition drive.[96] The MIC's Maika Holdings Bhd also grew in prominence, though through its access to government concessions, including the equity of privatized public institutions.[97]

This trend of parties in business was disrupted by serious allegations of corruption and political feuds over how government-generated resources were being distributed by governing elites. The large number of cooperatives that the MCA had established,[98] along with MPHB, were mired in scandals, with the latter subjected to a restructuring and takeover by a private enterprise. The MIC's leaders were heavily critiqued for abusing Maika Holdings' investments, much of which came from the poor.[99] However, the grimmest ramifications of this mix of politics and business were seen in UMNO. In 1987, a grand battle ensued among its leaders for control over this deeply divided party, with allegations that those in control of the government had abused public resources to serve their vested interests. There were

---

[96] Bruce Gale. 1985. *Politics and Business: A Study of Multi-Purpose Holdings Berhad*. Petaling Jaya: Eastern University Press.

[97] For an in-depth study of the rise and fall of the corporate enterprises incorporated by UMNO, MCA, and MIC, see Edmund Terence Gomez. 1994. *Political Business: Corporate Involvement of Malaysian Political Parties*. Townsville: Centre for Southeast Asian Studies, James Cook University of North Queensland.

[98] For an assessment of the controversies surrounding the numerous cooperatives established by the MCA, see: Edmund Terence Gomez. 1991. *Money Politics in the Barisan Nasional*. Kuala Lumpur: Forum.

[99] Lim Kit Siang. 1992. *Samy Vellu and the Maika Scandal*. Kuala Lumpur: Democratic Action Party.

also allegations that UMNO's vast corporate assets were being channelled to businessmen linked to party elites.[100] The many aftershocks of UMNO's contentious electoral contest included a massive purge of party dissidents while UMNO's corporate assets were transferred to private hands.

A variety of political–business relationships emerged after 1990, further distorting transparent and accountable market activities. Business allies of UMNO treasurer, Daim Zainuddin, were now corporate captains, holding assets that once belonged to the party, even figuring among the owners of Malaysia's top ten publicly-listed companies. Among these quoted enterprises were the Renong-UEM group and privatized firms such as Malaysia Airlines (MAS) and Celcom, both controlled by people reputedly close to then Prime Minister Mahathir Mohamad and Finance Minister Daim. Meanwhile, with privatization in vogue, UMNO politicians benefitted, many of them emerging as owners of business enterprises. A rather large group of UMNO politicians, who were reputedly close to leading party figures, including the then newly-appointed finance minister, Anwar Ibrahim, emerged as key business figures. This group of politician-cum-businessmen included the Deputy Prime Minister Ahmad Zahid Hamidi, particularly through a company called Kretam Holdings.

Another group comprised Bumiputera and non-Bumiputera businessmen, reputedly close to UMNO leaders, who had secured a major corporate presence. These well-connected businesspeople led enterprises such as Arab-Malaysian Corp, Astro, Advance Synergy, Berjaya, Diversified Resources, Genting, Hong Leong, KFC Holdings, Land & General, Magnum, Malakoff, Maxis, Metroplex, Nanyang Press, Sapura Telecommunications, Tongkah,

---

[100] For an incisive account of this epic battle between UMNO elites, see: Shamsul A.B. 1988. The Battle Royal: The UMNO Elections of 1987. *Southeast Asian Affairs*. Singapore: Institute of Southeast Asian Studies (ISEAS): 170–188.

and YTL.[101] Other enterprises were then emerging independent of federal politicians. These companies were associated with businesspeople from Sarawak and included the family members of Taib Mahmud, then this state's chief minister. The last group comprised companies that remained under the ownership of UMNO and MCA. These companies had a major presence in the media sector, through Utusan Melayu Press and Star Publications.

Political and business elites, in the peninsula and in Sarawak, were creating their own web of corporate networks, sometimes colluding with each other, at other times with competing agendas. The corporate sector was awash with different but interlaced political–business ties led by different elites who were soliciting government concessions and resources, such as land, as they jockeyed for pre-eminence—and visibility—on the stock exchange in order to secure foreign portfolio investments (FPIs), which were engulfing the market.[102] As political meddling in the corporate sector grew, governing elites appeared in different covert state–business relations, for example through party associates in business who they controlled, their families and proxies, and their personal ties with corporate elites.

A constant criticism in the early 1990s was that of the non-transparent public decision-making leading to the misallocation of privatized projects. Major privatized projects were being awarded based on private discussions between the

---

[101] The names of these companies were extracted from a long compilation of enterprises associated with UMNO leaders. For the complete list, see: Simon Johnson and Todd Mitton. 2001. Cronyism and Capital Controls: Evidence from Malaysia. NBER Working Paper No. w8521: https://ssrn.com/abstract=286193

[102] By the mid-1990s, Malaysia's stock exchange had emerged as Asia's third largest, after those in Japan and Hong Kong, while its market capitalization was over 300 per cent of its GDP, which, according to one study, was 'by far the highest in the world'. See: Prema-chandra Athukorala. 2010. Malaysian Economy in Three Crises. In *The Australian National University (ANU) Working Papers in Trade & Development No. 2010/12*. Canberra: ANU.

governing elites, their closest allies, and select businessmen.[103] By the mid-1990s, allegations abounded of abuse of power, conflicts-of-interest, and cronyism. A common concern about these highly-favoured well-connected businessmen and politicians-in-business was that they were either holding these corporate assets in trust for governing elites or acting at their behest in the corporate ventures they undertook.

This nexus between politics and business came to an abrupt halt when the Asian Financial Crisis (AFC) occurred in 1997. Numerous UMNO-linked businessmen who had emerged as corporate captains, given their easy access to loans from government-linked banks, found themselves mired in debt while others went bankrupt. Some were bailed out, at huge expense to the government, as these companies were nationalized. There were intense criticisms of these bailouts, with UMNO members also asserting that the AFC debacle had been caused by the rampant practice of cronyism, collusion, and nepotism. No one was charged in court for offences relating to these practices. Instead, another cataclysmic feud erupted in UMNO, with its president, Mahathir, ousting his deputy, Anwar, who subsequently spent about half a decade in jail for corruption, entailing abuse of power to prevent police investigations into his private affairs.[104]

Following this infamous 1998 UMNO feud, businesspeople aligned to Anwar lost control of their corporate assets. By the turn

---

[103] Apart from the controversial sale of MAS and Celcom, other contentious privatizations involved the award of mega-projects, such as the Bakun Dam and monorail ventures, as well as the sale of the Heavy Industries Corporation of Malaysia (HICOM), established to drive Malaysia's industrialization programme. Unsurprisingly, many of these privatized projects were dismal failures. See Jeff Tan. 2008. *Privatisation in Malaysia: Regulation, Rent-Seeking and Policy Failure*. London: Routledge.

[104] *Human Rights Watch*. 2000. Malaysia: Anwar Verdict 'A Step Backwards': https://www.hrw.org/news/2000/08/08/malaysia-anwar-verdict-step-backwards

of the century, monumental shifts had occurred in the ownership of major enterprises. Numerous enterprises in the hands of politicians-in-business and well-connected businessmen were brought under the control of the government and classified as GLCs. Corporate equity came to be concentrated in the hands of the government. In 2001, of the top ten publicly-listed companies, eight were GLCs. Bumiputera corporate captains fell away quickly, with none figuring among the top twenty companies. Prime Minister Mahathir went on to appoint himself as finance minister, an unprecedented move that smacked of gross misgovernance. Mahathir now had direct and indirect ownership and control over Malaysia's leading enterprises through the GLC ecosystem.

Clearly, an understanding of the past is imperative to appreciate the making of Malaysia's Political–GLC complex. A variety of political-business ties had emerged by the 1990s, resulting in hydra-like corporate empires controlled by governing elites, well-connected businesspeople, politicians, and political parties. These varied state–business ties eventually contributed to grand corruption and deeply divisive political feuds while the economic repercussions of this wide-ranging mix of politics and business became patently obvious when the AFC occurred. Until that point, arguments had been made by politicians and academics that 'developmental corruption', as opposed to 'degenerative corruption'—involving bribery, embezzlement, and kleptocracy—was permissible, as it facilitated rapid industrialization.[105] After the AFC, arguments in support of a developmental form of corruption ceased while many of these business empires came under government control, converting them from privately-owned enterprises to GLCs.

---

[105] For an incisive review of the debates in the 1990s about developmental and degenerative corruption, see: Andrew Wedeman. 2002. Development and Corruption: The East Asian Paradox. In Edmund Terence Gomez (ed.), *Political Business in East Asia*. London: Routledge: 34–61.

The core feature of this new intricate GLC structure was its complexity, which accorded it anonymity. A deeply troubling new concern was that of corporate concentration, with control over all this private equity in a structure that was under the charge of the executive arm of government. This profound change in ownership and control of business equity conferred on cabinet ministers enormous influence over the corporate sector as well as economic public institutions. This Political–GLC complex has been depicted in Figure 2.1.

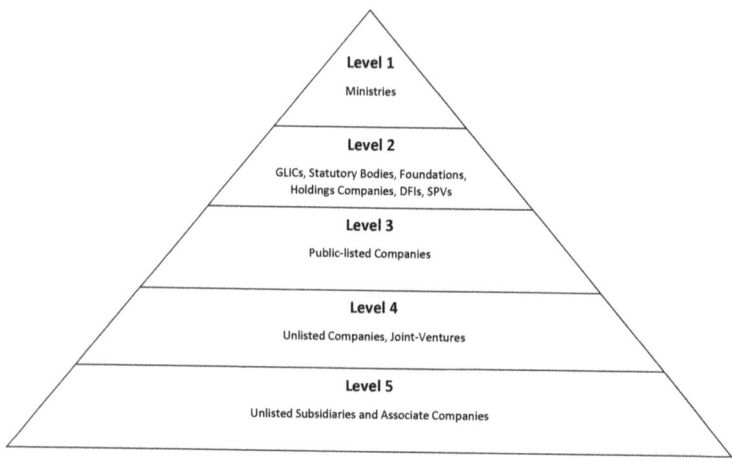

Figure 2.1: Power structure of the GLC ecosystem—five levels

Power Structure: Politicians, Institutions, Business Tools

Figure 2.1 indicates a structure of dominance, infused with power accorded to the prime minister and his cabinet, which has overwhelming control over a range of public institutions that have a business and regulatory purpose. In this structure, where the bureaucracy is subservient to the ministers, there is no need for governing elites to resort to excessive coercion to implement projects that serve their vested interests.

Malaysia's Political–GLC complex resembles that of large business groups or conglomerates, a five-tiered state–business pyramid structure—though it can go down many more levels—encompassing interlocked companies in different economic sectors. In the pyramidal ownership structures of conglomerates, their owners have enormous control over a large number of companies across different sectors while owning a relatively small volume of equity. A characteristic feature of these conglomerates is the use of holding companies that employ cross-holdings of enterprises situated in a multi-tiered pyramid. This method of corporate control facilitates bypassing the interests of minority shareholders while also undermining the transparent functioning of equity markets.[106]

Figure 2.1 indicates a similar governance system, though one not just with economic but political implications, too. This figure reveals how, in a wholly legal manner, power elites, public institutions, publicly-quoted companies, unlisted firms, and foreign and domestic joint ventures are directly and indirectly connected. Control over these interconnected public institutions and market-based enterprises, collectively known as GLCs[107], is concentrated in the cabinet (at Level 1), denoting an extremely asymmetrical distribution of economic influence. Since decision-making control is with the cabinet, it brings into question the volume of

---

[106] For an in-depth analysis of this method of corporate control from a political economy perspective, see: Ben Ross Schneider. 2009. A Comparative Political Economy of Diversified Business Groups, or How States Organise Big Business. *Review of International Political Economy*, *16* (2): 178–201.

[107] These different types of institutions, collectively referred to as GLCs, are reviewed in: Edmund Terence Gomez. 2017. *Minister of Finance Incorporated: Ownership and Control of Corporate Malaysia*. Basingstoke: Palgrave Macmillan.

autonomy accorded to public institutions at Level 2, hampering them from acting without favour or fear. Although the variety of business-based institutions at Level 2 and the publicly-quoted companies they control at Level 3 are annually accountable to parliament or to a regulatory body, suggesting public scrutiny, they have still been subjected to persistent political abuse.

It is, however, the multitude of unlisted companies at Level 4, as well as their subsidiaries and associate companies at Level 5 that are of primary concern. Though these unlisted enterprises at Levels 4 and 5 are required to submit their annual statements to the Companies Commission of Malaysia (CCM), it is unlikely that they are carefully vetted. It is, in fact, quite probable that there is little or no oversight of these unlisted companies. Indeed, it is unlikely that there is much public knowledge that these companies can be classified as GLCs, given their covert control by enterprises at Levels 2 and 3. It appears that even regulatory and oversight institutions have little knowledge of this GLC ecosystem, an indication of how vast, complex, and opaque it has become. That these companies at Levels 4 and 5 are GLCs is disclosed only when a major controversy occurs or if a whistleblower sheds light on them. Exposés of these sorts have revealed the volume of corporate power that politicians and the directors of GLCs wield at Levels 4 and 5, which can contribute to grand corruption.

When the foundations of this Political–GLC complex were laid in 1970, after the New Economic Policy (NEP) was introduced, its components were presented as agents for economic development and social provisioning; and, indeed, they did then serve these purposes. Subsequently, with the expansion of this structure, ownership of the government's vast business interests was situated in seven huge government-linked investment companies (GLICs), located at Level 2 of this pyramid, comprising financially well-endowed investment- and savings-based institutions, as well as a sovereign wealth fund and a holding company, Minister of Finance Incorporated (MoF Inc.). Also located at Level 2 are statutory bodies, development financial institutions (DFIs), foundations, and special purpose vehicles (SPVs). Since each statutory body at Level 2 falls under the administrative jurisdiction of a federal ministry, different cabinet members have control over the appointment of the directors of these powerful institutions. Some statutory bodies function as holding companies and GLICs, such as MoF Inc., indicating that public institutions can have multiple identities. The GLICs at Level 2 can be seen as 'super entities' because economic power is concentrated in them, given their ownership and control over Malaysia's leading publicly-listed enterprises and banks (at Level 3), as well as a host of unlisted companies (at Levels 4 and 5).

A business device employed at Levels 4 and 5 is that of shell and shelf companies, long abused in the corporate sector, for the most part to launder money and to conceal wealth. The use of proxies in business ventures is an alternative common method to ensure that beneficial ownership of corporate enterprises cannot be traced back to power elites. A core feature at Levels 4 and 5 is that of joint ventures. These encompass partnerships between GLCs and privately-owned domestic and foreign companies, as well as joint equity ownership with foreign state-owned enterprises (SOEs), including those from China—a growing trend.[108] Numerous controversies listed in Appendix 1 implicate obscure unlisted GLCs and a variety of statutory bodies, two institutions

---

[108] Edmund Terence Gomez, Siew Yean Tham, Ran Li, and Kee Cheok Cheong. 2020. *China in Malaysia: State-Business Relations and the New Order of Investment Flows*. Singapore: Palgrave Macmillan. This study assesses the mounting number of joint ventures between Malaysia's GLCs and China's state-owned enterprises.

hitherto seldom discussed in the literature on government-linked enterprises.[109]

The utilization of shell and shelf companies in corporate activities merits attention, given the exposés in the Panama Papers and Pandora Papers, as well as their covert use by government-controlled institutions.[110] A shell company, though formally incorporated, 'does not conduct any operations other than in a pass-through capacity'.[111] Shell companies can perform legal activities such as 'financing foreign operations, investing in overseas capital markets, or easing transfers of assets'. 'Taking advantage of the lack of beneficial ownership disclosure', they can be used to commit crimes such as tax evasion, bribery, drug trafficking, money laundering, and bankruptcy fraud.[112]

Shelf companies have been defined as unused 'aged corporations', which 'adds to their credibility' and offers an 'attractiveness [that] includes instant availability [and] immediate ownership.'[113] A major reason for using a shelf company is that once it is acquired, the buyer also obtains its 'established credit

---

[109] This volume provides case studies to examine how these two types of institutions function in the market. The case studies offer insights into how the cabinet's control over statutory bodies and unlisted companies can lead to major business controversies.

[110] In Chapter 3, the case study on MARA provides insights into how shell and shelf companies are employed by the directors of GLCs owned by this statutory body to facilitate the transnational flow of funds obtained through dubious means.

[111] This definition of shell companies is based on one provided by the OECD. See: José-de-Jesús Rocha-Salazar, María-Jesús Segovia-Vargas, and María-del-Mar Camacho-Mínano. 2022. Detection of Shell Companies in Financial Institutions Using Dynamic Social Network. *Expert Systems with Applications*, 207: 1–13.

[112] Ibid.

[113] Carl Pacini and Nate Wadlinger. 2018. How Shell Entities and Lack of Ownership Transparency Facilitate Tax Evasion and Modern Policy Responses to These Problems. *Marquette Law Review*, 102 (1): 111–166.

and tax history, which further enhances its credibility' while its 'lack of accurate and recorded information [. . .] can create almost insurmountable obstacles for auditors, forensic accountants [. . .] and regulators in any attempt to identify the beneficial owner[s].'[114]

Table 2.1 provides a list of the different types of public institutions routinely referred to as GLCs. The roles played by this diverse range of public institutions draw attention to a crucial point: their mixed social and business mandates, an issue that often poses performance and governance challenges. When undertaking their duties, these institutions have to strike a fine balance between these two roles, one being difficult to achieve. Moreover, governing politicians persistently talk of the need for these institutions to generate revenue while undertaking their social provisioning responsibilities.

---

[114] Ibid.

Table 2.1: Public institutions collectively classified as GLCs[115]

Types of Institutions	Definition	Names
Government-linked investment companies (GLICs)	The Treasury has deemed seven institutions as GLICs. They function as investment arms, pension funds, a sovereign wealth fund, and a holding company.	• Khazanah Nasional Bhd • Employees Provident Fund (EPF) • Kumpulan Wang Persaraan (Diperbadankan) (KWAP) • Lembaga Tabung Angkatan Tentera (LTAT) • Lembaga Tabung Haji (LTH) • Permodalan Nasional Bhd (PNB) • Minister of Finance Incorporated (MoF Inc.)
Statutory bodies	Established by various laws at the federal and state levels	• Majlis Amanah Rakyat (MARA) • Lembaga Kemajuan Tanah Persekutuan (FELDA) • Petroliam Nasional (Petronas) • Majlis Agama Islam Wilayah Persekutuan (MAIWP) • Iskandar Regional Development Authority (IRDA)

---

[115] For a lengthier list of the different types of GLCs controlled by the government, see: Edmund Terence Gomez. 2017. *Minister of Finance Incorporated: Ownership and Control of Corporate Malaysia*. Basingstoke: Palgrave Macmillan.

Types of Institutions	Definition	Names
		• Kedah Regional Development Authority (KEDA) • Terengganu Tengah Development Authority (KETENGAH) • South Kelantan Development Authority (KESEDAR) • Johor Tenggara Development Authority (KEJORA)
Foundations	Established for religious, educational, charitable, or social welfare activities under the Trustees (Incorporation) Act 1952 or Companies Act 1965	• Yayasan Ekuiti Nasional • Yayasan Pelaburan Bumiputera • Yayasan 1MDB • Yayasan Wilayah Persekutuan
Development financial institutions (DFIs)	Incorporated to execute specific projects serving the government's development policies	• Agro Bank • SME Bank • Export-Import (EXIM) Bank

Types of Institutions	Definition	Names
Special purpose vehicles (SPVs)	Institutions with a specific mandate to develop key sectors considered strategic for economic development	• KL International Airport • Pembinaan PFI • Pengurusan Danaharta Nasional
Holding companies	Enterprises created to hold the equity and assets of other companies	• MoF Inc. • CMI / MBI (Chief Minister Inc. / Mentri Besar Inc.) • Federal Land Commissioner (FLC)
Publicly-listed companies (GLCs)	Some of these quoted companies were statutory bodies that were corporatized and listed on the stock exchange	• Tenaga Nasional • Telekom Malaysia • Malayan Banking • Petronas Gas • Sime Darby
Unlisted companies (GLCs)	Companies registered under the Companies Act	• 1MDB • National Feedlot Corporation (NFC) • FELCRA

Concerns about the huge wastage of public funds through this colossal multi-faceted GLC ecosystem have been acknowledged by previous prime ministers, with Abdullah Badawi proposing reforms in 2005 through his ten-year GLC Transformation Plan (GLCT).[116] However, these reforms focused exclusively on the seven GLICs and the publicly-listed companies under their control, with attention on corporate—not public—governance. In 2010, when Najib Razak introduced his Government Transformation Programme (GTP),[117] one stated goal was the need to improve the performance of the GLCs. However, unlisted GLCs closely associated with Najib were subsequently mired in controversy.

Mahathir Mohamad, when aligned with opposition parties in 2018, was extremely critical of GLCs. As this ecosystem was a product of his tenure as prime minister between 1981 and 2003, Mahathir's view of the GLCs, as reported, merit mention:

> One thing that we did was to try to give the Malays more shares. But they didn't have the money and [whenever] we gave them the shares they sold them. So, we created GLCs, to ensure the money rests with the GLCs, which will be holding the shares for the Malays. But when we created GLCs, we never realised they were going to become a monster. Without supervision, GLCs have now become a monster, they are huge and rich.[118]

In this report, Mahathir went on to say that it 'seems like my past sin has caught up with me. I was one of the first few persons

---

[116] Putrajaya Committee on GLC High Performance. 2015. *GLC Transformation Programme Graduation Report*. Kuala Lumpur: Percetakan Nasional Malaysia.

[117] Government of Malaysia. 2010. *Government Transformation Programme*. Kuala Lumpur: Government Printers.

[118] *The Edge* (6 April 2018): https://theedgemalaysia.com/article/dr-m-says-glcs-not-serving-intended-purpose

accused of cronyism for giving contracts to cronies, but it is of course not really true. When we give contracts to anyone, we must be sure that they have the capacity to implement whatever that is given to them. Unfortunately, there are not many of them, even until today.'[119]

Following Mahathir's appointment as prime minister after his coalition's unexpected victory in the 2018 general election, he established a committee to, among other things, conceive a viable ownership and control model of GLCs that could be employed in an accountable manner. Mahathir did not release the report of this committee. When civil society organizations asked Anwar to make this report public when he took office as prime minister in 2022, he, too, did not do so.

No sitting prime minister has moved to introduce public governance reforms by instituting checks and balances in this vast GLC ecosystem. There is no indication of an attempt to curb collusive state–business relations that have led to cronyism, rent-seeking, selective patronage, and nepotism. The reforms that were implemented by Abdullah merely addressed management of publicly-listed GLCs (at Level 3), enterprises that were constantly in the public eye. A study in 2017 of quoted GLCs indicated that the politicians did not figure as directors, though control over these companies was in the hands of professional managers who were subservient to members of the cabinet.[120] As for government-controlled companies at Level 4, politicians could still shield abuse of power from the public eye, and even prevent prosecution, through their control over regulatory bodies.

What aids those in control of this Political–GLC complex, where power is concentrated at the apex, is their access to a

---

[119] Ibid.

[120] Edmund Terence Gomez. 2017. *Minister of Finance Incorporated: Ownership and Control of Corporate Malaysia*. Basingstoke: Palgrave Macmillan.

number of tools of control, indicating a form of state capture. Each of these tools of control merit review.

Control Tools in Place

Control Tool 1: Policies and Public Delivery System

Public policies matter, but they can also function as a key control device because they determine and justify methods of intervention in the economy. The best example of this is the longstanding policy endeavour to nurture a vibrant Bumiputera corporate class. Ethnic group-based patronage has been in place since the NEP was introduced in 1970. To implement the NEP, the government created a large number of public enterprises to help Bumiputeras secure 30 per cent of Malaysia's corporate wealth within two decades. After the NEP ended in 1990, other affirmative action-type policies were introduced, ostensibly because this 30 per cent equity ownership target had not been achieved.[121] However, the enduring practice of allowing only GLCs and Bumiputera-owned companies—usually coupled with intra-ethnic political patronage—access to public concessions, such as procurement contracts, has persistently compromised competition, as well as the quality and price of goods and services.

Major policies by different prime ministers to foster Bumiputera enterprise were Mahathir's Bumiputera Commercial and Industrial Community (BCIC), Najib's Bumiputera Economic Empowerment Plan (BEEP), and Muhyiddin Yassin's Shared

---

[121] Studies reviewing the NEP include: Just Faaland, Jack R. Parkinson, and Rais Saniman. 2003. *Growth and Ethnic Inequality: Malaysia's New Economic Policy*. Kuala Lumpur: Utusan Publications & Distributors; Edmund Terence Gomez and Johan Saravanamuttu (eds). 2013. *The New Economic Policy in Malaysia: Affirmative Action, Horizontal Inequalities and Social Justice*. Singapore: National University of Singapore Press; Lee Hock Aun. 2021. *Affirmative Action in Malaysia and South Africa: Preference for Parity*. London: Routledge.

Prosperity Vision (SPV). The Vendor Development Programme (VDP) and Global Supplier Programme (GSP) were promulgated to bring small- and medium-scale enterprises (SMEs) into domestic and global supply chains through the practice of mass selective patronage. One major non-interventionist policy employed to quickly create Bumiputera-owned enterprises was privatization. Although market-based policies served to reduce government intervention in the economy, they have similarly contributed to allegations of selective patronage, cronyism, and nepotism, with control furtively retained in the hands of their political patrons. The Private Finance Initiative (PFI), a policy akin to privatization, advocated private financing of public projects. However, PFI projects have been selectively awarded and funded by the government-controlled pension funds, EPF, and KWAP.[122]

A more recent policy, Jana Wibawa, similarly entailed the practice of patronage, targeting Bumiputera-owned SMEs, but was subsequently mired in controversy. Jana Wibawa was the government's response to the Covid-19 pandemic and the economic crisis that ensued. This pandemic so deeply undermined SMEs that public contracts were to be awarded through this policy to help them out. However, serious allegations of nepotism and cronyism were later levelled against Muhyiddin who, as prime minister, had introduced this policy.[123] A core issue surrounding these allegations entailed abuse of power by undermining strict bureaucratic regulations of the public procurement process. Political elites allegedly had 'allocation control' over the distribution of government-generated projects.

---

[122] For an in-depth assessment of the PFI policy and the controversies ensuing from its implementation, see Pushpan Murugiah and Edmund Terence Gomez. 2023. The Private Finance Initiative (PFI): Another Shocking Scam Unravelled. In Center to Combat Corruption and Cronyism (ed.), *State of Corruption: Power, Politics, and Policies in Malaysia*. Petaling Jaya: Center to Combat Corruption and Cronyism: pp. 85–120.

[123] A case study on the Jana Wibawa policy is provided in Chapter 3.

Control Tool 2: Ministries and GLCs

A feature unique to Malaysia is the bewildering number of business-based institutions under the control of federal ministries, over which cabinet ministers have jurisdiction. Of the twenty-six federal ministries, control over business-based institutions is concentrated with the PMD, Ministry of Finance (MoF), and Ministry of Rural and Regional Development (MRRD). Other ministries with a similar institutional structure, but on a smaller scale, are the Ministry of Defence (Mindef) and the Ministry of Agriculture and Food Security. Figure 2.2 provides the organizational structures of business-based institutions under the control of the PMD, MoF, MRRD, and Mindef. Though the organizational charts of these ministries go down only five levels, this is sufficient to indicate the considerable size of Malaysia's shadow GLC ecosystem.[124]

These complex interlocking state–business networks in Figure 2.2 going down five levels raise an important query. How did this GLC ecosystem become so huge and multifaceted, such that it is difficult to quantify the volume of assets under the control of the government? At their inception, these structures served as a mechanism for party elites to garner electoral support, with public institutions responding, in particular, to the needs of rural folk, UMNO's core constituency. These structures were then deployed to channel public concessions for party members, though with some trickle down to key electoral constituencies. The mode of employment of this GLC structure has now been expanded, with

---

[124] These organizational mappings constitute a segment of the GLC ecosystem because numerous ministries own or control business-based institutions. For example, the Ministry of Agriculture and Food Security controls several important statutory bodies located in rural areas, which, in turn, own numerous unlisted companies. The Ministry of Science and Technology has control over a large number of unlisted GLCs.

Figure 2.2: Corporate networks of four ministries: PMD, MoF, MRRD, & Mindef

Figure 2.2.1: Prime Minister's Department (PMD)

Grand Corruption and the Political–GLC Complex

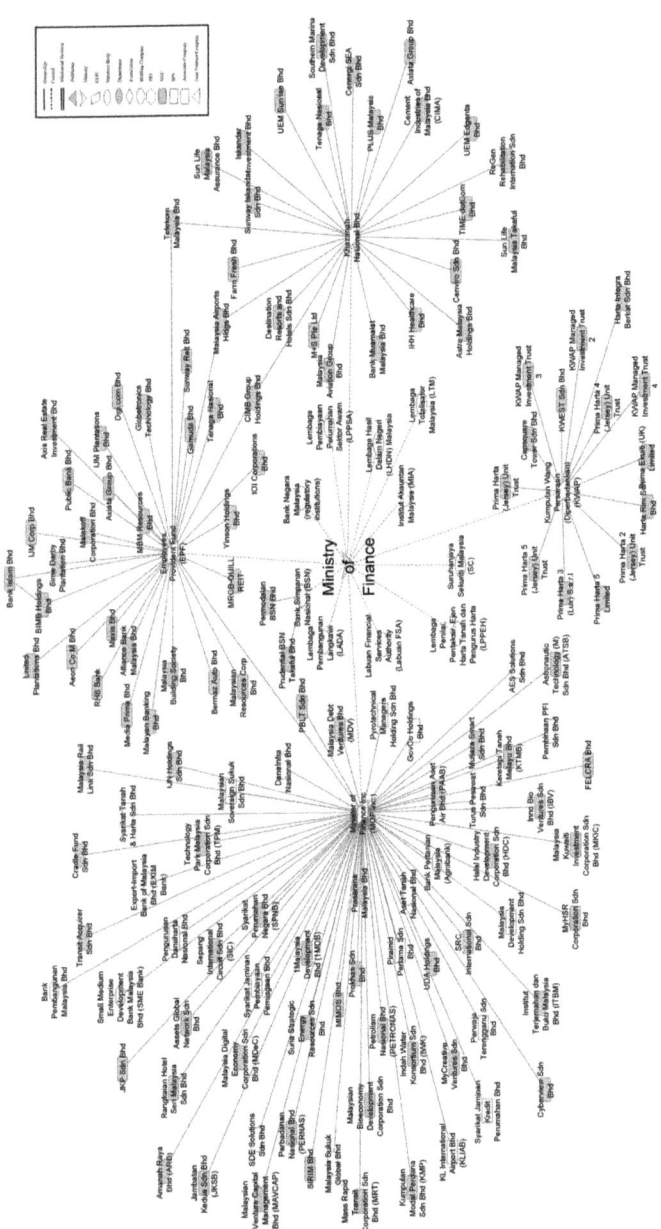

Figure 2.2.2: Ministry of Finance

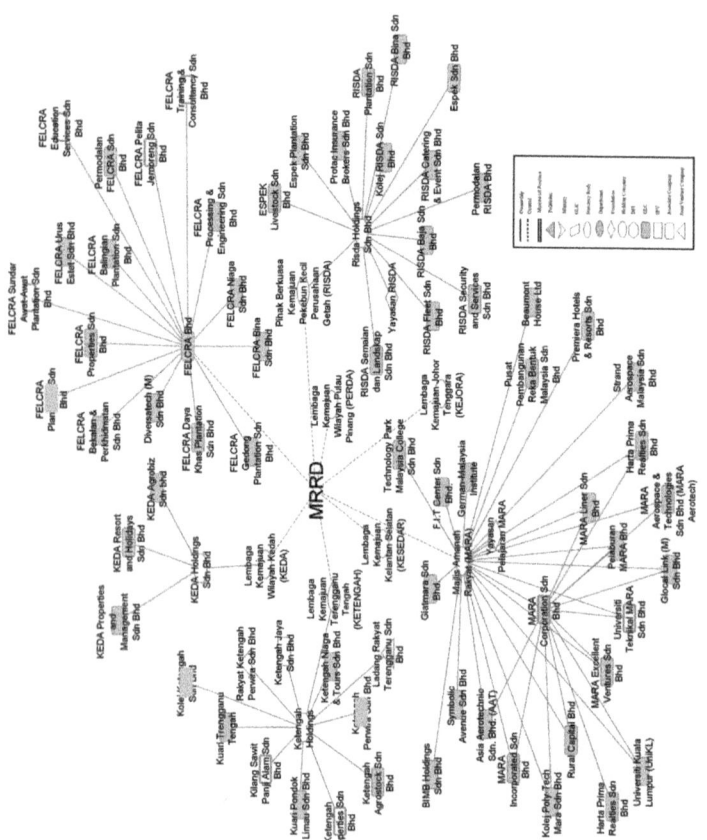

Figure 2.2.3: Ministry of Rural and Regional Development (MRRD)

Grand Corruption and the Political–GLC Complex

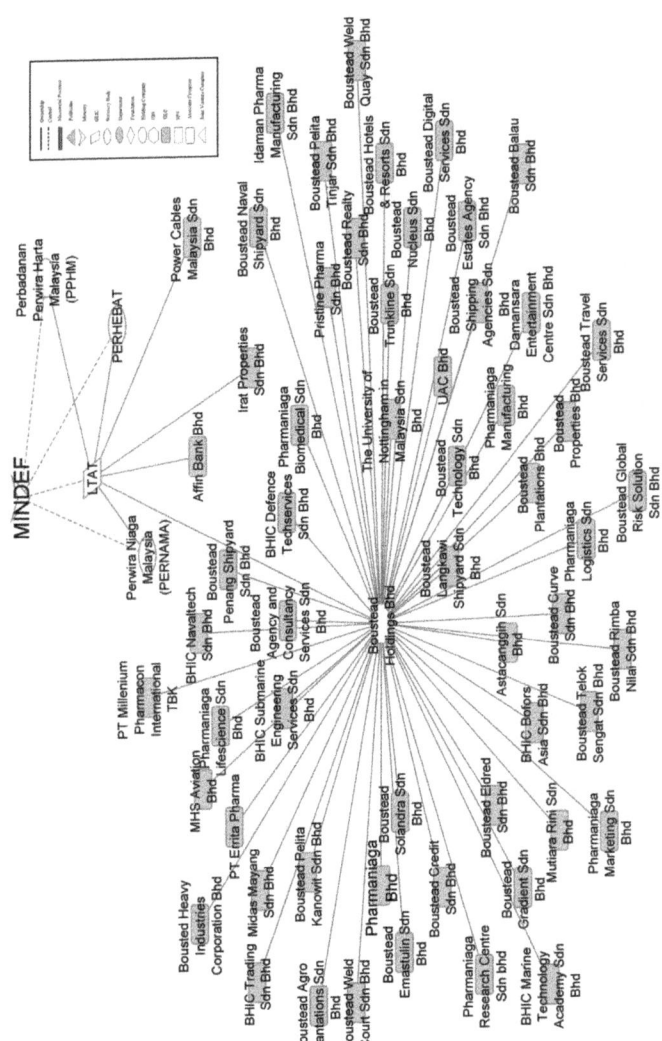

Figure 2.2.4: Ministry of Defence (Mindef)

directorships of major enterprises being offered as a strategy to secure cross overs.

Within the economy, the enterprises in this GLC ecosystem function as producers of key under-soil and above-soil resources—such as oil and gas and palm oil respectively—while offering a range of services, including private education and health services. This influential ecosystem cannot, however, be assessed independent of its economic and political contexts. Moreover, the sphere of influence of government institutions, particularly those that function as foundations, covers activities in religious domains.[125]

This catch-all 'umbrella system' has a dual method of corporate organization that can be directed by minsters. A well-structured and deeply centralized system is in place at Levels 1, 2, and 3, comprising the ministries, GLICs, statutory bodies, and quoted companies that are subjected to public scrutiny. At the bottom, however, is an extremely decentralized system that encompasses a colossal collection of subsidiaries, associate companies, and joint ventures, controlled by institutions at Levels 2 and 3. The companies at Levels 4 and 5, in turn, own a range of firms, with more levels of enterprises operating domestically and abroad far from the public eye.

The best example of an exposé involving levels of companies in this GLC ecosystem that functioned domestically and abroad, was 1MDB, a company that operated at Level 4, with a wide range of links to companies at Level 5. In this controversy, one analyst noted how 1MDB, then an unknown, unlisted GLC controlled by the MoF, was 'mired in RM42-46 billion of debt and a maze of dubious deals which resulted in at least US$7 billion (RM28 billion) being unaccounted for […and] as much as RM40 billion had been put at risk or lost through […]

---

[125] One federal-level institution, controlled by the PMD, is the Majlis Agama Islam Wilayah Persekutuan (MAIWP). A prominent state-level statutory body is the Penang Hindu Endowments Board.

theft, bond mispricing and overpayment for assets amongst others.'[126] The volume of wastage and extent of abuse of public institutions in this scandal was staggering. The exposé in the 1MDB fiasco provides some idea of the huge volume of funds sloshing around in this GLC ecosystem.

The scale—and scope—of the GLC ecosystem at Level 4 and below is unknown. What's more, there is inadequate knowledge of the volume of inter-organization relations between enterprises under the jurisdiction of different ministries, though it appears that there is little or no coordination between them. What is evident at Level 4 and below is a largely covert, unregulated, shadow economy, ultimately controlled by different federal ministers. It is at Level 4 and below that huge wastage of public resources and extensive patronage occur, all off-budget. A close nexus has been created between the political machinery of parties in power and the multitude of companies at the lower levels of this ecosystem. Through these unlisted companies, party leaders can offer their members and supporters jobs and public contracts, a crucial method to retain support during party, general, and state elections. Stacking the lower levels of the GLC ecosystem with partisan supporters is extremely wasteful, but dispensing patronage in this manner appears to have become a norm practised by politicians holding power in federal and state governments.[127]

Corporate control by ministers can also be exercised in the form of authority. Every ministry with a GLC ecosystem has a pyramid structure of subsidiaries denoting a fusion of

---

[126] Gunasegaram and KINIBIZ. 2018: 3.

[127] The GLC ecosystems in these state governments invest considerable economic power in the office their chief ministers. A study of similar state–business infrastructures, created by state governments in the Malaysian federation, was done in: Edmund Terence Gomez, Fikri Fisal, Thirshalar Padmanabhan, and Juwairiah Tajuddin. 2018. *Government in Business: Diverse Forms of Intervention*. Kuala Lumpur: Institute for Democracy and Economic Affairs (IDEAS).

government and corporate control under the authority of a powerful minister, a system that can lead to the furtive exchange of public resources. The authority vested in ministers can lead to misgovernance, resulting in different forms of corruption, such as personal enrichment and the practice of cronyism, collusion, and predation. The four vast government–business networks in Figure 2.2 further reveal the possible ways through which a torrent of undocumented cash can enter the political system.

Control Tool 3: Regulatory Institutions Under Politicians

Alarmingly, no public agency is responsible for determining how these deeply interlocked government-controlled institutions should function. Any public commission is also not responsible for assessing the collective performance of these enterprises, despite their enormous economic influence and the numerous corruption cases linked to them.[128] This serious public governance flaw prevails even though the government has acknowledged that it is unaware how many business-based institutions exist in this GLC ecosystem, particularly the total number of unlisted companies.

If one reason for systemic corruption is shoddy public governance, the response should comprise institutional reforms that create appropriate regulations and oversight institutions. However, a core factor contributing to flawed public governance is institutional capture by the executive arm of government and the ability of governing politicians to prevent enforcement of the law. As Figure 2.3 indicates, there is a clear absence of autonomous oversight institutions.

---

[128] In countries that have state-owned enterprises (SOEs), a lead agency normally monitors their activities. Indonesia, for example, has a Ministry of State-Owned Enterprises. In China, oversight of its numerous SOEs is through the State-Owned Assets Supervision and Administration Commission of the State Council (SASAC). For an assessment of institutions overseeing SOEs in Asian countries, see Edimon Ginting and Kaukab Naqvi (eds). 2020. *Reforms, Opportunities, and Challenges for State-Owned Enterprises*. Manila: Asian Development Bank.

Grand Corruption and the Political–GLC Complex 67

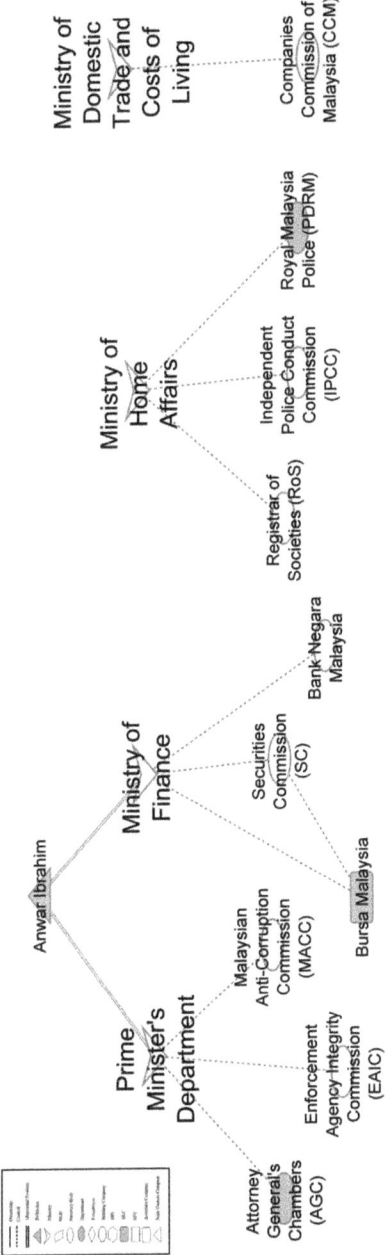

Figure 2.3: Executive control over regulatory institutions

Figure 2.3 further indicates why the issue of selective prosecution has been persistently raised. The prime minister has control of the Attorney General's Chambers (AGC) and the MACC while the finance minister oversees the Securities Commission (SC), Bursa Malaysia (the stock exchange), and Bank Negara, the central bank. The prime minister concurrently occupies the post of minister of finance, giving him enormous influence over these regulatory and oversight institutions. Although Anwar, as opposition leader, had been a strident critic of the prime minister controlling the treasury, he reintroduced this practice that had been stopped after the 2018 general election when UMNO lost power.

The Companies Commission of Malaysia (CCM), the other important oversight institution that monitors companies in the GLC ecosystem, is under the jurisdiction of the minister of domestic trade and cost of living. However, it is unlikely that the CCM closely monitors these GLCs given that there are about 1.2 million active companies in Malaysia.

Figures 2.2 and 2.3 indicate that the cabinet collectively has policy planning and implementation, GLC ownership and control, regulatory oversight, and budget expenditure under its direct charge, a combination that can facilitate corruption. This regulatory structure does not help curb opportunism by political elites, as the government can interfere, at will, in policy implementation, even if it leads to serious conflicts-of-interest, while ensuring that such misconduct is not dealt with when exposed.

Control Tool 4: GLC Directorships

In the business networks of the ministries, politicians, bureaucrats, and business professionals do not operate in isolation; they are inter-connected in a tightly-knit group. When directors of public institutions and GLCs share a common bond with a person at the apex of the pyramid, this governing politician can secure decisions that serve his interests or that of his party or the ruling coalition. Political control over directors can contribute to internal misgovernance of the enterprises in this pyramid. Such misgovernance can occur if these directors do not abide by their fiduciary duties, with an emphasis on full disclosure of decisions taken. Their decisions as directors should not impair public interests because they act as intermediaries between the government and the management, working with the latter to set strategies and implement them.[129] As directors of enterprises under the government's jurisdiction, they must be seen as public trustees and scrutinized greatly.

However, whether politically-connected directors abide by their fiduciary duties is in constant question because numerous corruption allegations implicate public institutions. Since directors are political appointees, they may be ill-equipped to fulfil their duties, with scant knowledge of the sector of the enterprise. This weakens their ability to recommend appropriate plans, thus undermining the management and operations of these enterprises while condoning or overlooking corrupt practices, a situation that contributes to normalizing such practices.

In this pyramid, comprising governing politicians at Level 1 and directors at Levels 2 (public institutions), 3 (quoted GLCs), 4 and 5 (unlisted GLCs, associate companies, and joint ventures), an important distinction needs to made between 'decision-making control' and 'operational control'. Decision-making control ultimately lies with political elites at Level 1, the members of the cabinet, though power is further concentrated with the office of the prime minister. Operational control, entailing day-to-day management, rests with the directors of the public institutions in Level 2 and companies in Levels 3, 4, and 5.

Since GLC directorships are politically-dictated, a common practice is for these directors to sanction the distribution of the

---

[129] OECD. 2013. *Boards of Directors of State-Owned Enterprises: An Overview of National Practices*. Paris: OECD Publishing.

resources of these enterprises to grassroots party members as a method to cultivate political support. GLCs have, inevitably, become sites of political struggles between elites attempting to consolidate federal and state power. This non-transparent selection of directors who are paid a huge stipend also serves as a method through which large amounts of public funds flow into the political system.

The importance of directorships in statutory bodies was made patently clear when Muhyiddin was controversially appointed prime minister in 2020 and sought to consolidate power in an extremely fragmented political system. Muhyiddin propped up his fragile government by unambiguously offering MPs directorships in major statutory bodies and the companies they controlled (see Table 2.2).[130] Additionally, Muhyiddin's allies were given control over key ministries, specifically MoF and MRRD, which control public institutions that could be deployed to muster electoral support in strategic constituencies, particularly in rural areas.

---

[130] *The Malaysian Reserve* (20 October 2020): https://themalaysianreserve.com/2020/10/20/glc-appointments-continue-apace-amid-power-tussle/

Table 2.2: Politicians appointed as GLC directors by Muhyiddin

No.	Name	Party	Institutions	Position
1.	Muhyiddin Yassin	Bersatu	Khazanah Nasional	Chairman
2.	Tengku Zafrul Aziz	UMNO	Khazanah Nasional	Board member
3.	Nelson Renganathan	BN-MIC	HRD Corp	Chairman
4.	Ruhaidini Abd Kadir	BN-UMNO	HRD Corp	Deputy chairman
5.	Mahdzir Khalid	BN-UMNO	TNB	Chairman
6.	Ahmad Fadhil Shaari	PAS	PTPK	Chairman
7.	Nik Mohamed Abduh Nik Abdul Aziz	PAS	KESEDAR	Chairman
8.	Nik Muhammad Zawawi Salleh	PAS	LPP	Chairman
9.	Ahmad Jazlan Yaakub	BN-UMNO	MPOB	Chairman
10.	Idris Jusoh	BN-UMNO	FELDA	Chairman
11.	Wan Hassan Mohd Ramli	PAS	SPAN	Chairman
12.	Che Alias Hamid	PAS	LPKMN	Chairman
13.	Ahmad Nazlan Idris	BN-UMNO	LGM	Chairman
14.	Mohd Salim Shariff	BN-UMNO	RISDA	Chairman

No.	Name	Party	Institutions	Position
15.	Yusuf Abd Wahab	GPS-PBB	CIDB	Chairman
16.	Wilson Ugak Kumbong	GPS-PRS	NIOSH	Chairman
17.	Lukanisman Awang Sauni	GPS-PBB	SEDA	Chairman
18.	Mohamad Alamin	BN-UMNO	MyIPO	Chairman
19.	Hajah Azizah Mohd Dun	Bersatu	MARA	Chairman
20.	Robert Lawson Chuat	GPS-PBB	BPA	Chairman
21.	Mohd Fasiah Mohd Fakeh	Bersatu	FAMA	Chairman
22.	Che Zakaria Mohd Salleh	Bersatu	KEJORA	Chairman
23.	Koh Chin Han	BN-MCA	MPA	Chairman
24.	Chong Sin Woon	BN-MCA	PKA	Chairman
25.	Tan Teik Cheng	BN-MCA	PPC	Chairman
26.	Razali Idris	Bersatu	KETENGAH	Chairman
27.	Khaled Nordin	BN-UMNO	Boustead	Chairman
28.	Ramli Mohd Nor	BN-UMNO	Amanahraya	Chairman
29.	Jalaluddin Alias	BN-UMNO	UDA Holdings	Chairman
30.	Ku Abdul Rahman	Bersatu	KEDA	Chairman
31.	Shabudin Yahaya	Bersatu	FELCRA	Chairman

No.	Name	Party	Institutions	Position
32.	Ahmad Johnie Zawawi	GPS-PBB	IWK	Chairman
33.	Anyi Ngau	GPS-PDP	MCB	Chairman
34.	Azman Ibrahim	PAS	LKTN	Chairman
35.	Osman Sapian	Bersatu	MPOC	Chairman
36.	Md Alwi Che Ahmad	BN-UMNO	MARA	Board member
37.	Mukhtar Suhaili	PAS	MPOCC	Chairman
38.	Kamaruzaman Muhammad	PAS	MTCC	Chairman
39.	Hasbullah Osman	BN-UMNO	SPNB	Board member
40.	Tajuddin Abdul Rahman	BN-UMNO	Prasarana Malaysia Bhd	Chairman
41.	Rais Hussin	Bersatu	MDEC	Chairman
42.	Noh Omar	BN-UMNO	PUNB	Chairman
43.	Kamarudin Md Noor	Bersatu	KEDA	Chairman
44.	Zakaria Mohd Edris	Bersatu	PNS	Chairman
45.	Yamani Hafez Musa	Bersatu	FELCRA	Chairman
46.	Mohamad Husain	PAS	FELCRA	Board member
47.	Mohd. Nizar Zakaria	BN-UMNO	LPPKN	Chairman
48.	Shaharizukirnain Abd Kadir	PAS	TEKUN	Chairman

No.	Name	Party	Institutions	Position
49.	Ahmad Tarmizi	PAS	MADA	Chairman
50.	Sabri Azit	PAS	ITMB	Chairman
51.	Syed Abu Hussin Hafiz	Bersatu	LKIM	Chairman
52.	Jugah Muyang	Independent (but Pro-Bersatu-PAS coalition)	MTIB	Chairman
53.	Mikai Mandau	GPS-PBB	TEKUN	Board member
54.	Fairuz Mohd Yatim	Bersatu	TEKUN	Board member
55.	Mizma Appehdullah	Bersatu	TEKUN	Board member
56.	Pirdaus Ismail	BN-UMNO	TEKUN	Board member
57.	Zambry Abdul Kadir	BN-UMNO	MAHB	Chairman
58.	Tuan Mohd Saripudin Tuan Ismail	PAS	KADA	Board member
59.	Ab Aziz Derashid	PAS	KADA	Board member

Politicians seek GLC-based directorships, as they can shape implementation of policies that favour their prospects of staying in power while availing substantial funds for their political activities, if not enriching themselves and channelling projects to those who have funded their electoral campaigns. GLC directors have decision-making control over where to invest, the selection of joint venture partners, who to channel subcontracts to, and the hiring of personnel who are usually members of their own political parties.

Based on the evidence presented during court cases against politicians who served in cabinet, different institutions in the GLC ecosystem used to support political patronage serve as a source of ready cash and help fulfil campaign promises. This is particularly true in rural areas, which constitute a majority of the parliamentary seats in Malaysia's acutely gerrymandered and malapportioned electoral system. For this reason, after the 2022 general election, which resulted in an unprecedented hung parliament, when Anwar took office as prime minister and leader of a coalition containing strange bedfellows, this practice of appointing politicians as directors of public institutions continued unabated, with a focus on statutory bodies located in rural areas (see Table 2.3). The directors of these statutory bodies were politicians from the Malay-based parties, such as UMNO and Parti Amanah Negara (Amanah, or National Trust Party). One year after Anwar came to power, it was reported that nineteen MPs and forty-two 'other politicians' were given directorial appointments in a variety of government-controlled institutions.[131]

A fundamental point that emerges in Tables 2.2 and 2.3 is that the MPs given directorships in public institutions serve as chairpersons. As chairpersons, these politicians have enormous influence over managerial decisions while taking instructions

---

[131] *Malaysiakini* (23 November 2023): https://www.malaysiakini.com/news/687525

Table 2.3: Politicians appointed as GLC directors by Anwar

No.	Name	Party	Institutions	Position
1.	Asyraf Wajdi Dusuki	UMNO	MARA	Chairman
2.	Ahmad Jazlan Yaakob	UMNO	FELCRA	Chairman
3.	Muhammad Bakhtiar Wan Chik	PKR	MYCreative Ventures	Chairman
4.	Reezal Merican Naina Merican	UMNO	MATRADE	Chairman
5.	Larry Sng	PBM	MTIB	Chairman
6.	Abdul Azeez	UMNO	KEDA	Chairman
7.	Syed Ibrahim Syed Noh	PKR	MDeC	Chairman
8.	Muhammad Husain	Amanah	KADA	Chairman
9.	Faiz Fadzil	Amanah	LKIM	Chairman
10.	Mahfuz Omar	Amanah	LPP	Chairman
11.	Aminuddin Zulkipli	Amanah	FAMA	Chairman
12.	Husam Musa	Amanah	SPNB	Chairman
13.	Wong Chen	PKR	MDV	Chairman
14.	Fauzi Abdul Rahman	PKR	MYHSR CORP	Chairman
15.	Ahmad Shabery Cheek	UMNO	FELDA	Chairman
16.	Noraini Ahmad	UMNO	RISDA	Chairwoman
17.	Charles Santiago	DAP	SPAN	Chairman

from the cabinet minister in charge of the institution they serve. As for other politicians serving as directors, it appeared that they had merely been rewarded for their support, with little to do except endorse decisions taken by the chairperson.

Control Tool 5: Ownership and Control of Banks

Another vital tool available to politicians is their control over finance-related institutions, specifically publicly-listed GLC-type banks and development financial institutions (DFIs). Control over financial institutions is crucial, as they facilitate the implementation of contracts awarded through political patronage. Executive capture of the banking sector occurred following an epochal government-directed bank consolidation exercise in 1999. This forced merger exercise undermined property rights and reduced the number of financial institutions from fifty-two to a mere ten anchor banks, most of which came under government control.[132] Although these financial institutions were owned by leading corporate figures in control of conglomerates, which conferred market power on them, they could not stand up to a government controlled by political elites seeking control of this important sector.

By 2021, there were only nine domestic banks, with ownership concentrated in the GLICs (see Figure 2.4). Malayan Banking (Maybank), the largest bank in terms of market capitalization, is controlled by PNB, while CIMB, the second largest, is owned by Khazanah Nasional. Bank Islam is controlled by Tabung Haji. Lembaga Tabung Angkatan Tentera (LTAT), the armed forces' pension fund, owns Affin Bank, the smallest bank by market capitalization.

---

[132] For an in-depth account of this controversial corporate exercise, see Edmund Terence Gomez. 2005. The State, Governance and Corruption in Malaysia. In Nicholas Tarling (ed.), *Corruption and Good Governance in Asia*, London: Routledge: 214–244.

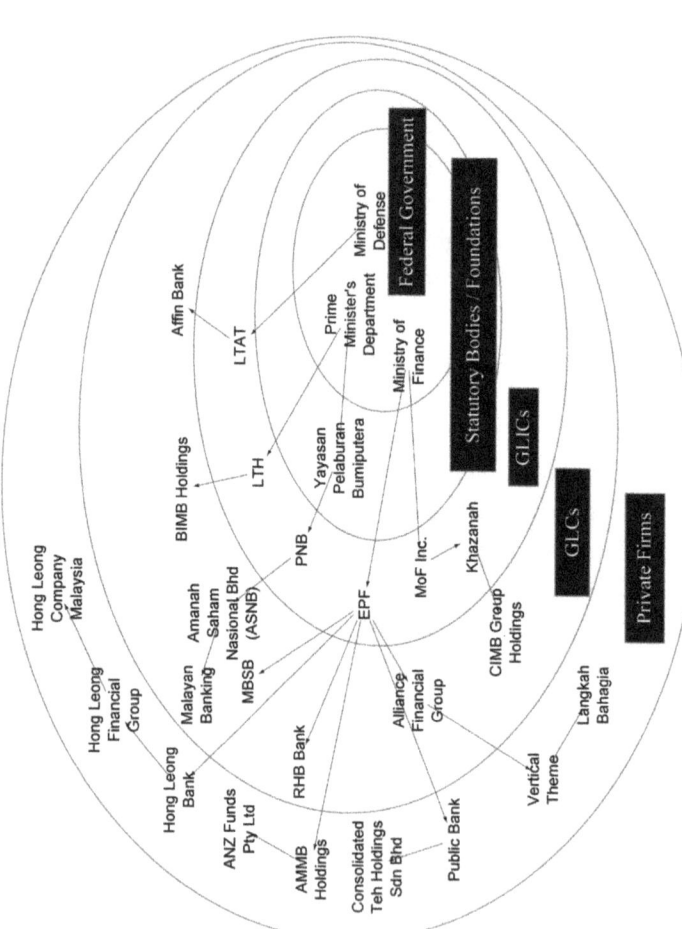

Figure 2.4: Control over the banking sector

A similar consolidation exercise, this time involving the DFIs, occurred in October 2021 when Bank Pembangunan was merged with the credit enhancement firm Danajamin Nasional. Later, the *Financial Sector Blueprint 2022* proposed that the Small Medium Enterprise Development Bank (SME Bank) and Export-Import Bank (Exim Bank) also should be merged with Bank Pembangunan.[133]

Political control over the capital market is now extensive, given this ownership structure of the financial sector. The GLICs, ultimately under MoF's jurisdiction, have majority ownership of the bank-based GLCs, giving the minister of finance significant influence over this sector. This minister also has regulatory control over this sector, as he has jurisdiction over Bank Negara and the Securities Commission (see Figure 2.3).

---

[133] *The Malaysian Reserve* (1 October 2021): https://themalaysianreserve.com/2021/10/01/bpmb-danajamin-the-1st-dfis-to-merge/

Chapter 3

Case Studies

The way the Political–GLC complex, with its range of control tools, has contributed to the emergence of systemic corruption can be better seen through a series of case studies dealing with the abuse of public policies, the procurement system, and statutory bodies. The case studies focus on assessing two major controversies: the manner of implementation of the Jana Wibawa policy and the award of procurement contracts through the Littoral Combat Ship (LCS) project. The third case study assesses allegations of criminal abuse of two major statutory bodies, the Federal Land Consolidation and Rehabilitation Authority (FELCRA) and the Majlis Amanah Rakyat (MARA).[134]

Each case study draws attention to different methods of corruption. Specifically, it focuses on corruption involving a secret exchange of formally allocated contracts (seen in the Jana Wibawa controversy); a situation where multiple business-based institutions, under the control of one GLIC, abuse publicly-generated

---

[134] Among the other statutory bodies that have been mired in business-related controversies are FELDA and Tabung Haji, which also functions as a GLIC. For a review of the controversies involving FELDA, see: Center to Combat Corruption and Cronyism. 2018. *The FELDA Crisis*. Petaling Jaya: Center to Combat Corruption and Cronyism: https://c4center.org/wp-content/uploads/Felda-Crisis-Booklet-BI-WEB.pdf. For a discussion on the history of Tabung Haji and controversies related to it, see Gomez. 2017: 31–33.

concessions contributing to a serious corporate debt crisis and the violation of the interests of minority shareholders and pensioners (seen in the LCS project); and a context where public funds are used to buy resources in domestic and foreign markets at an inflated price (as evident in the studies of FELCRA and MARA).

Each case study highlights the role of business-based institutions situated at Levels 2 to 5. In the controversies involving Jana Wibawa, LCS, and FELCRA, ministers holding different but key portfolios—prime minister, finance minister, and defence minister—(at Level 1) were implicated. In all four instances, these controversies implicated institutions at Level 2 and unlisted companies, both domestic and foreign, at Levels 4 and 5. The LCS controversy also implicated publicly-listed institutions at Level 2, including a GLC bank.

Case Study 1: Policy Creation and Power Abuse— Jana Wibawa

In November 2020, about eight months after the Covid-19 pandemic led to a lockdown of the economy in Malaysia, the government introduced the Program Jana Ekonomi Pemerkasaan Kontraktor Bumiputera Berwibawa, popularly known as Jana Wibawa. This policy was then Prime Minister Muhyiddin Yassin's response to this unprecedented global health crisis that had alarming socio-economic ramifications. Jana Wibawa constituted an endeavour to support Bumiputera-owned SMEs through the award of fifty-six projects with a total value of RM6.3 billion.[135]

---

[135] For a report on the history of the Jana Wibawa project, see *Free Malaysia Today* (26 February 2023): https://www.freemalaysiatoday.com/category/nation/2023/02/26/jana-wibawa-controversy-the-story-so-far. Jana Wibawa was reportedly also a continuation of the 'Program Pembangunan Kontraktor Binaan Bumiputera Berwibawa' introduced in 1993 as part of the government's attempt to nurture Bumiputera contractors. See also: *The Rakyat Post* (22 February 2023):

This policy concurrently aimed to accelerate economic recovery through the implementation of these projects.

Following a general election in November 2022, when a new government led by Anwar Ibrahim was formed, implementation of this policy was put on hold. Rural development projects amounting to RM5.7 billion were then still to be implemented. Subsequently, Muhyiddin was charged with four counts of power abuse and three counts of money laundering.[136] After these charges were made against Muhyiddin, he stressed that he had been accused of abuse of power, not for accepting bribes, 'because after an investigation, it was found that not a single sen of the rakyat's (people's) money went into my own pocket during my tenure as the PM (Prime Minister).'[137] Muhyiddin also contended that 'the prosecution against me is a form of organised political persecution'.[138] Not long after, two members of Muhyiddin's party, Parti Pribumi Bersatu Malaysia (Bersatu), was also charged in court. Bersatu's then information chief, Wan Saiful Wan Jan,[139] and Adam Radlan Adam Muhammad, a division deputy head,[140] were accused of money laundering and receiving bribes.

---

https://www.therakyatpost.com/news/malaysia/2023/02/22/tldr-jana-wibawa-what-is-it-and-whats-all-this-corruption-controversy-around-it

[136] *Al Jazeera* (10 March 2023): https://www.aljazeera.com/news/2023/3/10/malaysias-ex-pm-muhyiddin-charged-with-abuse-of-power; *The Edge* (13 March 2023):
https://theedgemalaysia.com/node/658801

[137] *The Edge* (10 March 2023): https://theedgemalaysia.com/node/658579

[138] Ibid.

[139] *The Malaysian Reserve* (21 February 2023): https://themalaysianreserve.com/2023/02/21/jana-wibawa-project-wan-saiful-charged-with-receiving-rm6-9m-bribe/; *New Straits Times* (25 October 2023): https://www.nst.com.my/news/crime-courts/2023/10/971131/wan-saiful-claims-trial-18-charges-money-laundering

[140] *The Edge* (22 February 2023): https://theedgemalaysia.com/node/656261
Adam Radlan, a businessman-cum-politician, was then serving as deputy chief of Bersatu's Segambut division, located in Kuala Lumpur.

When the Jana Wibawa controversy broke, there were intriguing comments about the implementation of this policy. The first, a series of quotes by Mohamed Fadzill Hassan, the president of the Malaysian Malay Contractors Association, published by the *New Straits Times* on 19 February 2023, drew attention to how ethnic patronage had been implemented while also providing insights into the governance system that dealt with the award of publicly-generated projects. Mohamed Fadzill was quoted in the *New Straits Times* as stating: 'We are not jealous of those who got the Jana Wibawa project, but the awarding of the project needs to be fair in terms of selection based on their ability, experience and professionalism. Not (just) anyone who is good with the prime minister or the minister who awarded the project.'[141] Mohamed Fadzill added that '(w)e also want action to be taken not only on the contractor companies involved in Jana Wibawa, but also government officials either in the Finance Ministry, Public Works Department (PWD) and the Department of Irrigation & Drainage (DID) who are involved in the contractor selection process.'[142] The *New Straits Times* went on to report that Mohamed Fadzill had revealed that the Jana Wibawa projects were awarded through 'direct negotiations', that 'the tender which is selected is an "open secret" known to Malay and Bumiputera contractors', and that Muhyiddin's successor as prime minister, Ismail Sabri Yaakob, had received a complaint about these issues and had given a 'commitment to investigate this matter'.[143] There is little evidence that Ismail acted on this allegation of corruption. Indeed, Ismail cut a dismal figure as a prime minister intent on eradicating corruption, probably because he belonged to UMNO, a party whose leaders were mired in numerous controversies.

---

[141] *New Straits Times* (19 February 2023): https://www.nst.com.my/news/nation/2023/02/881444/jana-wibawa-direct-nego-open-secret

[142] Ibid.

[143] Ibid.

Strict bureaucratic procedures were in place for the procurement processes of the award of Jana Wibawa projects. To qualify for the award of these projects, the applicant had to be registered with the government as a (G7) contractor, with the requisite financing facilities, as well as the technical ability and experience to implement the project.[144] The comments by Mohamed Fadzill suggest that these bureaucratic procedures were overlooked, or bypassed, when the projects were awarded.

The second set of important statements about Jana Wibawa came from Muhyiddin, with reference to the award process. Muhyiddin reportedly stated that he 'had no knowledge of the companies involved and only submitted the list of the companies given by the Bumiputra Wholesalers' Association to the Finance Ministry'.[145] Muhyiddin further stated that the 'Jana Wibawa project was Finance Ministry's idea, and it was headed by Tengku Zafrul [Aziz] to help affected Bumiputera contractors during the pandemic and I agreed to it.'[146] Muhyiddin made two more points. First, the '[r]ules for the programme were set by the Finance Minister to consider and evaluate whether the applicants were eligible or not. I was not involved in the process of reviewing or approving, as it was under Zafrul's ministry.'[147] Second, he stated that 'I only executed the decision of the cabinet, which required the Prime Minister's Office (PMO) to forward the request for

---

[144] *The Rakyat Post* (22 February 2023): https://www.therakyatpost.com/news/malaysia/2023/02/22/tldr-jana-wibawa-what-is-it-and-whats-all-this-corruption-controversy-around-it/

[145] *Sinar Daily* (18 February 2013): https://www.sinardaily.my/article/190488/malaysia/national/allegations-on-jana-wibawa-should-be-directed-to-zafrul-not-me---muhyiddin

[146] Ibid.

[147] Ibid.

projects to be considered by MoF in accordance with the rules and regulations in place.'[148]

While Muhyiddin was charged in court with a variety of offences following an investigation by the MACC, Zafrul was not, though he was interrogated as a witness. Muhyiddin's response to these charges were noteworthy. He stated that '(i)t is not fair! It was not my call on which companies were chosen for the project. It was the decision of the then Finance Minister,'[149] and that 'the prosecution against me is a form of organised political persecution.'[150]

Subsequently, Muhyiddin filed an application to quash four charges under the MACC Act relating to abuse of power. On this application, the high court judge ruled that he 'found that Muhyiddin was accused of an offence that was not provided for under the law. The four charges were flawed because they did not disclose any offence under Section 23(1) of the MACC Act, which is an injustice. The four charges also did not contain the details of how the offences were committed, as provided under Section 154 of the Criminal Procedure Code.'[151] This section of the MACC Act deals with the abuse of office or position by a public officer for 'any gratification, whether for himself, his relative or associate'. However, on appeal by the prosecution, a three-member Court of Appeal overturned this decision. These

---

[148] *The Edge Markets* (10 March 2023): https://ceomorningbrief.theedgemalaysia.com/article/2023/0536/Home/4/658541

[149] These quotes by Muhyiddin were obtained from this report by *Sinar Daily* (18 February 2023): https://www.sinardaily.my/article/190488/malaysia/national/allegations-on-jana-wibawa-should-be-directed-to-zafrul-not-me---muhyiddin

[150] *The Edge* (10 March 2023): https://theedgemalaysia.com/node/658579; *Malay Mail* (10 March 2023): https://www.malaymail.com/news/malaysia/2023/03/10/muhyiddin-claims-trial-to-two-charges-of-allegedly-laundering-rm195m-for-bersatu/58889

[151] *Astro Awani* (15 August 2023): https://www.astroawani.com/berita-malaysia/high-court-freed-muhyiddin-four-power-abuse-charges-432908

three judges unanimously decided that the 'High Court had erred in law when it ruled the charges were defective.'[152]

These series of quotes by Mohamed Fadzill and Muhyiddin, as well as the differing views about the four charges by the judges, draw attention to three key issues. First, they provide insights into how the system works (at Level 1); second, they indicate differing views with existing legislation that deal with abuse of power. Third, even genuine Bumiputera businesspeople running SMEs were not privy to these rents created by the government to help them during an economic crisis. These quotes, along with Muhyiddin's assertion about abiding by decision-making processes during the implementation of policies targeting Bumiputera-owned SMEs, specifically unlisted companies (operating at Levels 4 and 5), merit further attention as they deal with serious flaws in the award of projects.

Figure 3.1 charts how this system works based on the charges made in court. The creation of policies and the award of projects happen through the office of the minister of finance, who has to decide on how they are to be funded. At Level 1, how the commonly-held practice of selective patronage can be executed during the award of contracts to obscure companies at Level 4 is evident. Figure 3.1 further indicates how the system can be abused, specifically the nexus between direct negotiation for contracts and political funding, with money being channelled into the bank account of the party in power. The central business figures mentioned in the Jana Wibawa controversy are different—from Syed Mokhtar Syed Albukhary, the prominent well-connected business tycoon,[153] to Teo Wee Cheng, the relatively unknown

---

[152] *The Star* (28 February 2024): https://www.thestar.com.my/news/nation/2024/02/28/court-of-appeal-reinstates-muhyiddin039s-criminal-case-involving-rm232mil#:~:text=PUTRAJAYA%3A%20The%20Court%20of%20Appeal,down%20by%20the%20High%20Court

[153] Syed Mokhtar is among Malaysia's most prominent Bumiputera corporate figures. According to one tabulation, the value of his total corporate assets in

owner of a Johor-based publicly-listed furniture manufacturer, and the extremely obscure Lian Tan Chuan[154] and Azman Yusoff.[155] All four were mentioned when charges were made in court against these politicians.

Teo Wee Cheng was subsequently charged with two counts of soliciting bribes worth RM11.3 million and seven counts of receiving bribes amounting to RM1.5 million related to Jana Wibawa projects situated in Muhyiddin's home state of Johor.[156] According to one foreign report, Teo 'was previously named a "close friend" of the former premier (Muhyiddin) by one of the witnesses in Umno chief Zahid Hamidi's graft trial in 2022'.[157]

2023 was US$1.5 billion, with control of leading publicly-listed enterprises, including DRB-HICOM and MMC Corporation. See: *Forbes*: https://www.forbes.com/profile/syed-mokhtar-albukhary/?sh=2e5c9e4418ee

[154] Although an extensive search was done to obtain a profile of Lian Tan Chuan, no information was found about him.

[155] A search indicates that Azman Yusoff is the president of the Persatuan Kontraktor Bumiputera Malaysia (PKBM) (or the Bumiputera Contractors Association of Malaysia), which was established on 31 December 2018 (see: *PKMB*: https://www.pkbm.my/). This association is different from the Malaysian Malay Contractors Association led by Mohamed Fadzill Hassan. Azman is also a director of the Construction Industry Development Board (CIDB), a statutory body (see: *CIDB*: https://www.cidb.gov.my/eng/board-of-directors/). Azman retains his directorship of a government body though he was implicated in the Jana Wibawa controversy. For a report on Azman Yusoff's link to the Jana Wibawa project, see *The Vibes* (20 February 2023): https://www.thevibes.com/articles/news/85759/jana-wibawa-probe-macc-quizzes-tengku-zafrul-wan-saiful

[156] *The Edge* (22 February 2023): https://theedgemalaysia.com/node/656279; *New Straits Times* (22 February 2023): https://www.nst.com.my/news/crime-courts/2023/02/882567/jana-wibawa-project-company-director-charged-soliciting-receiving

[157] As reported in the Singapore-based *The Straits Times* (22 February 2023): https://www.straitstimes.com/asia/se-asia/more-graft-charges-issued-against-men-linked-to-ex-pm-muhyiddin

Case Studies 89

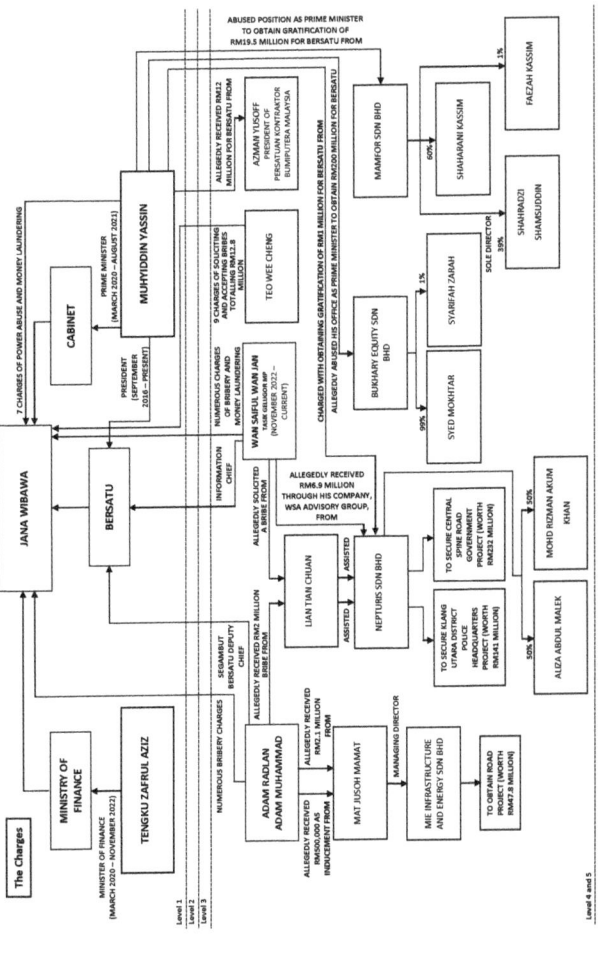

Figure 3.1: Charting the award of Jana Wibawa projects[158]

---

[158] This figure provides only a partial list of the charges against politicians and businessmen mentioned in this controversy. The information in this figure was obtained from the following sources: *The Malaysian Reserve* (21 February 2023): https://themalaysianreserve.com/2023/02/21/

A key point in these allegations is that the principal politicians implicated in the Jana Wibawa controversy are linked to Bersatu, the lead party in the then governing coalition. Bersatu had allegedly received funds from companies that had been awarded projects. The three politicians who were charged with accepting bribes, Muhyiddin, Wan Saiful, and Adam Radlan, held key positions in Bersatu at that point. In fact, when Muhyiddin was charged, the allegations against him were that he had abused his position as prime minister 'to obtain gratification[159] of RM200 million from Bukhary Equity and RM1 million from Nepturis', as well as 'RM19.5 million from Mamfor, and RM12 million from Azman Yusoff' for his party.[160] Muhyiddin confirmed that Syed Mokhtar had made a 'political donation that went straight into Bersatu's account',[161] which is not illegal in Malaysia, and he was not personally privy to these funds. Muhyiddin later claimed that the parties in Prime Minister Anwar's governing coalition had accepted donations from Syed Mokhtar 'for tens of years'. This raised the question why Bersatu was being probed for doing the same.[162]

Another issue in the court charges was that the recipients of the Jana Wibawa projects did not meet the criteria set by the

---

jana-wibawa-project-wan-saiful-charged-with-receiving-rm6-9m-bribe/; *The Edge* (10 March 2023): https://theedgemalaysia.com/node/658579; and *The Edge* (14 September 2023): https://theedgemalaysia.com/node/682525

[159] Table 1.1. provides a definition of the term 'gratification' under the MACC Act. An analysis of this term is provided in Appendix 2.

[160] *The Edge* (10 March 2023): https://theedgemalaysia.com/node/658579 This report also provides information of the shareholders of these three companies. As indicated in Figure 3.1, Bukhary Equity is an investment holding company owned by Syed Mokhtar and his wife Sharifah Zarah Syed Kechik. The two equal equity shareholders of Nepturis are Aliza Abdul Malek and Mohd Rizman Akum Khan. Mamfor's shareholders are Shaharani Kassim (60 per cent), Shahradzi Shamsuddin (39 per cent), and Faezah Kassim (1 per cent).

[161] *The Edge* (9 Mar 2023): https://theedgemalaysia.com/node/658541

[162] *The Edge Markets* (10 March 2023): https://ceomorningbrief.theedgemalaysia.com/article/2023/0536/Home/4/658541

government, suggesting that bureaucratic procedures had been violated, with decision-making left to private individuals. Moreover, the key people charged in court were not Bumiputeras. For example, Lian Tan Chuan, a core figure in this controversy, according to court charges, paid an RM2 million bribe to Adam Radlan to help a company, Nepturis, secure the North Klang District Police Headquarters Project, worth RM141 million, from the government (see Figure 3.1).[163] A related issue is the anonymity of people such as Lian and Azman Yusoff. There has been no public disclosure about Lian, despite his allegedly rather conspicuous role in the award of the Jana Wibawa projects. What these charges suggest is the relinquishing of government decisions to middlemen who have the power to determine who gets the contracts. Another noteworthy point is that, at the time when this case study was written, no charges were levelled in court against key business figures mentioned in the charges, such as Syed Mokhtar, Lian, and Azman.

Another contentious issue, one that had been reported on long before the Jana Wibawa controversy broke, is that of the family ties between Zafrul and Muhyiddin. This was noted when Muhyiddin, following his appointment as prime minister in 2020, appointed Zafrul as minister of finance.[164] At that time, Zafrul, who had developed a reputation as an investment banker, was not known to hold any political position, though he would subsequently disclose that he had long been a member of UMNO.

Figure 3.2 outlines the family ties between Muhyiddin and Zafrul. It indicates that Zafrul is related to Muhyiddin through Tengku Zuhri, his younger brother, who is married to Fara Nadia Abd Ibrahim, the younger sister of Muhyiddin's daughter-in-law Fara Ikma. More importantly, this mapping of the family ties of governing politicians draws attention to the key figures implicated in the Jana Wibawa controversy.

---

[163] *The Edge* (14 September 2023): https://theedgemalaysia.com/node/682525
[164] *Malaysiakini* (10 March 2020): https://www.malaysiakini.com/news/513968

92 Misgovernance

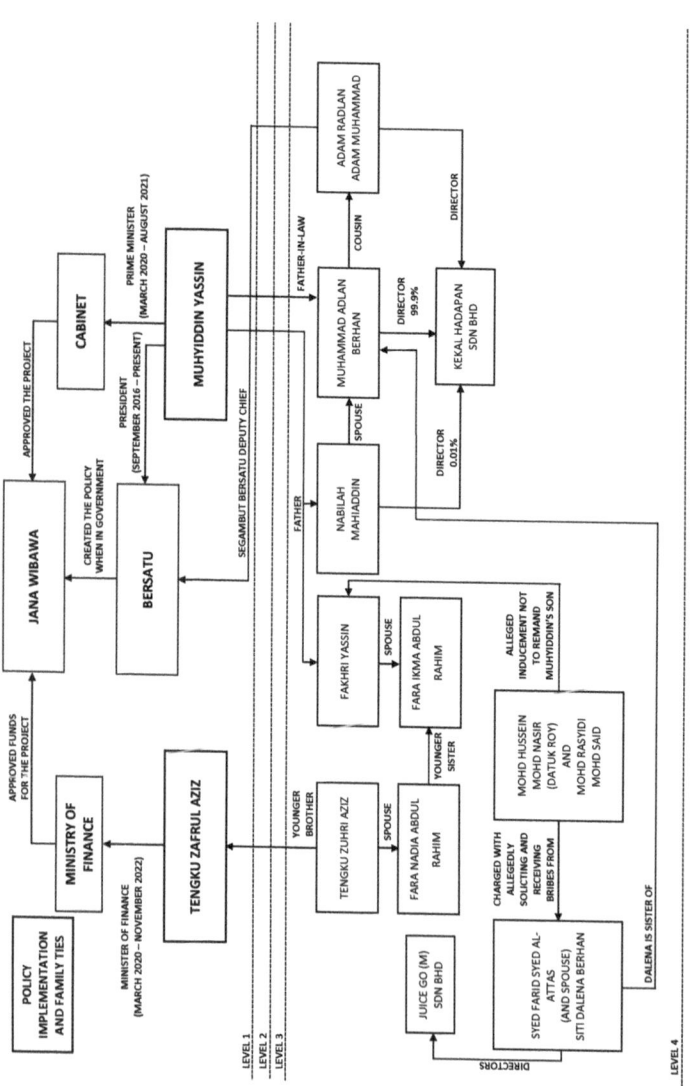

Figure 3.2: Mapping Muhyiddin–Zafrul family ties

Figure 3.2 indicates that a pivotal figure in the controversy is Dalena Berhan, the sister of Muhyiddin's son-in-law, Muhammad Adlan Berhan. Dalena and her partner, Syed Farid Syed Al-Attas, were charged with offering bribes to Mohd Hussein Mohd Nasir (known as Datuk Roy) and an MACC officer to not remand Muhyiddin's son, Fakhri Yassin, in relation to this case.[165] However, after extensive research of the corporate ties of Muhyiddin's children, no evidence of their ties to the implementation of the Jana Wibawa policy was uncovered. What was uncovered is that Muhyiddin's children hold positions as chairperson and shareholders of a large number of companies. It merits mention that in the Panama Papers, Fakhri Yassin was linked to two offshore enterprises incorporated in the British Virgin Islands.[166]

A reading of the court charges indicates that politicians in control of the procurement process created an intricate 'pay-to-get' system when awarding projects. Moreover, although these projects were meant for Bumiputera SMEs in need, the recipients were determined by obscure non-Bumiputera businessmen who appear to have had close ties with governing elites. The court charges indicate that politicians in control of the procurement process can shape how cash flows into the political system, channelling money to their parties or to themselves. The charges indicate that those responsible for promulgating a policy that entailed generating and distributing public projects also had discretionary allocation control, bypassing bureaucratic procedures. An outcome of allocation control being in the hands of cabinet members was

---

[165] *New Straits Times* (25 May 2023): https://www.nst.com.my/news/crime-courts/2023/05/913104/macc-senior-officer-datuk-roy-charged-over-bribes-linked-probe; *Malaysiakini* (25 May 2023): https://www.malaysiakini.com/news/666352

[166] *Malaysiakini* (13 May 2016): https://www.malaysiakini.com/news/341419

that those privy to these contracts had to, in turn, contribute a large volume of funds to the governing party. This act suggested serious conflict-of-interest and an abuse of government resources for personal gain.

If the charges against the politicians and businesspeople brought to court are proven valid, they will authenticate longstanding public apprehension of a well-entrenched system where governing elites and corporate figures exchange public contracts for money, which are used to finance electoral campaigns. If the charges against these politicians are proven, it would also indicate that the Jana Wibawa controversy is one about the excessive abuse of a much-required public policy to retain power.

Case Study 2: Sectoral Development and Corruption—Littoral Combat Ship (LCS)

The history of Malaysia's defence sector is riddled with a series of serious allegations of grand corruption. The first major defence controversy—the Pergau dam project—occurred in 1988 after then Prime Minister Mahathir Mohamad cultivated a close relationship with Britain's sitting Prime Minister Margaret Thatcher, an indefatigable advocate of the export of defence equipment by companies from her country. Given the close ties between these two prime ministers, Mahathir managed to secure a defence deal worth £1 billion in return for aid to finance the construction of the Pergau dam in Malaysia.[167]

---

[167] For an account of this controversial Pergau dam arms deal, see *The Guardian* (12 December 2012): https://www.theguardian.com/global-development/2012/dec/12/pergau-dam-affair-aid-arms-scandal
A detailed assessment of this affair was provided in: Tim Lankester. 2013. *The Politics and Economics of Britain's Foreign Aid: The Pergau Dam Affair*. Routledge: London.

Although Mahathir had been an ardent advocate of highly interventionist policies, he came to be profoundly inspired by the free market philosophy that Thatcher and Ronald Reagan, then president of the United States, had been zealously promoting in the early 1980s. Mahathir, who had long had a strong interest in business,[168] subsequently endorsed and actively employed the neoliberal ideas of these leaders. These ideas entailed advancing policies such as privatization, ostensibly to reduce government expenditure, and methods such as public–private partnerships (PPPs). Mahathir argued that privatization—and corporatization—of business-related public enterprises would enable them to function more efficiently as well as create a profit rather than focus only on their social obligations.

Privatization of public enterprises was also seen by Mahathir as a mechanism to speed up his policy endeavour to create conglomerates of global repute owned by Bumiputeras. In effect, there was an interventionist dimension to Mahathir's privatization policy. Thus began the drive to corporatize public enterprises that were subsequently partially-privatized—when they were listed on the stock exchange, leading to the rise of quoted GLCs—or projects and government assets that were routed to private hands through full privatization.

A major controversy subsequently emerged from this mixed policy agenda of privatizing projects to nurture Bumiputera capitalists. In 1995, Mahathir corporatized Limbungan TLDM, responsible for the maintenance of the fleet of the Royal Malaysian Navy (RMN), and then privatized it to Penang

---

[168] Before becoming prime minister, Mahathir authored a book entitled *Guide for Small Businessmen*. He also served as a director of a GLC, Kumpulan FIMA, owned by the government's holding company, Minister of Finance Inc., and incorporated in 1972 to venture into food processing. Mahathir held this directorship from 1972 until his appointment as prime minister. See: Gomez. 1990: 32-33.

Shipbuilding Corporation (PSC). Limbungan TLDM was renamed PSC-Naval Dockyard. PSC was then owned by Amin Shah Omar Shah, a UMNO member who was reportedly closely associated with then Finance Minister Daim Zainuddin.[169] In 1998, Amin Shah was awarded a RM5.4 billion contract to build six offshore patrol vessels (OPVs), a project he promptly subcontracted to a German enterprise. This project was the first consignment of a deal worth RM25 billion to build twenty-seven OPVs, then touted as the largest contract ever awarded by the Ministry of Defence (Mindef).[170] Amin Shah failed to fulfil his contractual obligations. With PSC on the brink of collapse, this debt-laden company, along with the OPV contract, was taken over in 2005 by Boustead Holdings in what was reported as a 'government enforced merger'.[171] The largest shareholder of Boustead Holdings, a highly diversified, publicly-listed GLC, was the Lembaga Tabung Angkatan Tentera (LTAT, or Armed Forces Savings Fund), a GLIC.[172] After this takeover, PSC Naval Dockyard was renamed Boustead Naval Shipyard Sdn Bhd (BNS).[173]

While the OPV contract was deeply mired in problems, another major navy-based controversy was brewing. In 2002, a year before the end of Mahathir's first administration, a French

---

[169] For a review of the links between Amin Shah and UMNO elites, see: Edmund Terence Gomez. 2002. Political Business in Malaysia. In Edmund Terence Gomez (ed.), *Political Business in East Asia*, London: Routledge: 82–140.

[170] *Asia Times* (25 August 2022): https://asiatimes.com/2022/08/najib-era-ship-scandal-resurfaces-to-sink-umno/

[171] *The Edge* (17 August 2022): https://theedgemalaysia.com/article/mindefs-weak-governance-led-lopsided-contract-and-lcs-woes-%E2%80%94-special-committee

[172] In 2023, LTAT had about 140,000 members on the pension roll, while 115,456 members were serving in the armed forces (*The Edge*, 9 October 2023): https://theedgemalaysia.com/node/685368

[173] Amin Shah was eventually declared bankrupt because he could not honour a personal loan of RM3.22 million that he had taken from Affin Bank also under the LTAT-Boustead group (*The Edge*, 19 October 2007).

enterprise, DCNS, renamed the Naval Group,[174] was contracted to build and deliver two Scorpene submarines, a project valued at €1.2 billion. In 2006, investigations into the murder of a young Mongolian translator, who was part of the negotiations for this deal, led to some shocking disclosures. An obscure company, Perimekar, controlled by close associates of then Defence Minister Najib Razak, had been paid €114 million in kickbacks during the negotiations for the Scorpene submarines.[175] As in the case of the OPV controversy, no one in the Malaysian government was held accountable for the transgressions in the Scorpene submarine deal.

This series of scandals since the late 1980s indicate that a structure was in place that allowed for the abuse of defence-based procurement projects. This structure involved sitting ministers, major GLICs, publicly-listed and privately-owned companies, foreign enterprises, and obscure firms. Figure 3.3 presents Mindefs complex business network. It indicates how the minister in charge of this ministry (at Level 1) has indirect control over numerous key institutions. These institutions include a GLIC-cum-statutory body-cum-pension fund (LTAT) (at Level 2) that functions as a conglomerate, with majority ownership of several publicly-listed GLCs—Boustead Holdings, Boustead Plantations, and Pharmaniaga—and a major financial institution, Affin Bank (at Level 3). This huge business group, in turn, has a multitude of unlisted companies and joint ventures (at Levels 4 and 5), facilitating the making of deals that escape the public eye, unless exposed by an unexpected event.

---

[174] DCNS, formerly known as Direction des Constructions Navales, was renamed the Naval Group in 2017. This enterprise had an international reputation in designing and constructing naval defence equipment.

[175] *Corruption Tracker* (12 November 2020): https://corruption-tracker.org/case/the-malaysian-scorpene-submarine-affair. It was during a court case in France that this issue of kickbacks in the Scorpene submarine deal was disclosed.

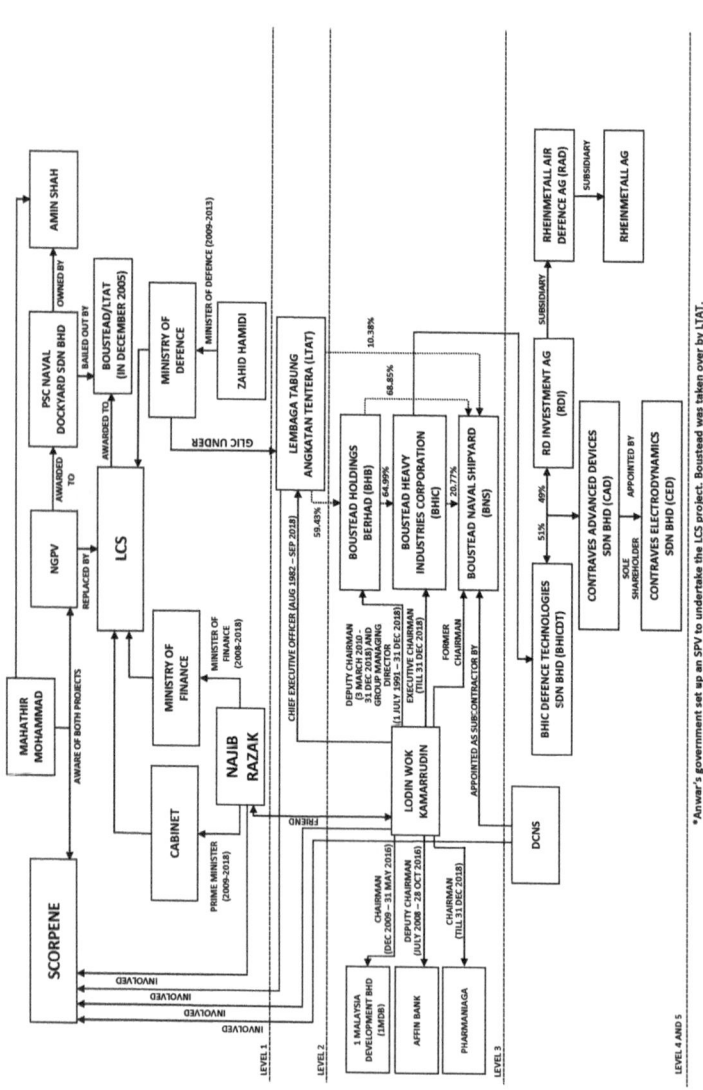

Figure 3.3: History of the LCS scandal

Figure 3.3 further indicates that, apart from Mindef, the two most important cabinet portfolios are the PMD and the MoF, both crucial ministries in the award of defence-related procurement projects. Moreover, when the Scorpene submarines controversy occurred, the posts of prime minister and minister of finance were held by the same person. A practice started by Mahathir in 2001, many critics argued it would give rise to conflicts-of-interest, which in fact happened. The controversies surrounding the OPV and submarine projects highlight insufficient oversight and ineffective checks and balances in decision-making for naval-based projects, a further indication of centralization of power in the cabinet. When the LCS controversy broke, it drew further attention to these public governance flaws.

The LCS controversy was directly linked to the LTAT-Boustead group's takeover of the privatized project awarded to Amin Shah. Following this takeover, BNS was deeply embedded (at Level 4) in the LTAT-Boustead group, as a subsidiary of Boustead Heavy Industries Corporation Sdn Bhd (BHIC). A year later, in 2007, a proposal was submitted to the Economic Planning Unit (EPU) in the PMD to build six combat ships. This proposal argued for the building of these ships, rather than acquiring them from abroad, to allow the government to continue with its long-running Vendor Development Programme (VDP). In the LCS proposal, it was projected that 2,000 Bumiputera companies would be incorporated into the project through product supply chains employed in the construction of these combat ships. BNS was evidently well aware of public policies, as the VDP had been introduced by Mahathir in the 1980s to nurture Bumiputera SMEs by integrating them into product supply networks controlled by publicly-listed GLCs and foreign enterprises. As for the LCS project, SMEs in the supply chain were expected to eventually be equipped with expertise in defence equipment manufacturing, allowing Malaysia to emerge as a regional hub in this sector.

It was, however, only four years later, in 2011, when Najib was prime minister and finance minister, that the LTAT-Boustead group was awarded, after direct negotiations with BNS, the project to build six combat ships at a cost of RM9.13 billion. The ships were to be delivered in stages, with the last handover in 2023.[176] The award of the LCS project to BNS served as a method for the LTAT-Boustead group to deal with the financial problems it had to incur as a consequence of the PSC bailout. This was disclosed by an LTAT executive who stated: 'BNS had the misfortune of inheriting hundreds of millions in liabilities from PSC-Naval Dockyard when Boustead took over the company in 2005. So, some of the money meant for LCS had to be used to pay off PSC's outstanding debt.'[177] Despite this, in a shockingly similar turn of events, a decade after BNS had secured the LCS contract, not one ship had been constructed, this too after it had received an advance of RM6 billion.

When the LCS project was awarded, Mindef was helmed by Ahmad Zahid Hamidi, who was the deputy prime minister as of 2024. It was reported that Zahid, in his ministerial capacity, had issued the following instruction to the procurement committee to award the contract to BNS: '*Sila laksanakan* (Please get this done).'[178] This suggests that bureaucrats did not have the autonomy to carry out their duties. It was reported that a 'declassified 2019 forensic audit showed handwritten instructions to the ministry's procurement division secretary to produce a letter of intent for

---

[176] *The Edge* (15 August 2022): https://theedgemalaysia.com/article/visit-lcs-site-hints-long-sail-towards-completion

[177] This was disclosed by LTAT's current CEO, Ahmad Nazim Abdul Rahman, during an interview. See: *The Edge* (19 May 2022): https://theedgemalaysia.com/article/cover-story-tribulations-lcs-project

[178] *New Straits Times* (17 August 2022): https://www.nst.com.my/news/nation/2022/08/823186/lcs-scandal-report-reveals-zahid-involved-procurement-process

BNS as proof of the government's mandate and consent for the LCS project.'[179]

Another tempest occurred after the LCS project was awarded when Zahid apparently altered the design of the ships. Mindef's original plan was that construction of the ships would be based on the Sigma design by a Dutch firm, coupled with the combat management system (CMS) of a French firm. This was the preferred choice of the navy. However, a few months later, Mindef abruptly amended the plan, following intense lobbying by BNS, to opt for the Gowind design and SETIS CMS—both from France.[180] The Gowind design was by the Naval Group, the same enterprise involved in the controversial Scorpene submarines project that was subsequently mired in serious allegations of corruption.[181]

Lodin Wok Kamaruddin, reputedly Najib's closest ally in the corporate sector, played a vital role in the implementation of the LCS project.[182] Lodin held multiple directorships in strategic enterprises under the LTAT group. Lodin also held chairmanship or directorship appointments in Boustead Holdings and its subsidiaries, BHIC and BNS, while serving as CEO of LTAT, a position he took up in 1982 and held until 2018. As a central figure in the LTAT-Boustead group, Lodin had considerable influence over project contracting and implementation by companies under his control. Significantly, too, Lodin was a pivotal figure in the Scorpene controversy in his capacity as a director of Perimekar,

---

[179] See: *Asia Times* (25 August 2022): https://asiatimes.com/2022/08/najib-era-ship-scandal-resurfaces-to-sink-umno/

[180] Then navy chief, Abdul Aziz Jaafar, sent about a dozen letters to Najib, Zahid, the government's chief secretary, and the secretary-generals of MoF and Mindef objecting this decision. Abdul Aziz argued that it was the navy, not the contractor, BNS, that should not be deciding the design of the combat ships.

[181] *The Edge* (15 August 2022): https://theedgemalaysia.com/article/rm9-bil-lcs-fiasco-simplified

[182] For an account of Lodin's close ties with Najib, see Gomez. 2017: 96–98.

and he was named as a director of 1MDB, a GLC under Najib's control that was mired in what came to be described as 'the world's biggest financial scandal'.[183]

Lodin was also the chairman of Affin Bank—Perimekar's bank. LTAT then owned 33.08 per cent of Affin Bank while Boustead Holdings owned 20.85 per cent (see Figure 3.3). BNS had promised all of its rights and future income to Affin Bank as collateral to obtain a huge loan. Affin Bank's presence in the LCS and Scorpene controversies was an indication of the role of financial institutions as enablers for projects awarded to well-connected companies.

To undertake the construction of the ships, BNS appointed two foreign companies, Contraves Advanced Devices Sdn Bhd (CAD) and Contraves Electrodynamics Sdn Bhd (CED). BHIC, which owned BNS, held a majority 51 per cent stake in both companies. Germany's Rheinmetall Group held the remaining 49 per cent. This joint venture agreement was highly irregular because BHIC, the majority shareholder, had conceded decision-making and management control to its minority partner, the Rheinmetall Group. Managerial control was placed, seemingly solely, in the hands of Gordon Hargreave, a long-time Rheinmetall employee, who headed CAD. It was not disclosed why the LTAT-Boustead group allowed a foreign enterprise to have managerial and decision-making powers over the mode of implementation of the LCS project.

Despite these controversies and the loss of a huge volume of public funds, no politician has been charged for abuse of power or other malfeasance while Gordon Hargreave has not been located. Only one person, Ahmad Ramli Mohd Nor, a former navy chief and the managing director of BNS, a company situated deep at Level 4, was charged with three counts of criminal breach

---

[183] *The Guardian* (28 July 2016):
https://www.theguardian.com/world/2016/jul/28/1mdb-inside-story-worlds-biggest-financial-scandal-malaysia

of trust (CBT) totalling RM21.08 million.[184] The problem with stopping the LCS project was disclosed by LTAT's current CEO, Ahmad Nazim Abdul Rahman, who pointed out that its 'economic impact in terms of technical capacities, job creation and the development of the supply chain has been enormous and far outweighs the cost.'[185]

Inevitably, the other outcomes of the LCS project have been dire. The number of ships to be delivered was reduced to five, though the total cost of the project was increased by RM2 billion, to RM11.2 billion. The government announced that a special purpose vehicle (SPV) had been created by MoF to complete the LCS project. This ministry's holding company, MoF Inc., through an enterprise named Ocean Sunshine, acquired BHIC's entire 20.8 per cent stake in BNS for a token one ringgit.[186] This was because, according to Prime Minister Anwar, 'we have no choice, we have spent RM6 billion, we can't close, we have to take over to complete the project.'[187] Meanwhile, Boustead Holdings was delisted from the stock exchange in June 2023, when LTAT made a general offer to take full ownership of the enterprise at a cost of RM703 million, with each share valued at a mere 85.5 sen.[188]

With LTAT now in full control of Boustead Holdings, in August 2023, it sold 33 per cent of its stake in Boustead Plantations for RM1.2 billion, after an open tender, to another

---

[184] *The Star* (17 August 2022): https://www.thestar.com.my/news/nation/2022/08/17/ramli-pleads-not-guilty

[185] *The Edge* (19 May 2022): https://theedgemalaysia.com/article/cover-story-tribulations-lcs-project

[186] *Free Malaysia Today* (21 August 2023): https://www.freemalaysiatoday.com/category/nation/2023/08/21/boustead-sells-naval-shipyard-stake-to-govt-firm-for-rm1/

[187] *The Edge* (30 May 2023): https://ceomorningbrief.theedgemalaysia.com/article/2023/0578/Home/3/668997

[188] *The Star* (23 June 2023): https://www.thestar.com.my/business/business-news/2023/06/23/boustead-to-be-removed-from-bursa-malaysia039s-list-june-28

leading enterprise in this sector, Kuala Lumpur-Kepong (KLK), owned by the Perak-based Lee family.[189] Following this sale, KLK secured a majority 65 per cent interest in Boustead Plantations with the remaining 35 per cent in the hands of the LTAT-Boustead Holdings group. However, two months later, the government blocked this move and announced its intention to inject RM2.3 billion in LTAT to help this GLIC deal with the problems in the Boustead group. This move by the government came under serious criticism with one editorial stating that this was 'effectively a bailout using taxpayers' money ... over a private investment by a successful home-grown company, which has been investing overseas and wanted to take up the government's call to invest more at home.'[190] In the event, LTAT took over Boustead Holdings' equity in Boustead Plantations and then made a mandatory takeover offer for all the latter's remaining shares at a cash price of RM1.55.[191] As for the LCS controversy, then Minister of Defence Mohamad Hassan, also the deputy president of UMNO, said that 'there is no use talking about the past'.[192]

This call to ignore the past is because extremely disconcerting trends are evident in the public governance of GLC-based institutions, controlled ultimately by the prime minister, finance minister, and defence minister. There has been serious and persistent dereliction of duty through the repeated abuse of LTAT, created as a pension fund but employed as a business group controlling a well-diversified conglomerate. Institutional changes have served to aid cronyism. Strategic public institutions,

---

[189] *The Edge* (28 August 2023): https://theedgemalaysia.com/node/679926

[190] *The Edge* (9 October 2023): https://www.klsescreener.com/v2/news/view/1214071/node/685275

[191] *The New Straits Times* (10 November 2023): https://www.nst.com.my/business/corporate/2023/11/977073/ltat-launches-unconditional-takeover-offer-boustead-plantation

[192] Quoted in *Focus Malaysia* (10 December 2022): https://focusmalaysia.my/no-use-talking-of-the-past-on-lcs-says-tok-mat/

such as Limbungan TLDM, have been corporatized and privatized and then channelled to politicians-cum-businessmen. This form of selective patronage, ostensibly part of policies to create Malay corporate captains, is facilitated by constant abuse of the procurement system coupled with inadequate monitoring of the implementation of public projects and no swift action when contractors fail to perform. These public governance flaws have inevitably compromised the execution of megaprojects, resulting in continuous and expensive bailouts.

A major feature of these defence-based controversies is their transnational dimension, comprising a lopsided joint venture agreement with a foreign (German) multinational that secured management control though it did not have majority equity ownership. Cabinet members also do not wish to answer a related question: Why was the French Naval Group incorporated into the LCS project though it was deeply implicated in the Scorpene submarine scandal a decade earlier? Multinationals in joint ventures with GLCs are required to transfer technical knowledge to domestic enterprises brought into the project as subcontractors or as part of the supply chains. And yet, despite the presence of multinational firms in this joint venture, there is little evidence of the award of contracts to well-qualified, Malay-owned enterprises. Professionals aligned with cabinet ministers have been incorporated to execute these projects, suggesting they have no managerial autonomy while control over a GLC bank was crucial to provide loans. Inevitably, the outcomes of these defence contracts include huge cost overruns and delays in completing projects, jeopardizing national security.

Case Study 3: Abuse of Statutory Bodies—Corporatization, Corruption, Political–Bureaucratic Ties

A recurrent issue in public controversies related to state-business ties and enterprises in the GLC ecosystem is how statutory bodies have persistently been mired in business controversies, including through publicly-listed companies (Level 3) and obscure unlisted enterprises (Levels 4 and 5) under their control. The most infamous of these controversies involved Tabung Haji, FELDA, and MARA, all statutory bodies that went on to incorporate numerous companies and currently function as well-diversified enterprises.

Although Malaysia's history of corporate controversies encompasses statutory bodies, these public enterprises have played a vital role in one area: reducing poverty in rural areas by promoting land redistribution and redevelopment. Public programmes to aid the landless poor resulted in a rural and semi-rural middle class, achieved particularly through statutory bodies such as FELDA, MARA, and FELCRA.[193]

These statutory bodies, as well as other types of public institutions, were established as the government's response to the 1969 riots.[194] The riots were attributed to inadequate government intervention to redress socio-economic inequities that had emerged during British colonial rule. Another core objective of the large number of public institutions introduced by the government was restructuring society to achieve inter-ethnic economic parity. One eventual method to achieve this objective was nurturing Bumiputeras in business. Related measures to address wealth and business inequities entailed increasing Bumiputera corporate

---

[193] FELDA and MARA were incorporated in the 1950s and were the first to promote Bumiputera welfare. Other public enterprises that were set up to aid rural folk were the Rubber Industry Smallholders Development Authority (RISDA) and the Federal Agricultural Marketing Authority (FAMA). For a history of the incorporation and development of statutory bodies between the 1950s and 1970s, see: Bruce Gale. 1981. *Politics and Public Enterprise in Malaysia*. Singapore: Eastern University Press.

[194] There are different perspectives on the riots. See: Tunku Abdul Rahman. 1969. *May 13: Before and After*. Kuala Lumpur: Utusan Melayu Press; Goh Cheng Teik. 1971. *The May Thirteenth Incident and Democracy in Malaysia*. Kuala Lumpur: Oxford University Press; Leon Comber. 2009. *13 May 1969: The Darkest Day in Malaysian History*. Singapore: Marshall Cavendish; and Kua Kia Soong. 2007. *May 13: Declassified Documents on the Malaysian Riots of 1969*. Petaling Jaya: Suaram.

equity ownership to 30 per cent and allotting to them publicly-listed shares at par value or with only nominal premiums. These objectives were outlined in the Second Malaysia Plan, 1971–1975, the foundation for the NEP, introduced in 1970, which constituted an affirmative action endeavour targeting poor Bumiputeras.

By the early 1970s, an outcome of the NEP was the proliferation of public institutions, of which there were three types: departmental enterprises responsible for public services, statutory bodies, and public limited companies incorporated under the Companies Act.[195] So large a number of enterprises were created that coordinating their activities became arduous. In 1974, the Ministry of the Coordination of Public Corporations was created to resolve this problem.[196] This ministry, which was renamed the Ministry of Public Enterprises in 1976, was always led by an UMNO minister until it was disbanded in 1995.[197]

The government fared remarkably well with these institutions, reducing poverty from nearly 50 per cent in 1970 to 5.6 per cent by 2020, while FELDA's land redistribution endeavour received global attention when it was acclaimed as a success story by the World Bank. However, the goal of Bumiputeras owning 30 per cent corporate equity ownership was not attained, even by 2018, standing then at only 16.9 per cent.[198] Furthermore, FELDA's

---

[195] For a review of the different types of public institutions created after the NEP was introduced, see Gomez and Jomo. 1997: 29–39.

[196] Gale. 1981. offers interesting insights into the problems that led to the setting up of this ministry, specifically the need to felicitously coordinate the activities of the public enterprises.

[197] During these two decades, from 1974 to 1995, the ministers of this ministry were Hussien Onn, Mohamed Yaacob, Abdul Manan Othman, Rafidah Aziz, Napsiah Omar, and Mohamed Yusof Noor.

[198] Edmund Terence Gomez. 2022. The Politics of Affirmative Action: Ethnicity, Equity and State–Business Relations in Malaysia. UNU-WIDER Working Paper 2022/104: https://www.wider.unu.edu/sites/default/files/Publications/Working-paper/PDF/wp2022-104-politics-affirmative-action-ethnicity-equity-state-business-relations-Malaysia.pdf

well-acknowledged corrective of socio-economic inequities was not sustained. By 2023, Prime Minister Anwar Ibrahim's government had to resort to 'the abolition of 80 per cent of settlers' loans worth RM8.3 billion', which, though a huge sum, constituted only a partial amount of the debts 'accrued by FELDA farmers when they borrowed extensively to participate in the 2012 listing of FELDA Global Ventures, now renamed FGV Holdings'.[199]

FELDA's restructuring, with the incorporation of FGV Holdings, led to the disempowerment of the settlers in terms of decision-making. If these settlers once had decision-making control as well as operational control of FELDA's assets, they lost both to governing politicians following corporatization.[200]

Legislative changes resulted in structural realignments in the way statutory bodies were managed. These legislative and structural shifts relocated managerial powers from bureaucrats (who oversaw these statutory bodies) to cabinet members (who vested operational control in the chairperson and board members they appointed of these enterprises), giving the latter enormous decision-making influence. However, legislative changes introduced to oversee the running of these enterprises did not have the necessary provisions to protect them from abuse once they began to operate as companies. After all, the professed aim of the legislative changes was to not oversee how they were managed but to convert the way statutory bodies functioned, that is as companies, not as government bodies.

These important power shifts in statutory bodies have contributed serious allegations of their abuse and corruption. This was evident in the well-exposed controversies of FELDA–FGV Holdings, where structural changes are now impoverishing the new rural middle class, returning them to a point where they are becoming, once again,

---

[199] *The Straits Times* (21 July 2023): https://www.straitstimes.com/asia/se-asia/malaysian-govt-writes-off-24-billion-in-felda-settlers-debts-with-eye-on-votes

[200] For an in-depth assessment of the controversial incorporation of FGV Holdings and the business controversies it was subsequently mired in, see: *Center to Combat Corruption and Cronyism*. The FELDA Crisis. 2018: https://c4center.org/wp-content/uploads/Felda-Crisis-Booklet-BI-WEB.pdf

highly dependent on the government. The case studies of two public enterprises, FELCRA and MARA, provide further insights into forms of corporate mishaps occurring through the private companies they have incorporated.

Case Study 3(1): FELCRA—Maladies of Corporatization: Inadequate Governance

The Federal Land Consolidation and Rehabilitation Authority was established in 1966, under the FELCRA Act. Under this legislation, FELCRA functioned as a cooperative, where its settlers and members had the power to direct this statutory body to rehabilitate or develop any piece of land, including how it was employed. The government's role was restricted to financing FELCRA's administrative expenses and providing loans to members who wished to develop their land.[201]

In 1997, then Prime Minister Mahathir Mohamad amended the FELCRA Act to allow for the corporatization of this statutory body. What this meant, as stressed on the company's website, is that 'FELCRA Berhad was incorporated and ceased to be a statutory body, evolving into a Corporate Organisation wholly-owned by the Minister of Finance Inc.'[202] The government had, in fact, announced in 2003, when the 2004 Budget was presented by then Minister of Finance Mahathir that it planned to list this corporatized body on the stock exchange.[203] It appeared that Mahathir's plan was to allow politicians to have a direct say in the corporate sector by controlling corporatized and partially-privatized publicly-listed companies that were important players in major sectors such as plantations.

---

[201] By 2022, about 1,370 projects covering 203,953 hectares of land had been developed on behalf of 107,130 participants. FELCRA Bhd also owned 31,613 hectares of estates. See: *FELCRA:* https://felcra.com.my/

[202] *FELCRA:* https://felcra.com.my/corporate-information/company-overview/

[203] See: *FELCRA May Be Listed On KLSE* (23 October 2003): http://lib.perdana.org.my/PLF/Digital_Content/Prominent_Leaders/Mahathir/News_1968-2004/2001-2005/2003aj/felcra%20ma.pdf

However, after Mahathir stepped down as prime minister in 2003, Abdullah Ahmad Badawi halted the proposal to publicly-list FELCRA. Under Najib Razak, who was responsible for the public-listing of FELDA's FGV Holdings, two attempts were made to list FELCRA. In 2013, there was a failed effort to launch an initial public offering (IPO), while in 2016 a plan to secure a 'backdoor listing' through a then ailing company, Kuantan Flour Mills Bhd, did not go through.[204] The plan was that, after its listing, FELCRA would venture beyond its focus on plantations and diversify into other sectors of the economy.[205]

As Figure 3.4 indicates, after its corporatization, FELCRA was turned into FELCRA Bhd, an unlisted GLC under the jurisdiction of the finance ministry. MoF Inc. owns 99 per cent of FELCRA Bhd's equity, while the remaining 1 per cent is owned by another statutory body, the Federal Lands Commissioner (FLC).

However, since MoF Inc. and FLC do not have boards of directors—both also do not have a management team—MRRD is responsible for overseeing FELCRA Bhd's operations. As Figures 3.4 and 3.5 indicate, FELCRA's corporatization led to a power shift. If FELCRA functioned as a cooperative, with decision-making power in the hands of the settlers, following its corporatization, the government now had direct control over the company that had been incorporated, FELCRA Bhd. Business decision-making in FELCRA Bhd was now solely in the hands of the company's board of directors (primarily its chairman) and MoF. Since the 1990s, this enterprise's chairmen—as opposed to when this statutory body was formed—have been government-affiliated politicians, as listed in Table 3.1. The settlers lost their say in FELCRA's operations and have now only been privy to annual dividends.

---

[204] *The Star* (14 December 2016): https://www.thestar.com.my/business/business-news/2016/12/14/felcra-plans-backdoor-listing

[205] *The Edge* (21 December 2016): https://theedgemalaysia.com/article/felcra-see-restructuring-considering-ipo; *The Star* (14 December 2016): https://www.thestar.com.my/business/business-news/2016/12/14/felcra-plans-backdoor-listing

Case Studies 111

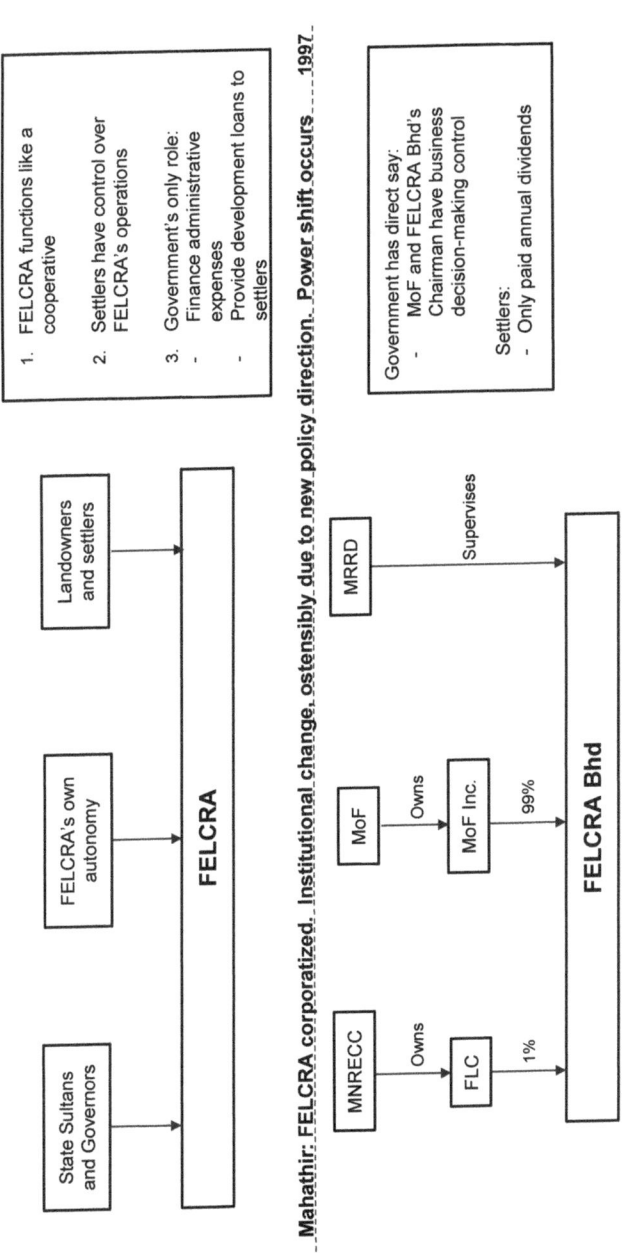

Figure 3.4: FELCRA: Before and after corporatization

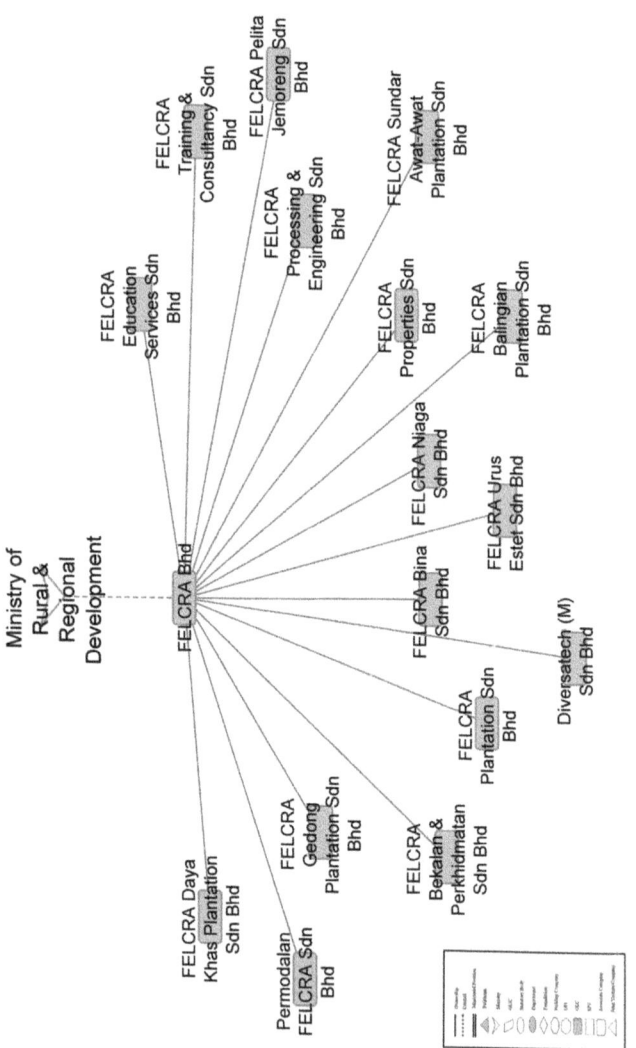

Figure 3.5: MRRD's control over FELCRA Bhd

Table 3.1: List of chairpersons of FELCRA

Prime Minister	Minister (MRRD)	Minister (MoF)	FELCRA Bhd Chairperson
Mahathir Mohamad (UMNO) (1997–2003) Abdullah Badawi (UMNO) (2003–2006)	Annuar Musa (UMNO) (1997–1999) Azmi Khalid (UMNO) (1999–2004) Abdul Aziz Shamsuddin (UMNO) (2004–2006)	Anwar Ibrahim (UMNO) (1997–1998) Mahathir Mohamad (UMNO) (1998–1999, 2001–2003) Daim Zainuddin (UMNO) (1999–2001) Abdullah Badawi (UMNO) (2003–2006)	Hamzah Zainuddin (UMNO) (2000–2006)
Abdullah Badawi (UMNO) (2006–2008) Najib Razak (UMNO) (2008–2013)	Muhammad Taib (UMNO) (2008–2009) Shafie Apdal (UMNO) (2009–2013)	Abdullah Badawi (UMNO) (2006–2008) Najib Razak (UMNO) (2008–2013)	Tajuddin Abdul Rahman (UMNO)

Prime Minister	Minister (MRRD)	Minister (MoF)	FELCRA Bhd Chairperson
Najib Razak (UMNO) (2013–2018)	Shafie Apdal (UMNO) (2013–2015) Ismail Sabri (UMNO) (2015–2018)	Najib Razak (UMNO) (2013–2018)	Bung Mokhtar Radin (UMNO) (2013–2018)
Mahathir Mohamad (Bersatu) (2018–2020)	Rina Harun (Bersatu) (2018–2020)	Lim Guan Eng (DAP) (2018–2020)	
Muhyddin Yassin (Bersatu) (2020–2021)	Abdul Latiff Ahmad (Bersatu) (2020–2021)	Tengku Zafrul Aziz (UMNO) (2020–2021)	Shahudin Yahaya (UMNO) (2020) Yamani Hafez Musa (UMNO) (2020–2021)
Ismail Sabri (UMNO) (2021–2022) Anwar Ibrahim (PKR) (2022–present)	Mahdzir Khalid (UMNO) (2021–2022) Ahmad Zahid Hamidi (UMNO) (2022–present)	Tengku Zafrul Aziz (UMNO) (2021–2022) Anwar Ibrahim (PKR) (2022–present)	Ahmad Jazlan Yaakub (UMNO) (2021–present)

Figures 3.4 and 3.5 reveal the key structural and governance transitions that have occurred since FELCRA moved from being a statutory body (Level 2) to an unlisted firm (Level 4), after its corporatization. FELCRA Bhd is governed by the Companies Act and is under the oversight of the Companies Commission of Malaysia (CCM). While statutory bodies are accountable to parliament, companies, even major GLCs, are seldom deeply scrutinized by CCM, given the huge volume of registered companies under this regulatory body. Importantly, too, CCM falls under the jurisdiction of the Minister of Domestic Trade and Cost of Living, a further indication that numerous cabinet members were directly or indirectly responsible for monitoring how FELCRA Bhd functioned.

With FELCRA Bhd directly controlled by MRRD, along with MoF, it secured control over a large number of unlisted companies. FELCRA Bhd's corporate structure indicates that it has control over a wide network of subsidiaries that are involved in a diverse range of industries (see Figure 3.5). It is unclear why there is a need for FELCRA Bhd to incorporate and manage such a large number of companies. Although FELCRA's focus has been in the plantations sector, and it has developed enterprises in upstream and downstream activities, the companies in the FELCRA Bhd group are involved in education, property development, agro-food, and consultancy and training services. Since its corporatization, there have been two controversies that speak to the implications of this structural—and power—shift. Both events occurred in 2015, when Najib was the serving minister of finance and a UMNO member was chairing FELCRA Bhd's board of directors.

In 2015, FELCRA Bhd allowed a property developer, the WZR group,[206] to fund the Semarak20 project. This entailed the construction of a high-rise office (Menara FELCRA), a

---

[206] The WZR group, a construction and property development enterprise, was incorporated in 1999.

forty-three-storey residential tower, a retail mall, and an international convention centre in the heart of Kuala Lumpur.[207] The project, originally listed at a cost of RM550 million, was to be implemented through mechanisms outlined in the Private Finance Initiative (PFI) policy. Under the PFI method, WZR was solely responsible for funding the project, though it would recoup its capital outlay through the sale of the residential units in the project and by leasing a segment of Menara FELCRA's office space.[208] However, a year later, FELCRA Bhd's subsidiary, FELCRA Properties Sdn Bhd, took over the financing of the project, turning the WZR group from funder to contractor (see Figure 3.6).

When one news outlet, *Malaysiakini*, published an account of this transfer of the financing of the project from WZR to FELCRA Properties, FELCRA Bhd issued a clarification.[209] In the company's clarification, interesting disclosures were made, including that the cost had increased to RM687.5 million because the project was revised to cover a larger area and that the board of directors, on the 'advice' of the MoF, had decided to take over its financing. The company's clarification went on to add that Pembinaan BLT Sdn Bhd, appointed by the ministry to evaluate the project, found that it was 'reasonably priced'.[210]

However, by 2018, with 42 per cent of the project completed, it was halted due to inadequate funds.[211] There were further disturbing revelations. In 2019, with Najib out of office, when then Deputy Economic Affairs Minister Mohd Radzi Md Jidin

---

[207] *The Star* (13 January 2020): https://www.thestar.com.my/business/business-news/2020/01/13/felcra-to-revive-stalled-rm1b-semarak20-project

[208] *Malaysiakini* (7 June 2016): https://www.malaysiakini.com/news/344319

[209] For the statement by FELCRA Bhd, see: *Malaysiakini* (7 June 2016): https://www.malaysiakini.com/news/344319

[210] Ibid.

[211] *The Malaysian Reserve* (20 January 2019): https://themalaysianreserve.com/2019/01/30/felcra-set-to-revive-rm1b-jalan-semarak-project/

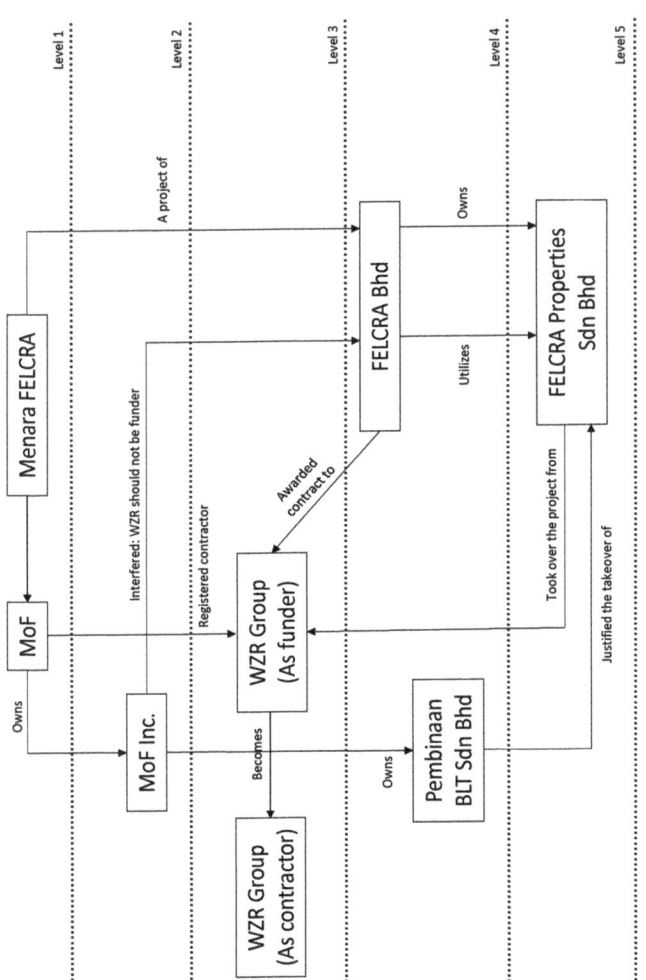

Figure 3.6: Menara FELCRA controversy

was asked in parliament 'how a once-cash rich FELCRA had fallen into debt', his shocking response was that it was 'currently in dire financial straits [. . .] because the company's finances have to be diverted towards the [Menara FELCRA] project'.[212] Radzi further disclosed that the 'discrepancies in the project, which goes against FELCRA's main cause for existence, have undergone a forensic audit and the new management has reported them to the MACC'.[213] To date, MACC has not issued a statement on this investigation. As for the project, *The Malaysian Reserve* quoted this view of an 'industry expert': 'What the project requires is a comprehensive revamp, but unfortunately the construction is at quite an advanced stage. It is a total loss on what has been sunk in to date.'[214]

Meanwhile, in the same year that the Menara FELCRA project commenced, another investment decision was made that resulted in a serious corruption allegation. Four years later, in May 2019, Bung Moktar, who was then the chairman of FELCRA Bhd, was charged with three counts of corruption amounting to total of RM2.8 million, which included him taking a bribe of RM2.2 million in 2015 from a Public Mutual investment agent through his wife Zizie Ezette. This bribe was allegedly given as an inducement to obtain approval from the minister of finance to allow FELCRA Bhd to invest RM150 million in Public Mutual unit trust products.[215]

---

[212] *Malaysiakini* (2 April 2019): https://www.malaysiakini.com/news/470524

[213] Ibid.

[214] *The Malaysian Reserve* (22 August 2019):
https://themalaysianreserve.com/2019/08/22/semarak20-a-difficult-sell-for-felcra-amid-property-overhang/

[215] To obtain a full account of the charges against Bung Mokhtar and his wife, see: *Berita Harian* (26 November 2021): https://www.bharian.com.my/berita/nasional/2021/11/892272/zizie-izette-terima-ganjaran-tunai-rm22-juta

During the court hearing, two pertinent points were made by one witness, a former general manager of this GLC, who provided crucial insights into what the government expected of a corporatized FELCRA. The first point was, 'FELCRA was a government body that was not allowed to engage in business, but after it was incorporated, FELCRA could generate its own income and increase productivity and was no longer a burden to the government.' The second point was, 'Before it was incorporated, FELCRA was answerable to the government and Parliament but after the incorporation, all became the responsibility of the board of directors.'[216] However, based on the general manager's testimony, the board of directors could only approve investments related to FELCRA Bhd's core businesses—plantations and manufacturing. In September 2023, a high court judge discharged Bung Mokhtar and his wife of all corruption charges because, to his mind, the sessions court had erred in ordering them to enter their defence.[217]

Evidently, based on these disclosures in court and the outcome of the Menara FELCRA project, none of the core objectives of the corporatization of FELCRA have been achieved, while monitoring of the operations of FELCRA Bhd has been abysmal. New vulnerabilities have been created to the detriment of the settlers, a point reinforced by other revelations in court, including that the board of directors having inadequate control over decisions taken by its chairman

---

[216] Both points were made by Adnan Yusof, and quoted in: *Malaysiakini* (3 January 2020): https://www.malaysiakini.com/news/505825

[217] For a report the high court judge's ruling, see *New Straits Times* (7 September 2023): https://www.nst.com.my/news/crime-courts/2023/09/952193/bung-and-wife-freed-all-corruption-charges-involving-rm28mnsttv#:~:text=KUALA%20LUMPUR%3A%20Datuk%20Seri%20Bung,couple%20from%20the%20case%20today

and the MoF. The board erred in employing the PFI policy to construct the Menara FELCRA, a project that was soon transferred back to FELCRA Bhd, resulting in the company carrying a huge financial burden with the project stalled. The PFI, introduced in Britain, was discarded by its government in 2018 because the policy, though seen as a form of public–private partnership, was being abused by companies.[218] However, in Malaysia, PFI continues to remain in place and is still considered when implementing major projects.

There was now too much cabinet control over FELCRA Bhd, a core factor that contributed to these two controversies. Legislative changes have led to institutional and managerial changes that have been detrimental to this once thriving statutory body. After FELCRA's corporatization, parliamentary oversight was removed and decision-making and operational controls over it were vested in politicians and a seemingly subservient board. This clearly undermined the ability of this institution to support rural-based settlers and help them develop their land. Crucially, too, these controversies underlined problems with cabinet—or ministerial—directives on business-related matters concerning institutions they control.

Case Study 3(2): MARA—Statutory Bodies and Transnational Crime

The Majlis Amanah Rakyat (MARA, or Council of Trust for Indigenous People), was originally known as the Rural and Industrial Development Authority (RIDA), which was established in 1950 to alleviate rural poverty and enhance Malay participation in business by giving them access to credit facilities and the requisite training to develop an enterprise. RIDA constituted

---

[218] *The Guardian* (29 October 2018): https://www.theguardian.com/uk-news/2018/oct/29/hammond-abolishes-pfi-contracts-for-new-infrastructure-projects

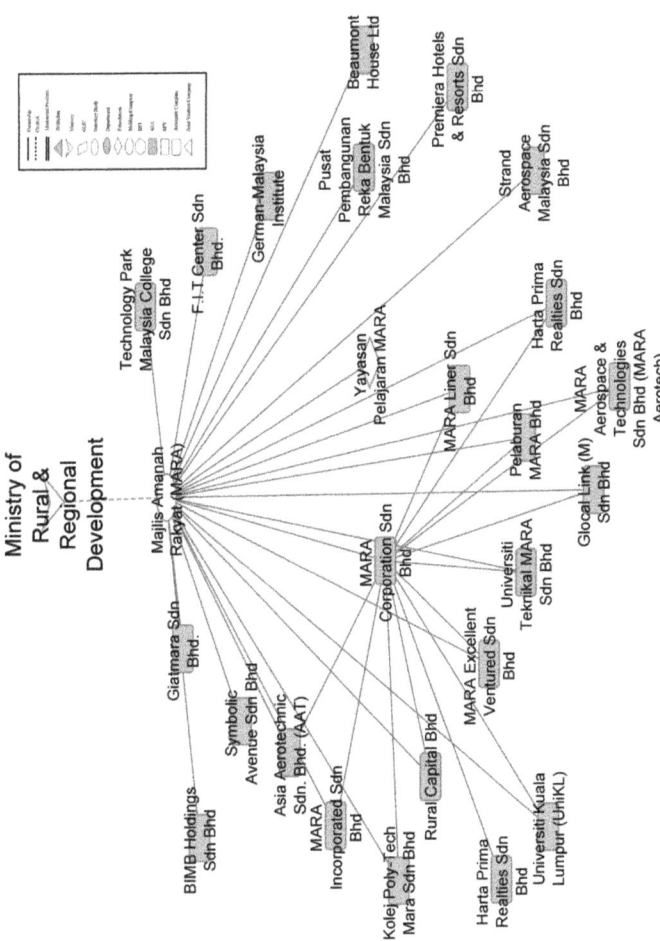

Figure 3.7: MARA's control over companies

the first concerted public endeavour to develop rural-based, Malay-owned small enterprises. In 1966, the MARA Act was introduced in response to UMNO's strong criticism that RIDA had failed to nurture thriving Malay-owned businesses. MARA was created to establish and manage new industrial enterprises to later be transferred to the Malays.[219] By 2022, the net worth of the companies under MARA was estimated at RM1.4 billion (see Figure 3.7).[220]

MARA has two major holding companies, MARA Corporation Sdn Bhd and MARA Incorporated Sdn Bhd (Mara Inc.). It is unclear why MARA required two holding companies of a similar sort. Clearly, a Level 2 enterprise (MARA), under the jurisdiction of the MRRD, owned and controlled a vast expanse of companies (Levels 4 and 5), regulated by the Companies Act and far removed from the attention of the general public. MARA Corporation also owned companies situated in two foreign countries—England and Australia—that had acquired properties such as hotels and student residential buildings (see Figure 3.8). However, convoluted property scams in Australia exposed by its media, implicated MARA's subsidiaries.[221] The Australian media also exposed that this statutory body was associated with shell companies in the British Virgin Islands, a tax haven where such enterprises are known to be incorporated by corrupt government leaders to hold their ill-gotten wealth.

In 2013, MARA Inc. spent RM375.4 million to purchase four properties in Melbourne, one of which was Dudley International House, a student residential apartment complex. The sale of

---

[219] Gale. 1981. provides a history of MARA.

[220] *The Malaysian Reserve* (7 February 2022): https://themalaysianreserve.com/2022/02/07/mara-corp-crisis-far-from-over/

[221] *The Age* (23 June 2015) (https://www.theage.com.au/national/corrupt-malaysia-money-distorts-melbourne-market-20150622-ghu6a0.html) and *The Sydney Morning Herald* (27 July 2020) (https://www.smh.com.au/national/man-charged-with-bribing-malaysian-official-over-22m-property-deal-20200727-p55fub.html).

Dudley International House[222] was described by an Australian newspaper, *The Age*, in a major exposé as 'part of a global money laundering and bribery scheme engineered by greedy local developers and powerful officials overseas who pocketed A$4.75 million in bribes on this single deal.'[223] MARA Inc. had used Thrushcross Land Holding Ltd, established in the British Virgin Islands, to acquire Dudley International House.[224] *The Age* further disclosed that this A$4.75 million had been 'wired to a mysterious Singapore shelf company.'[225] The MARA Inc. officials named in this controversy were its former chairman, Mohd Lan Allani, as well as two senior executives, Abdul Halim Rahim and Zainal Zol Kulop Alang, who reportedly bribed a Singaporean to use a company in that country for transferring funds.[226] A complex web had been spun comprising companies in foreign countries that dealt in funds originating from MARA (see Figure 3.8).

---

[222] Dudley International House was constructed by a group of developers comprising two Australians and three Malaysians. When construction of the building was completed, these five individuals had it valued at A$17.8 million but agreed to inflate its price to A$22.5 million to provide kickbacks to a group of Malaysian officials. One member of this group of five, Dennis Teen Boon Lye, was later charged with bribing a Malaysian official to secure the sale of this building. See: *The Sydney Morning Herald* (27 July 2020): https://www.smh.com.au/national/man-charged-with-bribing-malaysian-official-over-22m-property-deal-20200727-p55fub.html

[223] For an in-depth and insightful account of this controversy, see *The Age* (23 June 2015): https://www.theage.com.au/national/corrupt-malaysia-money-distorts-melbourne-market-20150622-ghu6a0.html

[224] Thrushcross was also used to acquire another piece of property in Melbourne valued at A$23.5 million. See: *The Age* (23 June 2015): https://www.theage.com.au/national/corrupt-malaysia-money-distorts-melbourne-market-20150622-ghu6a0.html

[225] *The Age* (23 June 2015): https://www.theage.com.au/national/corrupt-malaysia-money-distorts-melbourne-market-20150622-ghu6a0.html

[226] Ibid.

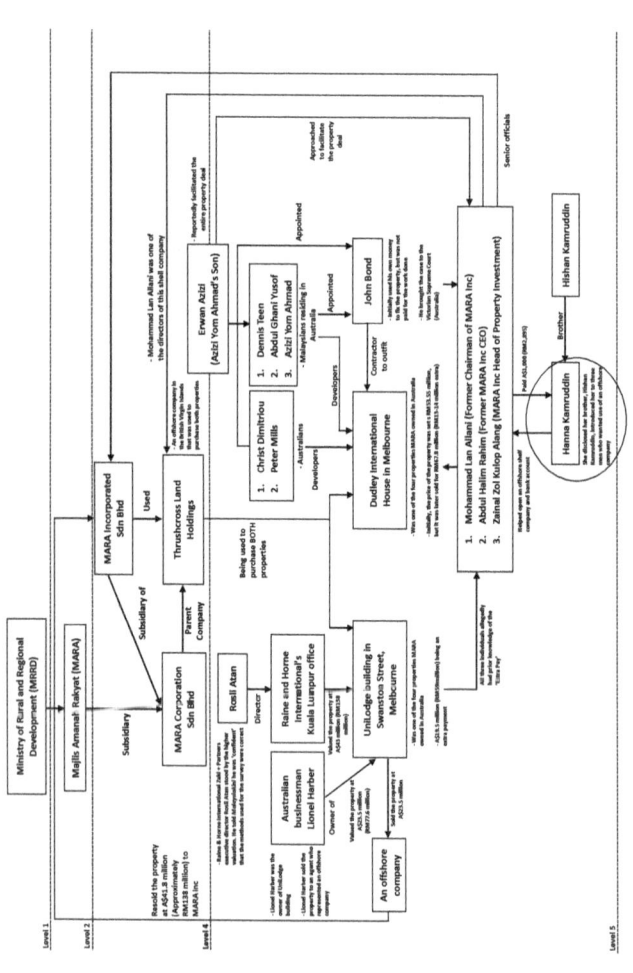

Figure 3.8: MARA's foreign enterprises in Australia and the British Virgin Islands[227]

---

[227] The information for this figure was obtained from: *The Age* (23 June 2015): https://www.theage.com.au/national/corrupt-malaysia-money-distorts-melbourne-market-20150622-ghu6a0.html; *The Sydney Morning Herald* (27 January 2018): https://www.smh.com.au/

Later, *The Sydney Morning Herald* reported that the acquisition of another one of these four properties—UniLodge, an accommodation complex for foreign students in Melbourne—was similarly mired in allegations of 'flipping property' for a vast sum of money—A$18.3 million—that benefited people associated with MARA. The Panama Papers disclosed that this deal was done by creating 'two secretive front companies in the British Virgin Islands and the Isle of Man', which 'were used, in turn, to set up a Melbourne company'.[228]

When the Dudley International House scandal was exposed, the MRRD Minister Shafie Apdal (then a UMNO member), along with the chairman of MARA, Annuar Musa (also then a UMNO member and a former minister), denied knowledge of these business transactions that had occurred through MARA's companies in Australia, Singapore, and the British Virgin Islands. Annuar reportedly stated that then Prime Minister Najib Razak was involved in approving the acquisition of the student accommodation as the 'purchase of any property by the council had to go through procedures, including a final approval by the Finance Ministry or the Economic Council [EC]. Najib is finance minister and chairs the EC.'[229] Najib did not rebut Annuar's

---

politics/federal/the-australian-building-that-made-almost-20m-for-corrupt-malaysians-20180126-p4yyxd.html; *The Sydney Morning Herald* (27 July 2020): https://www.smh.com.au/national/man-charged-with-bribing-malaysian-official-over-22m-property-deal-20200727-p55fub.html

[228] This controversy is analysed and reported by *The Sydney Morning Herald* (27 January 2018): https://www.smh.com.au/politics/federal/the-australian-building-that-made-almost-20m-for-corrupt-malaysians-20180126-p4yyxd.html

[229] These quotes by Annuar were as reported in *The Malaysian Insider* (25 Jun 2015): https://theedgemalaysia.com/article/aussie-cops-launch-raids-after-mara-property-buy-expose?type=Latest%20News

comment, stating that the decision was 'made based on consensus by the Economic Council'.[230]

What can be inferred from the statements by the Prime Minister, the MRRD Minister, and MARA's Chairman—all then UMNO members—is, despite the procedures in place and a well-structured chain of command in this statutory body to ensure checks and balances, transnational crimes had occurred without their knowledge! If these statements are to taken at face value, another concern arises. The government was allowing its statutory bodies to unnecessarily create multiple holding companies whose directors had too much decision-making power, allowing them to abuse these obscure unlisted GLCs domiciled abroad. What was obvious was that this complex ecosystem allowed for the extensive practice of corruption many levels down, far removed from the ministry and MARA.

After this scam was exposed, the only person who was charged in Malaysia with corruption was MARA Inc.'s chairman, Mohammad Lan, who had admitted that 'he was involved in setting up offshore companies in tax havens as a "convenient" way of selling property bought by the Malaysian government.'[231] Mohamad Lan, like those in positions of authority in institutions in each level of MARA's chain of command, was a UMNO member. He had served as a state assemblyman in Sabah between 1999 and 2008, in the Sulabayan constituency.

Mohammad Lan's admission was fraught with other deeply disquieting concerns:

1. Why did the government need to allow a statutory body to incorporate a shell company in a tax haven?
2. Did MARA need to acquire foreign property when its objectives are developing rural enterprises and aiding Bumiputeras mired in poverty?

---

[230] Ibid.

[231] *The Age* (23 June 2015): https://www.theage.com.au/national/corrupt-malaysia-money-distorts-melbourne-market-20150622-ghu6a0.html

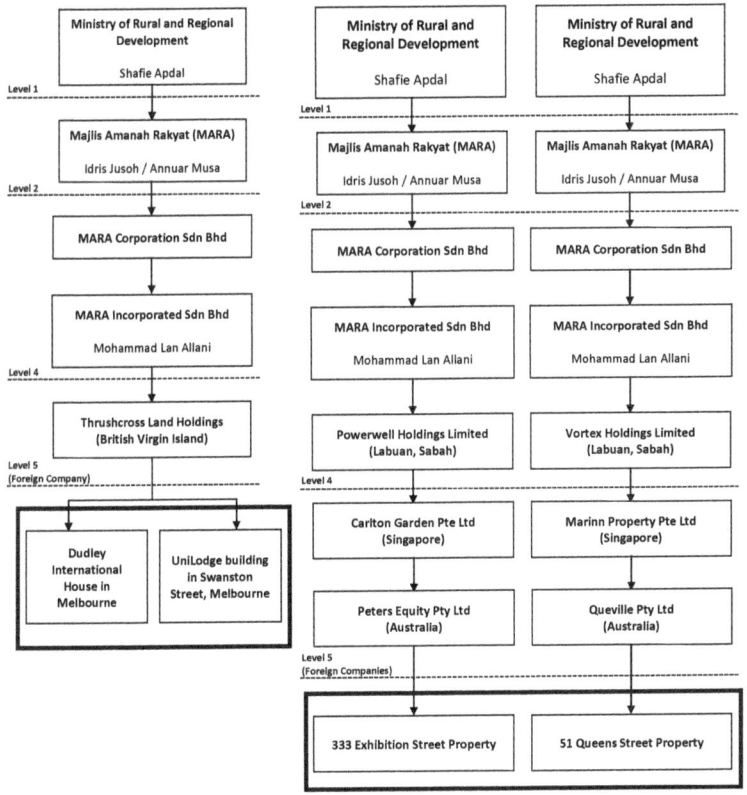

Figure 3.9: MARA's chain of command

3. Though a variety of corrupt practices involving large sums of money from MARA were occurring simultaneously, how were these issues missed by those in-charge of MARA, i.e. the Minister, the Economic Council, and the chairman of MARA, who was reported to have visited Dudley International House?[232]

4. How many more obscure companies, at Levels 4 and 5, owned by statutory bodies like MARA are involved in

---

[232] *The Star* (26 June 2015): https://www.thestar.com.my/News/Nation/2015/06/26/Annuar-Musa-Mara/

dubious foreign projects with government approval that are contributing to huge leakages of public funds?

The manner in which the corporatized subsidiaries of this statutory body were operating was not in tandem with the public policy it was supposed to serve.

Evidently, Mohammad Lan unequivocally admitted that the use of tax havens for acquiring foreign properties with public funds happened with the knowledge, and even approval, of those in MARA's chain of command. Equally disconcerting was the presence of politicians at every level of this system, i.e., the cabinet and the board of directors of MARA, and in its holding company, a core contributing factor to the corporate controversies of this statutory body as well as its subsidiaries incorporated abroad.

In 2021, Mohammad Lan was charged in a Kuala Lumpur Sessions Court with twenty-two counts of bribery and money laundering amounting to RM20.45 million that involved properties in Australia, including Dudley International House.[233] However, Mohammad Lan was granted a discharge not amounting to an acquittal (DNAA) when the judge was informed that he would face similar charges in Sabah. In March 2022, Mohammad Lan was charged with two counts of money laundering involving RM10 million by the Kota Kinabalu Sessions Court.[234]

---

[233] *The Malaysian Reserve* (5 February 2021): https://themalaysianreserve.com/2021/02/05/ex-mara-inc-chairman-charged-with-corruption-money-laundering/

[234] *The Edge* (15 March 2022): https://theedgemalaysia.com/article/exmara-inc-chairman-charged-again-money-laundering-involving-rm10m

Chapter 4

The Lessons Learned

Structure and System: State of Play

The most effective mechanism to curb grand corruption is deconstructing this well-entrenched Political–GLC complex. As Appendix 1 and the case studies indicate, multiple avenues exist for governing politicians to mismanage this vast GLC ecosystem while various ownership and control methods facilitate misgovernance of these public enterprises.

The case studies reveal the workings of this shadow Political–GLC complex which governing politicians use to shape corporate activities. State–business ties within this opaque complex comprise a multitude of interlocking corporate webs spun in the multifaceted GLC ecosystem that allow politicians to access funds through the abuse of public resources. Inadequate criminal and disclosure laws facilitate the process to selectively award government-generated concessions. In this context, when decisions are made, there appears to be little consideration of the massive waste incurred. Moreover, the government's response to one defence scandal has produced actions that shape the way the next scandal occurs, suggesting appalling political elite impunity to commit graft.

When politicians from different coalitions secure power, they adopt, even adapt, this GLC ecosystem to suit their political and economic objectives. Mahathir Mohamad, for example, called this ecosystem a 'monster', one that he admitted he had a hand in creating, but when he returned as prime minister in 2018, he did not move to dismantle it. Instead, he reframed the GLC infrastructure to consolidate his position and manoeuvred it to hamper Anwar Ibrahim from taking over as prime minister. Mahathir also placed key statutory bodies under the control of his allies to enhance his party's presence in rural Bumiputera-dominant parliamentary constituencies.[235] Abdullah Badawi introduced corporate governance-type reforms within government-linked enterprises in the public eye—the GLICs and publicly-listed GLCs—ostensibly in response to his call to deal with corruption. These reforms have done nothing to prevent the LCS controversy that implicated a GLIC, LTAT, and its publicly-listed conglomerate, the Boustead Holdings group. Anwar, too, did not announce any reforms for this GLC ecosystem after declaring that curbing systemic corruption was his government's principal agenda.

There are undoubtedly inadequate regulations binding ministers from abusing decision-making in the public procurement process, as well as the distribution of concessions through the public delivery system. Politicians in public office have influence over policy-making, which they voice as a means to address social and economic problems. They use this influence to create concessions that they control and can allocate, consequently securing electoral and party support. Furthermore, ethnic-based policies allow for selective patronage, which is legal, though there is serious travesty of power in the discharge of public duties when the concessions are channelled to party members from this ethnic group. Checks and balances are hamstrung by cabinet hegemony over bureaucratic and regulatory institutions.

The implementation of other policies has had alarming outcomes, such as the corporatization or privatization of public

---

[235] For an account of this restructuring of the GLCs under different ministries, see *The Star* (12 January 2019): https://www.thestar.com.my/business/business-news/2019/01/12/patronage-is-king/

enterprises. Statutory bodies that have been corporatized include FELCRA. Decision-making control over FELCRA was taken away from its settlers when it was converted into a company, with plans to privatize it through public-listing, an endeavour that failed to materialize on two occasions. Decision-making control was situated in the hands of politicians—the cabinet minister in-charge of this enterprise and the chairman of its board of directors. FELCRA has since fallen significantly in its public standing, marred by business controversies taken by its directors, leaving its settlers in a precarious situation. In the case of MARA, the decision taken by politicians sitting as chairmen of this statutory body as well as its holding companies have resulted in investments abroad, in property, through dubious deals. MARA, however, was established to aid the plight of disenfranchised communities, particularly those in rural under-developed areas. These case studies unambiguously substantiate the long-held criticism that the directors of the GLCs, specifically the chairpersons, have operational control of public funds obtained annually through the budget. These GLC chairpersons take orders from the minister on the implementation of public policies and projects, aided by scant monitoring by bureaucrats.

Table 4.1 captures the lessons learned from the case studies of the core themes running through this book:

1. the types of corruption;
2. how the governance structure, comprising the GLC ecosystem and key regulatory institutions, has been abused by key actors situated at each of the five levels in the pyramid;
3. the outcomes of this abuse of political and economic power.

It offers insights into how public governance is compromised and patronage-based processes, which serve as mechanisms to resolve social inequities, are misused by politicians to accumulate wealth and support family members and business allies.

Table 4.1: Lessons from case studies

Jana Wibawa			
Level	Type of Corruption (Alleged)	Institutions	How Misgovernance Occurred	Key Problems
Level 1	Abuse of power Conflict-of-interest Nepotism	Prime Minister's Department Ministry of Finance	PMD and MoF initiated; the cabinet gave final approval **Policy abuse:** Concessions not reaching targeted group **Bureaucracy / procurement system:** Award process abused during direct negotiation	No limits on power of ministers in the procurement process No transparency in every segment of the procurement process No protection for bureaucrats to whistleblow on decision-making misconduct

Jana Wibawa

Level	Type of Corruption (Alleged)	Institutions	How Misgovernance Occurred	Key Problems
			Bureaucrats appear to have been hampered from adhering to directives	No requirement that politicians and their families declare their assets
Level 4	Bribery Selective patronage Rent-seeking Collusion Cronyism	Massive number of obscure companies	**Policy implementation:** Distributing contracts directly from Level 1 to Level 4. Private sector individuals determining who gets public contracts	No transparency and public access to the award of procurement projects; abuse of direct negotiations

Jana Wibawa

Level	Type of Corruption (Alleged)	Institutions	How Misgovernance Occurred	Key Problems
			Policy outcomes: Concessions channelled to obscure companies who may subcontract to non-Bumiputeras Funds channelled to party and politicians allegedly related to Jana Wibawa-based projects	No law that companies securing public projects cannot donate to party in government

LSC				
Level	Type of Corruption (Alleged)	Institutions	How Misgovernance Occurred	Key Problems
Level 1	Abuse of power Collusion	Cabinet of Ministers Ministry of Finance Ministry of Defence	**Ministerial abuse:** Relevant need in navy abused for apparent personal gain Minister helped BNS obtain contract and change design of ships without consulting the stakeholder (RMN) Posts of prime minister and finance minister held by one person (Najib)—centralization of decision-making power	Prime Minister occupying more than one portfolio Unlimited powers of ministers in procurement process No law to hold key ministers accountable

LSC				
Level	Type of Corruption (Alleged)	Institutions	How Misgovernance Occurred	Key Problems
			Loss of bureaucratic independence: Did the costing, but price was inflated	
			Unnecessary direct negotiation—orders from minister (*sila laksanakan*)	
Level 2	Abuse of institutions: statutory body / GLIC	Lembaga Tabung Angkatan Tentera	**Public institutions abused:** Government has indirect control of projects through state-controlled institutions (LTAT and Boustead); can dictate how projects are implemented	Public institutions diverted from their objectives when they function as businesses

The Lessons Learned

LSC				
Level	Type of Corruption (Alleged)	Institutions	How Misgovernance Occurred	Key Problems
			Pension fund (LTAT): Abused to bailout failing GLCs and projects	
Level 3	Collusion CBT Abuse of procurement process	Boustead publicly-quoted, but now delisted Chairmanship roles in GLIC, listed GLC, & unlisted GLCs	**Key Actors / institutions:** Appointing allies as chairman of multiple companies (Lodin—close Najib associate)—making crucial decisions on behalf of principals Banks (enablers)—Affin Bank provides a huge loan	Allies sitting as chairmen of numerous companies Key figures in defence controversies since 1980s: prime ministers (Mahathir and Najib); defence ministers (Najib and Zahid); professionals (Lodin of LTAT / Boustead)

LSC Level	Type of Corruption (Alleged)	Institutions	How Misgovernance Occurred	Key Problems
			Procurement process: Appointing contractors via direct negotiations (BNS)—misappropriating project funds and poor financial management	No politician—and Lodin—was charged, despite major controversies, suggesting inadequate legislation, possibly selective prosecution Compromised institutions—MACC; AG's Chambers
Level 4	Creating multiple layers of contracting Transnational collusion	Joint ventures (CAD) Foreign firms (DCNS)	**Strategic partners:** Deliberately creating numerous layers of contracting to inflate cost (CAD / CED)	No transparency in procurement process—particularly subcontracts

LSC

Level	Type of Corruption (Alleged)	Institutions	How Misgovernance Occurred	Key Problems
			Appointing foreign contractor with poor track record (DCNS–Scorpene); questions raised of kickbacks to UMNO Ceding management control of local companies to foreign firm (BHIC to Rheinmetall)	No monitoring of projects

MARA

Level	Type of Corruption (Alleged)	Institutions	How Misgovernance Occurred	Key Problems
Levels 1 and 2	-	Ministry of Rural and Regional Development MARA	-	Apex (minister and MARA chairman) claimed no knowledge of activities of holding company (MARA Inc.) Statutory bodies unnecessarily creating multiple holding companies
Level 4	Money laundering Money muling Collusion Conflict-of-interest Price inflation	MARA Incorporated	**Directorship:** Chairman (Mohammad Lan Allani) and CEO (Abdul Halim Rahim) deal with foreign developers to purchase foreign properties at an inflated price	Absence of checks and balances after creation of multiple holding companies Directors have too much decision-making power

MARA

Level	Type of Corruption (Alleged)	Institutions	How Misgovernance Occurred	Key Problems
			Chairman and CEO also directors of BVI (tax haven) company	
Level 5	Money laundering Money muling	Thrushcross Land Holding Ltd (BVI company)	**Shell companies:** Being abused to launder money	Legislation on employment of shell companies is weak
	Collusion			
	Bribery	Shelf Company (in Singapore)	Creating multiple layers of offshore shell companies to purchase foreign properties at an inflated price	Only exposed when Australian contractor informed the press
	Abuse of Power			
	Conflict-of-interest			

FELCRA

Level	Type of Corruption (Alleged)	Institutions	How Misgovernance Occurred	Key Problems
Level 1	Abuse of power	Ministry of Finance Ministry of Rural and Regional Development Statutory body (FELCRA)	**Ministry:** Shift of power—from settlers to MoF and chairman of holding company (FELCRA Bhd) **Public institutions:** Structural change: FELCRA–statutory body (Level 2) to FELCRA Bhd–Business group (Level 4)	Ministries have enormous control over corporatized bodies Corporatized bodies not answerable to parliament and settlers CCM has not shown capacity to monitor corporatized bodies Corporatization policy has failed

FELCRA

Level	Type of Corruption (Alleged)	Institutions	How Misgovernance Occurred	Key Problems
			FELCRA Bhd creating diverse number of subsidiaries (Level 5)	Appointment of politicians to chairmanship of FELCRA Bhd
			Proxy: Political appointments: Chairman of corporatized statutory bodies (UMNO members appointed as FELCRA Bhd's chairman)	No transparency in implementing PFI (selection of funders and contractors)
Level 2	Abuse of power	Statutory body (MoF Inc.)		
Level 4	Bribery	Corporatized body (FELCRA Bhd)	**Policy abuse:** Was PFI policy abused to inflate project price (Menara FELCRA)?	

Table 4.1 illustrates corruption at the apex of Malaysia's governance system being aided by a range of control tools available to political elites. Cabinet members can control the mode of implementation of these public concessions by placing politicians on the boards of institutions at Level 2—GLICs, statutory bodies, and key foundations that have direct and indirect control over companies at the lower rungs of this pyramid. In extremely covert rent-distribution cases, politicians at Level 1 bypass institutions at Levels 2 and 3 and channel concessions to obscure companies at Level 4. The workings of the GLCs at Levels 4 and 5, where there is no transparency and accountability, drive down the entry of new firms and marginalize those in business. This is a key factor contributing to the current crisis of developing SMEs in Malaysia.

Such discreet methods of distributing concessions, through ownership and control networks in this Political–GLC complex, have resulted in corruption that is most pervasive at Levels 2 and 4. Once corruption reaches Level 4, it permeates and spreads deep into society. Once there, it is often seen as a form of petty corruption, primarily bribery, and kickbacks, while those charged for corporate malfeasance are company directors situated in this level, as seen in the LCS, MARA, and FELCRA controversies. Meanwhile, the outcomes of investments emerging from collusive ties, particularly in the LCS case study, include low quality products, poorly maintained services, and perversely priced products.

The case studies point to the need to identify the decision-making power elites in this Political–GLC complex of rent creation, distribution, and implementation. In each case study, this group was different and made more complex with regime changes. In the Jana Wibawa controversy, although it was Muhyiddin Yassin who was charged in court following a regime change, he pointed to the role of the then finance minister, Tengku Zafrul Aziz, in the award of these contracts. Zafrul, who was appointed minister of trade and industry when Anwar took office as prime minister, was not charged with any offence related to the implementation of the Jana Wibawa policy. The LCS controversy occurred during Najib Razak's premiership, though the problems related to this project emerged during Mahathir's first administration. The problems in MARA and FELCRA began under Mahathir, related also to his active endeavour to corporatize statutory bodies, though abuse of their subsidiaries continued well into the late 2010s.

In all cases, when these politicians were in office, they worked closely with different business figures, some prominent, others quite obscure. In the Jana Wibawa case, it is difficult to identify some business figures who obtained control over the projects created by the government. In the LCS controversy, a primary person helping to implement the project was Lodin Wok Kamaruddin, a well-known corporate figure linked to Najib, who had also been involved in other controversial defence deals and the 1MDB scandal. However, the LCS project was undertaken by a joint venture led by a little-known figure (also a political appointee) and a foreign manager (appointed by the German enterprise contracted to implement the project). Yet, in both the Jana Wibawa and LCS controversies, based on the court charges, the people dictating the allocation of the concessions and how they were to be implemented were members of the cabinet.

Since institutions created to check the excesses of government have been compromised and are unable to act impartially, this has contributed to the accumulation of extreme unaccountable wealth by political—and business—elites, thus undermining public trust in government. Another disconcerting outcome has been rural development being undermined despite hardcore poverty persisting in these areas—a point quite evident in the case studies on MARA and FELCRA. This is a particularly unfortunate outcome, as the largest of these public enterprises were established to redress rural underdevelopment and tackle hardcore poverty. Similar rural-based statutory bodies have been mired in Malaysia's most notorious scandals, as noted in Appendix 1.

Legal Inadequacies and Low Prosecution Rate[236]

A recurring theme in the case studies is that of non-permissible practices in public governance, specifically favouritism, leading to nepotism, cronyism, and selective patronage. Enterprises in the GLC ecosystem have been subjected to allegations of embezzlement, bailouts, and rent-seeking. Ironically, there are laws and regulations that can hush up bureaucrats from exposing these irregularities, if they become aware of it. In fact, no protection is accorded to bureaucrats who report misgovernance.

Undoubtedly, the rampant abuse of different GLCs happens due to the presence of legislation such as the Official Secrets Act and the Sedition Act, which severely hinder, and even prevent, whistleblowing. Although a Whistleblowers Protection Act was introduced in 2010, critics contend that whistleblowing is a 'rare occurrence'.[237] Two reasons have been attributed to this reluctance to whistleblow. Under this Act, first, the 'whistleblower will not be afforded protection' if the person goes public using 'channels other than what is stipulated under the provision to reveal the information, or reveals the information to a third party after disclosing it to the enforcement agency'; such agencies, as noted, are under the jurisdiction of the cabinet. Second, a whistleblower 'could face criminal prosecution if the information revealed is classified under the Official Secrets Act 1972', while the 'Penal Code criminalises public officials for revealing the

---

[236] An in-depth review of the legal inadequacies that need to be addressed is provided in Appendix 2, given the technical details that have to be considered when addressing different types of corruption. This section reviews the lessons learned about Malaysia's legal system and its capacity to deal misgovernance of public resources that has contributed to grand corruption.

[237] Christopher Leong. 2017. A Critical Look into the Whistleblower Protection Act 2010. *Policy Ideas No. 36*. Kuala Lumpur: Institute for Democracy and Economic Affairs (IDEAS).

information obtained while executing their duties or functions'.²³⁸ Confidentiality evidently serves a useful purpose in covert state–business relations.

However, these political–business ties emerging from the abuse of the GLCs are of concern, as court charges have exposed how the political system has come to be awash with dark money, that is covert political donations by businesspeople who have secured public contracts. Neither is there a law regulating political donations to curb the murky flow of funds into electoral contests nor is there one banning the beneficiaries of public projects from giving side payments to politicians or parties in power.²³⁹ Inevitably, the gush of dark money flooding the political system is deeply corroding political institutions and undermining the integrity and trustworthiness of elections. This was most evident in the 2013 general election when funds—it was later revealed—from 1MDB, then a little-known GLC controlled by the sitting prime minister, were unrestrainedly used during the campaign period.²⁴⁰

Other troubling matters have been occurring. Appendix 1 indicates persistent allegations of corruption and abuse of power directed at politicians who have served in the cabinet or as backbenchers in parliament. Although, in numerous cases,

---

²³⁸ Both quotes are from the following report: *Center to Combat Corruption and Cronyism*. 2021 Gaps in the Act: A Legal Analysis of Malaysia's Current Whistleblower Protection Laws: https://c4center.org/wp-content/uploads/C4-Center-Whistleblower-Protection-Report_.pdf

²³⁹ Since 2018, the numerous court cases embroiling prominent politicians revealed an embarrassing and alarming account of abuse of public projects that were allegedly awarded in return for huge kickbacks. In one case, when a former cabinet minister was questioned in court whether the RM2 million given to him by a 'close' business associate, purportedly over a land deal, was 'considered valuable', his astonishing response was: 'No it was not. To me it's like my pocket money, you know.' Quoted in: *The Edge* (5 March 2020): https://theedgemalaysia.com/article/rm2-just-pocket-money-%E2%80%94-ku-nan

²⁴⁰ Edmund Terence Gomez and Joseph Tong. 2021. Financing Politics in Malaysia: Reforming the System. *Journal of the Malaysian Parliament* 1: 69–97.

they have not been tried in a court of law. In other instances, these allegations have been withdrawn before or during the trial. One reason why governing elites have not been charged is the inadequacy of the laws to deal with forms of corruption that feature favouritism through cronyism, nepotism, even selective bailouts during economic crises. As the case studies indicate, even though cabinet members have decision-making control over corporate activities that result in allegations of corruption, there is no direct chain-of-command to prove this.

When politicians are charged with corruption, there is now a constant use of DNAAs (discharge not amounting to an acquittal) and NFAs (no further action). Some politicians have been given DNAAs when their parties became crucial to keep a coalition in power. This use of DNAAs has become serious enough for one prominent civil society organization, Bersih, to issue a strong statement on this matter. Bersih called for a 'moratorium on application of DNAA on high-profile cases involving politicians, namely Najib's ongoing and outstanding cases, his wife Rosmah Mansor's ongoing cases, Lim Guan Eng, Syed Saddiq and any other cases,' while entreating that the judiciary be allowed to 'determine their guilt or innocence without any interference from the AG (Attorney General) or his political master'.[241]

A year prior to Bersih's statement, in September 2022, Abdul Azeez Abdul Rahim, a UMNO leader, had been given a DNAA. He was reportedly facing 'three charges of accepting bribes amounting to RM5.2mil and six charges of money laundering in the amount of RM972,414.60, in relation to road projects in Perak and Kedah,' the latter his home state where he had served

---

[241] *The Malay Mail* (16 September 2023): https://www.malaymail.com/news/malaysia/2023/09/16/bersih-urges-pause-on-dnaa-in-high-profile-cases-calls-to-maintain-appeal-against-zahids-visa-system-case-acquittal/91171.

as an MP for the constituency of Baling.[242] Abdul Azeez also served as chairman of one of Malaysia's seven government-linked investment companies, the controversy-ridden Tabung Haji.

In June 2020, the prosecution dropped forty-six charges of corruption and money laundering against Musa Aman, another UMNO leader who had been the long-serving chief minister of Sabah, from 2003 to 2018. It was reported that the 'corruption charges alleged that Musa in his capacity as Sabah chief minister and chairman of the Board of Trustees of the Sabah Foundation had received US$50.1 million from eight logging concessionaires as an inducement to approve logging concessions for 16 companies.'[243]

One well-known politician was given a DNAA after securing a senior position in the cabinet. UMNO's current president, Ahmad Zahid Hamidi, who was facing numerous charges of corruption was given a DNAA in September 2023, less than a year after being appointed as deputy prime minister following the 2022 general elections. Zahid's trial commenced in 2019, and during those four years, since a prima facie case was established, there was a public backlash against his DNAA. Malaysia's Bar Council subsequently filed for a judicial review of Zahid's DNAA arguing that it had 'taken this recourse as part of its statutory duty to uphold the cause of justice, uninfluenced by fear or favour'.[244] Zahid's response was that the Bar Council was a 'mere busy body' because 'only a party who is adversely or gravely affected by the decision of the public prosecutor in this case may apply for leave

---

[242] *The Star* (23 September 2022): https://www.thestar.com.my/news/nation/2022/09/23/abdul-azeez-gets-dnaa-for-nine-graft-money-laundering-charges-over-road-projects

[243] *The Edge* (9 June 2020): https://theedgemalaysia.com/article/prosecution-drops-all-charges-against-musa-aman-judge-grants-acquittal

[244] *New Straits Times* (4 December 2023): https://www.nst.com.my/news/crime-courts/2023/12/986437/bar-council-files-judicial-review-ags-dnaa-decision-zahid

to file judicial review'.[245] Zahid went on to add that 'looking at the legal cases in the past where similar decisions were made, the applicant (the Bar Council) had been keeping silent or rather cowed or muted in their response'.[246]

Zahid's latter contention brought to the fore, once again, serious misgivings about 'selective prosecution.' There were numerous complaints of selective prosecution by politicians in the opposition when charged for offences that occurred when they were in government. These trends indicate the need for an autonomous Attorney General's Chamber, beyond the control of the cabinet, failing which corruption can be weaponized to indict powerful political figures in the opposition or to drop charges to forge political alliances to sustain or secure power.

Evidently, the abuse of institutions and GLCs persists under different government leaders because of inadequate legislation to deal with public misgovernance, while the Political–GLC complex offers the cabinet enormous control over the government's vast corporate base. As the LCS study indicates, this outrageously large network of cross-shareholdings comprises subnetworks where enterprises own each other directly or indirectly through chains of ownership relations. A similar trend of using multiple holding companies and cross-shareholdings is evident in the MARA case study. These cross-holdings and interlocking ownership ties allow for covert transactions that can be missed by regulatory institutions, the media, and investors—a reason why such corporate pyramid structures comprising numerous holding companies are banned in some countries.

Since these networks are riddled with graft and the flow of dark money, a core question that should be taken into consideration

---

[245] *New Straits Times* (11 January 2024): https://www.nst.com.my/news/crime-courts/2024/01/999865/zahid-calls-malaysian-bar-busy-body-challenging-his-dnaa

[246] Ibid.

when dealing with corruption is this: Who controls these institutions issuing orders that have to be followed by directors of GLCs down the pyramid? Since this question is not adequately tackled when dealing with corruption allegations linked to GLCs, as seen in the MARA controversy, power elites have near-total impunity when they misgovern during the distribution of public concessions. There is also no law that prevents politicians from being funded by any type of GLC. And, as the 1MDB scandal suggests, a politician can run a campaign entirely funded by a GLC.

With power concentrated in the cabinet, what is extremely disconcerting is that the review of Malaysia's statutes, in Appendix 2, indicates that the country is confronted with a 'curious paradox'. In this country, as argued in Appendix 2, politicians do not fall under the 'jurisdiction of any of the Service Commissions established under Part X of the Federal Constitution for the purposes of disciplinary control, but are deemed to be public servants when it comes to criminal offences. There are generally no codes or regulations to dictate how a Minister or elected representative is supposed to conduct themselves within the scope of their official functions.' This problem is even more acute when there is no abuse of power-related legislation to curb, or even prevent, nepotism, cronyism, and selective patronage, all allegedly widespread practices in the political system.

It is, however, difficult to precisely determine political favours because the forms through which they occur are often subtle and even concealed. Since obtaining evidence to conclusively prove favouritism is difficult, criminalization of such practices merits thought. Indeed, a more viable response would be to introduce administrative preventive measures. Meanwhile, to address other root causes of corruption, additional crucial reforms are required.

Chapter 5

Conclusion: The Reforms Malaysia Needs

Reviewing Public Governance: State Structure

What history teaches is that the federal and state governments are flirting with disaster by allowing this covert Political–GLC complex to persist in its current form, a lesson that can be gleaned from the disastrous outcomes of governing political parties controlling major enterprises. An inevitable consequence is poor market confidence in public governance, a core factor that has long hampered domestic investments.

There are three major paradoxes in the structure of the Malaysian state, which features extensive state–business relations that function through this Political–GLC complex. First, what is in place is a deeply corrupt system that can function legitimately. Second, the persistent rhetoric of government leaders has been of the need to tackle endemic corruption, a palatable statement for a nation deeply concerned about this debilitating problem. However, no politician, whether in government or in opposition, has called for the dismantling or even restructuring of the GLC ecosystem. Third, power is overwhelmingly concentrated in the cabinet that controls an ecosystem whose misuse can have major economic and political ramifications. And yet, legal avenues to curb ministerial misgovernance of the government's vast control over deeply-interlocked public and private enterprises are inadequate.

Reforms are required to stop the predatory options open to politicians through this ecosystem. To deal with grand corruption, cabinet hegemony must be checked through devolution of power and the introduction of appropriate checks and balances. As for the GLC ecosystem, it must be restructured to allow public institutions to autonomously carry out their social and economic roles. A core aspect of these two major reforms is the need to separate ownership and control of GLC-based enterprises. This issue of ownership and control also matters because the extent of GLC control can vary, taking the form of full ownership, minority ownership, and indirect ownership.[247]

Reforming this powerful and well-entrenched political-economic system encompasses dealing with corruption of different sorts, not merely bribery. Each form of corruption requires careful analysis to identify its distinctive features, the part of the body politic it affects, and what its specific causes are—an endeavour that will take time. Legislative reforms will be required to deal with the different types of favouritism leading to power abuse occurring in the GLC ecosystem and public governance. To undertake these reforms effectively, there is a need to strip away the shroud blanketing the enigmatic GLC ecosystem, quantify the number of enterprises within it, and determine how the public delivery system is abused to allow for the illegitimate flow of projects and funds to private hands.

These reforms are vital because, in countries where corruption is systemic, politicians in power are known to be extremely proactive in creating and distributing concessions

---

[247] Wilfred Dolfsma and Anna Grosman. 2019. State Capitalism Revisited: A Review of Emergent Forms and Developments. *Journal of Economic Issues*, 53 (2): 579–586: 10.1080/00213624.2019.1606653

through public policies.²⁴⁸ This is particularly disconcerting in the context of Malaysia because a core component of public policy implementation and rent distribution is a GLC infrastructure that connects the corporate sector and the political system.

Moreover, institutions remain in place even after one set of politicians is replaced by another following a power shift or regime change. A new regime can also comprise political elites from the old regime, though different government leaders differently employ the institutions in the GLC ecosystem. In essence, what has emerged is competing political elites attempting a form of state capture of an economic system created by an interventionist government to address serious socio-economic inequities, leading to various forms of state–business collusion.

Clearly, the full extent of corruption related to these public institutions and the enterprises that they control is difficult to quantify, with Appendix 1 providing only a snapshot of state–business-based controversies in Malaysia. The case studies offer insights into methods of abuse of this multi-level Political–GLC complex in the pursuit of vested political and business interests. A refined and nuanced definition of corruption is urgently required.

Interestingly, in this complex, the well-structured and deeply-centralized ties between the behemoth, moneyed GLICs and the publicly-listed GLCs are subjected to constant public scrutiny. The number of politicians as directors of quoted GLCs is extremely small, suggesting some adherence to good public and corporate governance.²⁴⁹ However, below these listed GLCs is

---

[248] John Joseph Wallis. 2006. The Concept of Systematic Corruption in American History. In Edward L. Glaeser and Claudia Goldin (eds). *Corruption and Reform: Lessons from America's Economic History.* Chicago: Chicago University Press: 23–62.

[249] However, as noted in Chapter 3, despite this, in the LCS scandal, a publicly-listed GLC controlled by a GLIC was mired in business controversies emerging from the close ties between one professional director and the then sitting prime minister.

an unstructured, near invisible, mountain of unlisted enterprises going down many levels, areas where colossal wastage is occurring, extensive patronage prevails, and varieties of corruption feature. At the lower levels of this pyramid, politicians appointed as directors of these obscure, unlisted companies can abuse public resources without difficulty.

The struggle to secure access to this vast and veiled patronage system is contributing to political fragmentation at the apex. Persistent feuding among the political elite has exacerbated exploitation and misuse of the GLC infrastructure, leading to the covert flow of considerable public funds into the political system, undermining its legitimacy. Moreover, with control over this shadow economy, political elites can become economic elites, a principal factor contributing to grand corruption. As this confluence of political and economic power permeates down many levels into the corporate sector and society, this contributes to equally debilitating petty corruption.

Checking Corruption

The case studies offer insights into complex cross-holdings and control tools that can be exploited, which result in different forms of corruption. Constructive reforms to deal with this hugely defective GLC ecosystem must focus on three core areas:

1. **Prevention**: Structural reforms (power devolution and checks and balances), primarily at Level 1
2. **Corrective public governance**: With focus on institutions at Level 2 and the multitude of GLCs at Levels 4 and 5
3. **Criminalization**: New laws and amendments to existing legislation are required to curb corruption.

Prevention: Structural Reforms

In the numerous proposals by civil society to curb corruption, the focus has been on prevention through structural reforms, amendments to laws, and the introduction of legislation dealing with freedom of information, the procurement process, and fiscal responsibility. These reform demands are among those listed in the well-structured National Anti-Corruption Plan 2019-2023,[250] introduced before the fall of the Mahathir administration in 2020. Most of these reforms have not been instituted. One structural reform long demanded by civil society that was instituted, but only between 2018 and 2022, was that the prime minister should not concurrently serve as the minister of finance.

A fundamental fear in the context of a highly interventionist government is executive usurpation of the GLC ecosystem, a form of state capture. The cabinet's control over the GLC ecosystem has persistently led to the misuse of bureaucracy, policies, and public delivery system. Enterprises in the GLC ecosystem serve as strategic avenues for the practice of selective patronage, deemed permissible, since policies are structured for implementation in a targeted manner. However, policies targeted at one ethnic group have been exploited to primarily benefit the well-connected.

In public governance, apart from devolving power concentrated in the office of the executive, an accompanying need is for an arms-length relationship between the cabinet and oversight institutions, specifically the MACC, Bank Negara, and the Securities Commission. The autonomy of the Attorney General's Chambers is imperative or, if it is to retain its role as legal advisor to the government, an office of the public prosecutor that has no ties with the cabinet should be established.

---

[250] Apart from the reforms listed below, which pertain principally to curbing corruption within the GLC ecosystem, the recommendations in the National Anti-Corruption Plan have to be considered when discussing methods to tackle this problem.

Relevant monitoring institutions should have the autonomy to screen the award and execution of public projects. These regulatory and enforcement authorities need to be equipped with personnel who have the training, funding, and tools required to fight corruption. Preventive reform measures must include delineating the role of economic public institutions and how they allocate government-generated concessions.

Corrective Public Governance: Dismantling the Political–GLC Complex

This book has focused on two issues: first, providing an assessment of Malaysia's complex GLC ecosystem comprising many interacting or interconnected business-related public institutions; second, outlining how this ecosystem is controlled and misgoverned by ministries through an analysis of major corporate controversies. This dual approach to analysing state–business relations in Malaysia has exposed how a well-entrenched Political–GLC complex contributes to the woeful governance of the government's vast economic resources. This scrutiny of types of corruption, as perpetrated through institutions in the GLC ecosystem, offers insights into the wide-ranging public governance reforms that are required.

Two core findings emerge from the case studies. First, a common denominator in all three cases is the presence of politicians with the authority to control. Second, the concessions created by the government are awarded to beneficiaries who are not selected based on bureaucratic procedures. Power abuse in public office takes the form of selectively allocating publicly-generated concessions and then imposing obligations on the beneficiaries, including channelling money into the coffers of governing parties or the bank accounts of political elites.

In this context, the principal institutional reform, one that can lead to momentous and meaningful change, is to subject the entire GLC ecosystem to public scrutiny. Uncovering and quantifying the whole GLC ecosystem and flattening its pyramidal structure is hardly controversial and will play a vital role in curbing corruption and ensuring transparent and accountable implementation of policies and projects. Casting light on this shadow GLC ecosystem, which serves as a difficult-to-trace source of funds, will keep politicians accountable during the distribution of public concessions while appreciably reducing the flooding of the political system with dark money.

The control tools of this ecosystem, situated in the hands of the cabinet, must be appraised. The government's role when promoting economic and corporate development through its business-related institutions must be publicized to prevent public concessions from being channelled to well-connected companies, party members, and the electorate in strategic constituencies. This is obligatory to dispel concerns that the resources in the GLCs are expended to fund the party machinery—a covert form of colossal public funding for governing parties.

To curb these forms of misgovernance, the economic and social roles played by different types of government-linked institutions must be clearly demarcated. The copious use of GLCs—which operate covertly in the corporate sector, including to fund parties—will then be checked. There are no laws to prevent the financing of politics by GLCs. The dismantling and reshaping of the GLC ecosystem will curb the abuse of public resources that has contributed to improper parcelling out of land and equity, embezzlement, money laundering, and the creation of slush funds.

Limit cabinet authority and develop transparent political–bureaucratic relations

The cabinet controls critical resources, such as land and equity, as well as funds from the pension funds, development financial institutions (DFIs), and GLC banks. Ministers have allocation and operational control, with decision-making authority over the promulgation of policies and the distribution of the concessions accruing from them. The cabinet's allocation control over public concessions is a core factor contributing to allegations of cronyism, nepotism, and selective patronage, with no protection for bureaucrats who report misconduct.

Since there is considerable concentration of economic power at the apex, boundaries that cabinet members cannot cross must be created. Anti-corruption reforms must focus on controlling the actions of the ministers. Cabinet members should not dictate the manner of implementation of these policies and projects, a role that should be left to the bureaucracy. The cabinet, in fact, should be controlled by law to ensure it does not interfere in policy and project implementation.

A parliamentary select committee should review complaints of policy and project implementation as a check on bureaucracy. This will encourage scrutiny of policy implementation while also safeguarding transparency in every segment of the procurement process (Levels 1 and 2) and when components of a project need to be subcontracted (in Levels 4 and 5).

Moreover, cabinet members—or their family members—have a prominent presence in the corporate sector, including owning major enterprises. There is evidence of the revolving door phenomenon—of businessmen appointed to cabinet who later return to running their companies.[251] While ministers must relinquish their corporate holdings when in office, their equity interests can be channelled to family and proxies, with public contracts subsequently awarded to them. And they can introduce policies and regulations that favour their companies. Two issues require attention here. First, address the absence of a mandated asset declaration by elected representatives and their

---

[251] For a review of the revolving door phenomenon in Malaysia, see: Edmund Terence Gomez. 2023. Business in Politics: Seeking Control of Malaysia's Political System. In *State of Corruption*: 121–156.

family members. This asset declaration should be issued annually and made publicly available. Second, to deal with the use of proxies, beneficial ownership requirements must be enhanced to ensure disclosure of the ultimate owners of companies securing government concessions.

Reform the ecosystem

The core elements of a well-functioning, GLC-based institutional system are responsible political decisions, deliberation and coordination boards, and transparent and accountable implementation of public policies and projects. A well-constructed institutional structure, designed to foster effective state–business ties, should stress three essential functions: meaningful information exchange, accountable allocation, and minimal rent-seeking.[252] Two issues, thus, need to be addressed: transparency and coordination.

Coordination is crucial because figuring prominently in this ecosystem are GLICs, statutory bodies, SPVs, and holding companies, as well as quoted or partially-privatized GLCs and their privately-incorporated subsidiaries, while transparency curbs misgovernance of these enterprises. These government-controlled public and private enterprises have different goals, ranging from operating in sectors with natural monopoly characteristics, to supplying goods and services and supporting national strategies or social policies. An appraisal is required of the implications of this restructuring on the market, as it necessitates distinguishing between competitive partially-privatized GLCs and statutory bodies whose primary role is fulfilling their social obligations. These reforms entail determining the necessity of a variety of enterprises, as well as the hazards of reforming them, and addressing both. This assessment includes deciding how they

---

[252] Ben Ross Schneider. 2015. *Designing Industrial Policy in Latin America: Business-State Relations and the New Developmentalism*. New York: Palgrave Macmillan.

should be structured and controlled, and how they should function, as well as what the relationship between them will be.

The core institutions that require review are the GLICs, as these seven institutions hold in trust a large volume of corporate equity. In August 2023, the MoF disclosed the fund size of each of these GLICs: EPF (RM1.096 billion), PNB (RM332 billion), Khazanah (RM122.5 billion), KWAP (RM167 billion), Tabung Haji (RM91 billion), and LTAT (RM10.5 billion). These six GLICs collectively owned RM451.3 billion worth of listed corporate equity, which constituted 25.63 per cent of the total market.[253] The GLICs are the hub of this huge, interlocked network of public enterprises, and listed and unlisted GLCs. This concentration of corporate control has contributed to numerous controversies, with three of these GLICs——Tabung Haji, LTAT, and KWAP—being persistently and deeply mired in major corporate scandals. This plainly indicates that Tabung Haji and LTAT should not function as business groups. Meanwhile, MoF Inc., which ultimately owns these GLICs, neither has directors nor is it under the management of professionals. Control is vested in the office of the minister of finance, which severely undermines the principle of checks and balances.[254]

There is a long list of statutory bodies, most of which are out of the public eye and constantly open to misgovernance. These statutory bodies play a vital role in different areas of the economy and society while their activities are dictated by the minister in-charge, though a board of directors ensures implementation of policies and projects. Since statutory bodies are governed by their respective statutes, these legislations require review to ensure

---

[253] *The Edge* (21 November 2023). The total volume of listed corporate equity held by the seventh GLC, MoF Inc., was not disclosed in this report.

[254] There are provisions in the statutory acts of LTAT and Tabung Haji that give the minister of defence and minister of Islamic affairs, respectively, some jurisdiction over them.

loopholes are covered to prevent them from being subjected to exploitation. Numerous statutory bodies function as business groups, a practice that must cease. Evidently, neither do these statutory bodies need corporatization nor should they be required to establish companies because their role is not to generate revenue. The corporatization of public agencies has blurred the line between the public and the private while changing the objectives of socially-inclined government institutions to one where they are asked to focus on revenue generation and profit maximization, even going into competition with the SMEs that they are supposed to aid.

There are holding companies that function as statutory bodies. On the other hand, numerous holding companies, incorporated under the Companies Act, serve to own and control the subsidiaries of GLICs and statutory bodies. The level of prominence of these holding companies differs, depending on where they are situated in the pyramid. These holding companies are most visible at Level 2 and near invisible at Level 4. The need for holding companies should be questioned, as they have been associated with allegations of money laundering and money muling as seen in the case study of MARA. Moreover, enterprises under the control of holding companies can be directly managed by the relevant GLIC or statutory body.

Some foundations play an important, though complex, role in terms of ownership and control of public institutions. For example, the National Equity Corporation or Permodalan Nasional Bhd (PNB) a major GLIC, is wholly-owned by the Bumiputera Investment Foundation (Yayasan Pelaburan Bumiputera or YPB). However, the use of foundations in more obscure ways is widespread, as seen in the institutional structures of four ministries—PMD, MoF, MRRD, and Mindef. There is no law stipulating how foundations should function.

The institutions in urgent need of reform within the GLC ecosystem are those that function as companies or what correctly constitute GLCs. The number of GLCs within this ecosystem must be quantified, as the government appears unaware of how many of them have been incorporated. This is vital because the figures of the four core ministries reveal the existence of extremely bloated infrastructures (at Level 4) where huge fund wastage and corruption occur. In this segment of the GLC ecosystem, misgovernance is out of control and in dire need of an in-depth evaluation. This review entails determining if these unlisted GLCs are required and, if there is a need for them, how they are to be owned, managed, and monitored. Reforming this section of the ecosystem has to be handled carefully because these GLCs, collectively, employ many people, a large volume of whom probably belong to the lower income bracket and are based in rural areas.

When determining which institutions are necessary, the related issues are their location, volume of physical assets, quality of personnel, and ability to carry out their responsibilities. This is necessary to address the problem of numerous enterprises doing similar things, thus reducing overlap and enhancing coordination. Internal reorganization of personnel—the directors, management, and employees—is essential to remove political appointees who contribute little or nothing to the enterprise.

Restructure institutional governance

The current system of federal ministries controlling a multitude of public and private enterprises that function actively in the corporate sector must cease. A major institutional governance change entails creating a commission to monitor all types of institutions in this vast GLC ecosystem. The commission's initial role will be to identify, list, and assess the enterprises in this ecosystem, then move to improve coordination between them while enhancing their governance. The volume of corporate equity—and other assets—owned, ultimately by the MoF must be publicly available while control and management methods should be clear. This GLC commission will advance endeavours to enhance financial transparency and administrative coordination of the enterprises under its watch. This commission must be independent of the cabinet, as it will serve as the location of all forms of government-linked, business-based institutions.

When determining the structure of this commission, guardrails must be built in to prevent executive interference. This will accord the commission the autonomy and administrative control to enforce changes in this ecosystem and act independently when monitoring the performance of these enterprises. For example, each statutory body would need to have an unambiguous economic or social strategy while enterprises that function under the Companies Act must be carefully monitored with the aid of the Companies Commission of Malaysia. This GLC commission will address the reasons why GLCs are not operating as per their role.

The commission has to be accorded coordinating authority to reduce non-transparent transactions that lead to selective patronage, cronyism, and collusion. Transparency will also be improved by ensuring asset disclosure and well-defined employment procedures, while guaranteeing the public and civil society organizations access to information, enforcing regular audits, and monitoring the management and financial performance of GLC-based institutions. The reasons for contracting out must be transparent and publicly disclosed. This will trim the cost of projects and decrease the volume of transactions, specifically unnecessary subcontracting that reduces quality and augments profits, considered crucial for kickbacks.

This commission, inevitably, has to monitor the appointment process of directors and senior management of GLC-based institutions, with an emphasis on limiting the number of companies functioning in Level 4—and, inevitably, in Level 5. There is also a need to monitor if joint ventures, domestic and foreign, are necessary. A core work of the commission is ascertaining that the resources of GLC-based institutions are not deployed to serve political interests in key constituencies while also banning them from financing party activities.

The nomination process of members of the commission has to be codified, with the selection committee comprising the prime minister, the opposition leader, head of the relevant parliamentary select committee, and the chief secretary of the government. The commission's members will play an advisory role to the cabinet on operational and technical issues, given their knowledge of how the institutions in the GLC ecosystem are controlled and function. Moreover, the cabinet will have to rely on the commission's members and the directors they appoint to implement and accomplish policy goals. The commission will provide information on individual enterprises when there is a public request for them.

Directorships and managerial control

A fundamental question in the public domain has long been whether politicians should sit on the boards of GLC-based institutions. The appointment of politicians as GLC directors ostensibly ensures that these institutions implement policies as expected by the cabinet, though there is little evidence of this. However, even professionals have been subservient to the cabinet when securing a GLC directorship. The right question to then ask is this: What mechanisms should be put in place so that the directors of GLCs are independent of political influence? A related issue is the need to keep the conduct of these directors under public scrutiny.

The only institution where politicians can be appointed as directors is Khazanah Nasional, the country's only sovereign wealth fund (SWF). The core functions of a SWF include investment decisions in new industries in the economy, a reason why the prime minister and minister of finance can serve on Khazanah Nasional's board. However, adequate checks and balances are necessary. For example, the prime minister and minister of finance should have no voting rights on proposals tabled for consideration. The board members cannot be removed and must have a fixed term limit. For the other GLICs, specifically the pension and investment funds, politicians should not serve as directors. An independent board of directors is required for MoF Inc., the government's equity holding company.

As for statutory bodies created and deployed to serve economic, educational, and social needs, there is no need for politicians to serve as their directors. Banning politicians from the boards of statutory bodies is imperative given their roles and where they are primarily located. In numerous instances, the function of a statutory body is spatially determined, that is they are situated in rural areas. Statutory bodies also have a class-based dimension, in that they target the poor and those in the lower-income bracket. Currently, statutory bodies are abused through the practice of ethnic-based patronage to secure the support of key constituencies during elections. Public universities are statutory bodies with politicians appointed to the boards of these tertiary education institutions as a method to control students and even academics.

The guidelines for the appointment of directors of institutions in the GLC ecosystem should be based on several criteria to guarantee competent enterprise management. Incumbent public officials directly linked with the cabinet cannot be appointed as directors. Politically-exposed persons should not be inducted as directors or management of these institutions. Board appointments should happen through an open selection process. Members of these boards should have control over the organizational structure and the appointment of the senior management. These boards must evidently comprise a well-credentialed technocratic group that has the know-how to develop these enterprises.[255] This is crucial because the boards of these

---

[255] Identifying these technocrats will not be easy. In fact, those who are qualified may not accept the government's offer to manage the GLCs because this entails being summoned to parliament to account for their business decisions while also constantly being in the public eye. This does not justify the argument that politicians should be appointed to lead these GLCs.

enterprises have overall responsibility for long-term strategic planning and budget supervision. Crucially, too, board decisions can be of a commercial nature, which necessitates expertise and transparency in decision-making.

The cabinet should not be allowed to intervene in decision-making by these boards, particularly in matters relating to the implementation of policies and projects, but can voice their concerns, if any, to the commission monitoring the GLC ecosystem. The current practice where statutory bodies submit their annual reports to parliament for scrutiny and debate should be maintained.

Criminalization?: Legislative and enforcement reforms

Given the variety of state–business relations and the large scale of the GLC ecosystem, what is required is well-designed and enforceable regulations and protection from abuses by those in government. Since politicians are escaping conviction when brought to court, and some cases cannot be prosecuted, a root concern is whether the laws are comprehensive enough to deal with grand corruption. Evidently, the laws overseeing these ties need to be reviewed, with a focus on whether amendments or new legislations are required. Legislative reforms require careful attention, starting with outlining how corruption, a polyvalent concept, is defined or how it should be redefined.

A thoughtful review is required of actions emerging from the award of public concessions that feature favouritism in all its forms—selective patronage, cronyism, nepotism, and collusion. These forms of favouritism must be criminalized, given their rampant practice, seen particularly in the procurement process. While a legal definition of favouritism encompassing cronyism, nepotism, and collusion is critical, such terms can be difficult to define in a way that ensures they are unambivalent and enforceable. It needs to be decided if these definitions can be woven into existing legislation such as the MACC Act or if a new law needs to be created.

For example, Prime Minister Anwar Ibrahim has, correctly, spoken of a 'policy and legal strategy to curb rent-seeking activities',[256] as well as his intent to introduce a Government Procurement Act.[257] The proposal to separately legislate on rent-seeking and on monitoring the procurement process merits careful consideration, specifically when dealing with a concept such as 'rent', which can be difficult to define. Furthermore, rents created by the government, if openly and properly deployed in the economy, can generate growth and create new, vital, industries. The focus, then, should be on the process of determining how publicly-generated rents are awarded to curb rent-seeking. Two matters merit consideration: first, precise, unambiguous use of terms when drafting a law; second, since bribes are given during the procurement process, the focus should be on a well-constructed Procurement Act to curb rent-seeking. The core point is the need to avoid over-legislating, particularly when all that is required is amendments to existing legislation, thus instituting reforms speedily.

Other covert and unbridled practices that should be proscribed include the laundering of proceeds of corruption, as well as concealment. There is also a need to better understand and respond to the transnational dimensions of corruption, including tax evasion through the use of offshore accounts in tax havens, a practice that has to be banned. There is an important reason for this. A number of prominent Malaysian politicians and businesspeople, as well as their family members, were named

---

[256] *The Star* (11 July 2023): https://www.thestar.com.my/news/nation/2023/07/11/pm-law-being-mulled-to-end-ali-baba039-culture

[257] *New Straits Times* (24 February 2023): https://www.nst.com.my/news/nation/2023/02/883248/2023-budget-govt-will-table-postponed-government-procurement-act-improve

in the Panama Papers and the Pandora Papers. The Malaysians named in these two exposés included:

1. the children of three former prime ministers—Mahathir Mohamad's son, Mirzan; Najib Razak's son, Naziffudin; and Muhyiddin Yassin's son, Fakhri Yassin;[258]
2. the family members of former finance minister Daim Zainuddin, specifically his wife, daughter, and two sons;
3. two children of former Sarawak Chief Minister Taib Mahmud—his son, Mahmud Abu Bekir, and his daughter, Hanifah Taib, currently a deputy minister; and
4. the son of former Sabah Chief Minister Musa Aman, Yamani Hafez Musa.

Since the children of former prime ministers, chief ministers, and a finance minister were named in the Panama Papers and Pandora Papers, this has inevitably led to serious questions about the issue of nepotism and the storing of huge sums of money in secret locations. Other concerns were raised after the release of these papers. The substantial volume of funds held by shell companies in offshore accounts suggested tax evasion while raising the possibility that this was money accrued from illegal activities that had been channelled out of the country. There was also the likelihood that offshore accounts served as slush funds for politicians during electoral contests within the party and during federal and state elections. In some cases, it appeared that nominees or proxies of politicians were being used to hold assets on their behalf.[259]

---

[258] *Astro Awani* (13 May 2016): https://www.astroawani.com/berita-malaysia/three-more-malaysian-politicians-sons-named-panama-papers-105246?

[259] According to one news outlet, the name of Daim's close associate, Josephine Premla Sevaretnam—reported to be 'a former lawyer and deputy public prosecutor, who served alongside Daim in the service before holding key positions in his various ventures'—appeared in foreign companies associated

Conclusion: The Reforms Malaysia Needs

Politicians and their family members have been investigated by the MACC in relation to their offshore accounts, including Mahathir's sons and Daim, his wife, and his children. However, by early 2024, not all politicians named in the Panama Papers and Pandora Papers were similarly subjected to an investigation, including Taib Mahmud and his family. Deputy Prime Minister Zahid Hamidi and another cabinet member, Zafrul Aziz, have similarly not been investigated though both were named in the Pandora Papers. These two ministers are UMNO members.

In this reformed public governance system, there must be precautions to curb the confluence of political and economic power if corruption is to be checked. This entails ending anonymity and imposing safeguards to restrict working with certain types of firms, including enterprises that do not properly report their beneficial owners. One important legislative revision on beneficial ownership did occur when the Companies (Amendment) Bill, 2023, was passed in parliament, though this was a response by the government to the Financial Action Task Force (FATF),[260] of which Malaysia is an observer. FATF, an inter-governmental agency, was established in 1989 by the G7 to tackle, among other things, money laundering and financial crime.[261] In the amendment to this bill, a beneficial owner is defined as a person who 'ultimately owns or controls over a company and includes a person who exercises ultimate effective control over

---

with him. These companies included a Swiss bank, ICB Banking Group, in which Daim has a substantial equity interest, Newton Invest & Finance Limited (in the BVI), and Splendid International Ltd (in the BVI). See *Malaysiakini* (4 October 2021): https://www.malaysiakini.com/news/593919

[260] See the statement by the central bank, *Bank Negara Malaysia* (7 June 2023): https://amlcft.bnm.gov.my/documents/6312201/10624487/Preparation+of+Malaysia%27s+MEE+2024-2025.pdf/ea9e1196-17bb-db01-2614-c9902446dc58?t=1686211932154

[261] Details of the activities of FATF can be obtained at its website: *FATF*: https://www.fatf-gafi.org/en/the-fatf/what-we-do.html

a company'.[262] All information on beneficial owners of private enterprises is to be lodged with the Companies Commission of Malaysia (CCM), which is under the jurisdiction of the Minister of Domestic Trade and Cost of Living (see Figure 2.3).

Three notable points emerge from this legal amendment dealing with this important issue of beneficial ownership. First, the government's response to repeated calls for greater transparency on beneficial owners of companies only occurred following pressure from a foreign agency. Second, information from companies about their beneficial owners is to be given to a government agency, the CCM. The public does not have open access to this information, thus undermining the call for transparency on the issue of ultimate beneficial owners. Third, the minister in charge of CCM has the authority to 'exempt any class of companies from the application of this Division either unconditionally or subject to such terms as the Minister may impose'.[263] This provision to allow the minister to selectively exempt companies from disclosing their beneficial owners can be subjected to abuse.

These amendments indicate how legislative changes need not necessarily lead to greater transparency and accountability. In fact, cabinet members may be vested with more power to decide how to selectively use information that they are privy to about the beneficial owners of companies. This issue of not publicly disclosing ultimate beneficial owners of companies is of particular concern, as a large number of GLCs function as private enterprises. In the amendment to this bill, no restrictions were placed on enterprises whose key personnel or beneficial owners include a public official with a potential conflict-of-interest. Such a provision is imperative because GLC-based institutions should not deal with politically-exposed third parties and should publicly commit to avoiding inappropriate partnerships. Only

---

[262] Companies (Amendment) Bill, 2023: Section 60A(2).
[263] Companies (Amendment) Bill, 2023: Section 60E.

with appropriate legislative reforms will there be an increased likelihood of detection and the certainty of punishment, making it harder to commit a corrupt act.

Closing Remarks

The ramifications of allowing this Political–GLC complex to remain in place are evidently troubling, given the scale and scope of government intervention in the economy. Meanwhile, politicians have not learned the lessons from persistent state–business controversies. Although, among their horrendous outcomes are the massive abuse of the meagre savings of the poor, the continued marginalization of rural Bumiputera communities though affirmative action-based policies have targeted them over the past five decades, the persistent destabilization of the political system because of acrimonious intra-power elite feuds over the spoils of the government, and the murder of an auditor and a foreign interpreter.[264] This situation is made worse by the fact that there is no playbook to deal with problems stemming from this ecosystem, most clearly seen when the LCS and 1MDB scandals erupted, the repercussions of which continue to haunt the nation.

Moreover, because of this Political–GLC complex, equitable development is at risk, market entry is limited, and competition is fettered, while policies do not redress social, spatial, and economic inequities. A GLC ecosystem created by the government to solve socio-economic inequities and promote justice now functions as a method for power elites to expropriate public resources and finance a political system heavily embedded in the practice of patronage and mired in monied politics.

---

[264] During the BMF controversy, Jalil Ibrahim was sent to Hong Kong to audit the accounts of this GLC. He was found murdered in Hong Kong in 1983. Altantuya Shaariibuu, a Mongolian national who served as a translator in defence deals, was murdered in 2006. For a discussion of these two murder cases, see: Teh Yik Koon. 2018. *From BMF to 1MDB: A Criminological and Sociological Discussion*. Petaling Jaya: Strategic Information & Research Development Centre (SIRD).

What aids this resistance to change by governing elites is that there is little public knowledge or understanding of this dense multi-layered GLC ecosystem and of its extensive misgovernance. The public also knows little about the serious undermining of a once well-functioning bureaucratic structure and of the staggering influence that governing politicians have over the corporate sector through this GLC ecosystem, which can be abused in numerous ways to suit their interests.

A redeeming factor in this dismal situation is the active role played by civil society to educate the public about these issues, even when confronted with a highly authoritarian government. Among the key NGOs that have persistently and vigorously campaigned to promote accountable and transparent governance are the Bar Council; Bersih (which began its crusade for fair elections in 2005,[265] including by curbing the use of dark money in electoral contests); the Center to Combat Corruption and Cronyism, and Transparency International (Malaysia), both strident anti-corruption advocates; and the Institute for Democracy and Economic Affairs (IDEAS), a think tank that has strongly campaigned for, among other things, rule of law. Another civil society institution that has been rigorously pursuing reforms is the Malay news daily, *Sinar Harian*, whose owner, Hussamuddin Yaacub, created a movement, 'Rasuah Busters' (Bribery Busters), that serves to educate the public on the repercussions of corruption.[266]

---

[265] An account of the launch of Bersih, as the Coalition for Clean and Fair Elections, is provided by Khoo Ying Hooi. 2020. *The Bersih Movement and Democratisation in Malaysia: Repression, Dissent and Opportunities*. Lanham, Maryland: Lexington Books; Danny Lim. 2022. *We Are Marching Now: The Inside Story of Bersih 1.0*. Petaling Jaya: Matahari Books.

[266] An e-media institution that has been at the forefront of calls for accountable governance and freedom of the press is Malaysiakini, a pioneering online news portal that was established in 1999. See Janet Steele. 2023. *Malaysiakini and the Power of Independent Media in Malaysia*. Singapore: National University of Singapore Press.

These institutions have also worked collectively and with academics, ex-bureaucrats, and business figures to propose a series of well-structured proposals to curb corruption and illicit financing of politics, devolve power, and enhance the institutional efficacy of parliament. These civil society members have collaborated to make a joint demand for the introduction of legislations on public procurement and political financing, the amendment of laws to better protect whistleblowers and guarantee the autonomy of the MACC, the creation of the office of the public prosecutor separate from the Attorney General's Chambers whose role is to advice the cabinet, and the reinstatement of the Parliamentary Services Act to free parliament from its control by the executive arm of government.[267] Interestingly, social media has emerged as an important medium that constantly exposes public misgovernance, though it has also been covertly used by governing elites to discredit dissenting voices.

Regulations, thus, must be in place to control the actions of politicians entrusted to hold public office, while bureaucrats must be free to expose abuse of power. However, power concentration and flawed or deficient legislation are not the only drivers of systemic corruption. Reforms are required of the institutions in this ecosystem. These institutional reforms differ, depending on the role and mode of governance of each enterprise, but ultimately must lead to all of them functioning transparently. Clarity of purpose is crucial, as the mixed mandates of GLC-based enterprises often pose performance and governance challenges. What's more, with serious misallocation of public resources to low productivity GLCs, output is reduced, which can jeopardize economic growth

---

[267] The Parliamentary Services Act was introduced in 1963 to allow parliament to function as an independent body with adequate funds to manage its own affairs. In 1992, this Act was repealed, bringing parliament under the control of the PMD. Mahathir Mohamad was serving as prime minister when parliament was placed under the control of the executive arm of government, a clear violation of checks and balances in governance.

while hampering the development of domestic entrepreneurial enterprises, a longstanding government endeavour.

These institutional, legislative, and regulatory reforms can only be done properly if governing politicians are willing to rectify the problem of power concentration in the cabinet. Strong political will is required if this Political–GLC complex is to be dismantled, as governing elites are highly dependent on this vast GLC ecosystem, as a political and economic tool, to win electoral support in a situation where no party has a commanding presence. Incumbent governing elites, including those who once strongly advocated *reformasi*, must show this political will if they hope to inspire public confidence that their call to curb systemic corruption is much more than a mere grand narrative.

Acknowledgements

This project was undertaken under the auspices of the Center to Combat Corruption & Cronyism (C4 Center). I owe a huge debt to its members, as it was with them that the idea of a study on the nexus between corruption and GLCs emerged. When we embarked on this project, we had an article in mind, but it has since evolved into this book. Given the voluminous data that we gathered, a deeper analysis of what needs to be done to help rid Malaysia of corruption was required.

I thank the Board of Directors of C4 Center, Ashrul Mohd Khalib, Cynthia Gabriel, and Sutinah Sutan, for supporting this project. Pushpan Murugiah, the CEO of C4 Center, constantly stressed the importance of this work and was behind the project from conception to completion.

I am indebted to the researchers at C4 Center, as each member of the team was assigned different tasks. Responsibility for each case study was undertaken by Nabila Syuhada Zulkeflee (Jana Wibawa—policy creation and power abuse), Keiran Dass (Littoral Combat Ship [LCS] project—sectoral development and corruption), Lew Guan Xi (FELCRA—abuse of public enterprises), and Johnson Tay (MARA—transnational crime). The extremely tedious work of compiling the large number of state–business controversies listed in Appendix 1 was ably and diligently undertaken by Claire Chin and Yusra Mahmoud Mohamad El Sayed. The figures were prepared by Juwairiah Tajuddin and Sherilyn Pang, who also compiled a number of the tables and coordinated the research. Sangeetha Niscinta Nandini was responsible for fact-checking and the final editing of Appendix 1, while she and Harmit Singh checked and improved the figures. All of them actively participated in the many discussions we had as we ploughed through the massive database to determine what to retain. Another round of long discussions was held to analyse the draft case studies and the state–business controversies in Appendix 1. I applaud this team's willingness to put in long hours to get the work done, their desire to learn, and their commitment to their research. I feel privileged to have worked with this bright and dynamic group of young Malaysians.

Prishanth Linggaraj, Bryan Cheah, and Arief Hamizan, the lawyers at C4, were responsible for preparing the legal discussion in Appendix 2, as well compiling the information on the legislative issues listed in Table 1.1. One of the most gratifying aspects of this project was the opportunity afforded to me to learn about Malaysia's legal system and its capacity to deal with corruption in its numerous forms. I thank them and Pushpan, also a lawyer by training, for their legal insights and for their vetting of the manuscript. A few other lawyers also went through the manuscript and provided sound feedback for which I am grateful.

When the research was completed, the core findings were presented at a public seminar held in July 2023. This seminar was well attended, offering us the opportunity to present our core arguments. The participants raised numerous questions, which forced us to think through how we were navigating this slippery Political–GLC-corruption terrain. Indeed, many of the arguments in this book are appreciably different from those presented at this forum.

My final debt is to my family—my wife, Sharmani, and our children, Evie, Eric, and Eshward—for supporting this project in manifold ways.

Appendix 1

Public Controversies: State–Business Ties and Enterprises in the GLC Ecosystem, 1980–2023

No.	Title and year	Brief description
1	Bumiputra Malaysia Finance Bhd 1979–1983	In the 1970s, BMF, a subsidiary of Bank Bumiputra, provided three Hong Kong property speculators with loans amounting to RM2.5 billion. These loans could not be serviced following a property market crash between 1981 and 1982. Petronas, the oil-based government-controlled cash rich conglomerate, was used to bailout Bank Bumiputra that was mired in bad loans.[268] It was further alleged that funds provided for these property deals were channelled back to certain leaders of the UMNO, the leader of the governing multi-party coalition, BN.[269] This scandal occurred at a point when

---

[268] Teh Yik Koon (2018). *From BMF to 1MDB: A Criminological and Sociological Discussion*. Petaling Jaya: Strategic Information & Research Development Centre (SIRD).

[269] Lim Kit Siang (1986). *BMF: Scandal of Scandals*. Kuala Lumpur: Democratic Action Party.

No.	Title and year	Brief description
		money was beginning to be used garner support during UMNO elections, a practice that contributed to the deep monetization of the political system and the rise of the phenomenon of money politics.[270]
2	Maminco–Makuwasa 1981	Maminco Sdn Bhd, a RM2 company, was created by the government to secretly corner the world tin market. This activity was funded through a RM1.5 billion loan, obtained from government-owned Bank Bumiputra, which could not be serviced when the tin market collapsed in 1985. To cover up the losses from this speculation exercise, the government set up another RM2 company, Makuwasa Sdn Bhd, which took over newly-issued shares (at par value), reserved for Bumiputeras and allocated to the EPF, and sold them at market prices, thus securing a huge profit.[271] The Maminco–Makuwasa scandal indicated inadequate checks and balances in the cabinet, which allowed for the abuse of a GLC bank institution for speculative activities and then the misuse of a savings-cum-pension fund to institute a bailout.

---

[270] Edmund Terence Gomez (2012). Monetizing Politics: Financing Parties and Elections in Malaysia. *Modern Asian Studies*, 46 (5): 1370–1397.

[271] *New Straits Times* (17 September 2017): https://www.nst.com.my/opinion/columnists/2017/09/280648/how-dr-m-abused-epf-money-london-tin-market

Appendix 1

No.	Title and year	Brief description
3	Perwaja Steel Project 1982–1995	In 1982, Perwaja Steel, a joint venture between a GLC, Heavy Industries Corporation of Malaysia (HICOM) and Nippon Steel, was created to increase domestic production of steel. In 1987, when Nippon Steel pulled out, Eric Chia, closely associated with Mahathir, was brought in to lead the enterprise. Government funds and loans from Bank Bumiputra and EPF were pumped into Perwaja Steel. After Chia resigned in 1995, it was revealed that the company was in crippling debt due to mismanagement and misappropriation of funds.[272]
4	Multi-Purpose Holdings Bhd 1975–1989	MPHB was incorporated in 1975 by the Malaysian Chinese Association (MCA), UMNO's partner in the BN. MPHB was the MCA's attempt to venture into business, with funds raised from the public, to increase national corporate equity ownership among the ethnic Chinese, ostensibly to counter the growing impact of public enterprises in the economy through the implementation of the NEP. MPHB was subsequently deeply mired in corporate controversies due

---

[272] *Asiaweek* (19 April 1996): http://edition.cnn.com/ASIANOW/asiaweek/96/0419/nat7.html; Barry Wain. 2009. *Malaysian Maverick: Mahathir Mohamad in Turbulent Times*. Basingstoke: Palgrave Macmillan: 172–177.

No.	Title and year	Brief description
		to the business deals undertaken by its president, Tan Koon Swan, and was subjected to a takeover.[273]
5	Maika Holdings Bhd 1984	Maika was incorporated to serve as the investment arm of the Malaysian Indian Congress (MIC), another member of the BN. This holding company managed to raise about RM106 million from 66,400 shareholders, primarily poor Indians, to increase this ethnic group's ownership of corporate equity. Maika benefited from the privatization policy during the IPO of partially-privatized public institutions such as the corporatized telecom service, Syarikat Telekom Malaysia (STM), and as a shareholder of TV3, the country's first private television network. However, Maika was subsequently mired in controversies, including allegations of gross mismanagement.[274]

---

[273] Edmund Terence Gomez. 1994. *Political Business: Corporate Involvement of Malaysian Political Parties*. Townsville: James Cook University: 198–219.

[274] Lim Kit Siang (1992). *Samy Vellu and Maika Scandal*. Kuala Lumpur: Democratic Action Party.

Appendix 1

No.	Title and year	Brief description
6	Promet Bhd 1984	A mega development project in Langkawi, amounting to US$1 billion (Tanjung Rhu Resort), that led to the displacement of people and serious harm to the environment. The project was eventually substantially scaled down and subsequently sold off.[275]
7	Sports Toto 1985	This highly profitable gaming enterprise owned by MoF Inc. was privatized to Melewar Corp (controlled by Tunku Abdullah) and B&B Enterprise Sdn Bhd (owned by Vincent Tan Chee Yioun), both then well-connected with then Prime Minister, Mahathir Mohamad, and his Finance Minister Daim Zainuddin.[276]
8	Pan-Electric Industries 1985	Pan-Electric Industries Ltd, in which Tan Koon Swan had a huge interest, was involved in 'forward contracting' that subsequently resulted in the stock exchanges of both Singapore and Malaysia shutting down for three days.[277]

---

[275] Bella Bird (1989). *Langkawi – From Mahsuri to Mahathir: Tourism for Whom?*. Kuala Lumpur: Insan.

[276] Edmund Terence Gomez. 1999. *Chinese Business in Malaysia: Accumulation, Ascendance, Accommodation*. Honolulu: University of Hawai'i Pess: 112–127.

[277] Clad. 1989: 131–132.

No.	Title and year	Brief description
9	UMBC–Pernas 1986	In 1984, just before he was appointed minister of finance, Daim Zainuddin acquired a huge stake in the United Malayan Banking Corporation (UMBC), then Malaysia's third largest bank. Two years later, Daim sold off his stake in this bank to Pernas, then a major GLC, for what was reportedly a 'huge profit', an issue that then came to be referred to as the UMBC–Pernas scandal.[278]
10	Deposit-taking Cooperatives 1986	Twenty-four deposit-taking co-operatives were suspended by Bank Negara for fraud and mismanagement involving numerous leaders from the MCA.[279]
11	Cooperative Central Bank (CCB) 1986	Audited accounts indicated a huge loss suffered due to undocumented and unauthorized transactions. This included granting large loans to various non-performing small groups of borrowers.[280]

---

[278] *Asian Wall Street Journal* (31 May 1988). For a detailed account of the 'UMBC Saga', see: Gomez and Jomo. 1997: 56–59.

[279] Edmund Terence Gomez. 1991. *Money Politics in the Barisan Nasional*. Kuala Lumpur: Forum: 47–104.

[280] *Consumer*. https://consumer.org.my/history-of-cooperative-scandals/

Appendix 1

No.	Title and year	Brief description
12	Hatibudi–UEM–North-South Highway project 1987	The government privatized the North–South Highway project to United Engineers Malaysia Bhd (UEM), a company then owned by an UMNO holding company, Hatibudi Sdn Bhd.[281]
13	Pergau Dam Affair 1988	A secret defence agreement linking the promise of aid by Britain to Malaysia to build the Pergau Dam in return for a major arms export deal.[282]
14	Hatibudi Nominee–Time Engineering–Renong 1989	Following UMNO's deregistration in 1988, UMNO's shares in Hatibudi and UEM were placed in the hands of the Official Assignee's office under the Ministry of Home Affairs controlled by Mahathir. In 1989, Time Engineering Bhd acquired convertible unsecured loan stocks (CULS) worth RM37.5 million from Hatibudi Nominees Sdn Bhd for RM281.25 million. Hatibudi Nominees and Hatibudi were both controlled by the same people.[283]

---

[281] Gomez. 1994: 90–94.

[282] Tim Lankester. 2013. *The Politics and Economics of Britain's Foreign Aid: The Pergau Dam Affair*, London: Routledge.

[283] Gomez. 1994: 94–99.

No.	Title and year	Brief description
15	Celcom 1989	Tajudin Ramli secured 51 per cent of Celcom, the first company to obtain a licence to operate a cellular telephone network. Celcom was originally a joint venture between UMNO's Fleet Group and the government's Syarikat Telekom Malaysia (STM), which was then being prepared for privatization. Celcom then had virtual monopoly of the cellular telephone network.[284] Celcom was later taken over by Telekom Malaysia, a listed GLC.
16	Mycom Ltd Sabah 1990	In 1990, Mycom, a rather unprofitable enterprise, obtained control over Lotteries Corporation (Sabah) Sdn Bhd, which operated the Sabah Big Sweep lottery with a licence issued by the state government. The chairman of Mycom was Tamrin Ghafar, the son of then Deputy Prime Minister Abdul Ghafar Baba. In 1990, Mycom's profits were projected at RM54 million.[285]

---

[284] Gomez and Jomo. 1997: 95.

[285] Searle. 1999. *The Riddle of Malaysian Capitalism: Rent-Seekers or Real Capitalists.* Honolulu: University of Hawai'i Press.

No.	Title and year	Brief description
17	Bank Negara Forex 1991–1994	Bank Negara became active in foreign exchange trading in the late 1980s. Bank Negara speculated that the British Pound would appreciate. When it did not, this resulted in a loss of RM31.5 billion between 1991 and 1994. Bank Negara was criticized for gambling with Malaysian taxpayers' money.[286]
18	Malaysia Airlines Bhd 1994	In 1994, MAS was privatized without an open tender to Tajudin Ramli, reputedly a close associate of former Finance Minister Daim Zainuddin, at a value of RM1.79 billion. This MAS equity was acquired from Bank Negara, reportedly to help the central bank deal with the forex crisis it was involved in at that time (see above).[287] Tajudin obtained loans from several banks to acquire this MAS equity, bought at a higher price than the market value, following which he took charge of the enterprise.[288]

---

[286] *Malay Mail* (22 June 2017): https://www.malaymail.com/news/malaysia/2017/06/22/what-was-the-bnm-forex-scandal/1405201

[287] *Asia Sentinel* (6 March 2012): https://www.asiasentinel.com/p/mahathirs-disastrous-financial-speculation

[288] *The Edge* (2 February 2012): https://theedgemalaysia.com/article/saga-tajudin-ramli

No.	Title and year	Brief description
19	Indah Water Konsortium 1993	The government privatized the national sewerage project to IWK, a consortium led by Berjaya Group, controlled by the well-connected Vincent Tan. In 2000, this project was renationalized, with a government compensation of RM200 million for the takeover, which was seen as a bailout.[289]
20	United Malayan Banking Corporation controversies 1986–1998	UMBC had been persistently embroiled in controversies. In 1986, when then Finance Minister Daim Zainuddin, divested his controlling stake in the bank to a government enterprise, Pernas, allegedly at an inflated price, the incident came to be known as the 'UMBC scandal'. This equity was channelled, in 1992, to an ailing publicly-listed Datuk Keramat Holdings, whose primary shareholder was Mohd Noor Yusof, once the political secretary of then Prime Minister Mahathir Mohamad. Another shareholder of the bank was UMNO's cooperative, Koperasi Usaha Bersama (KUB). In 1995, following numerous allegations of corruption, another government-owned enterprise, Sime Darby, acquired the bank and renamed it Sime Bank. In 1997, since

---

[289] Jeff Tan. 2007. *Privatisation in Malaysia: Regulation, Rent-Seeking and Policy Failure*. London: Routledge: 78–105; *Malaysiakini* (19 April 2001): https://www.malaysiakini.com/news/2133

No.	Title and year	Brief description
		Sime Bank was laden with huge non-performing loans, it was taken over by Rashid Hussain, a well-connected businessman who renamed it RHB Bank. Following a fallout between Rashid and Mahathir, ownership of the bank was shifted to family members of the then chief minister of Sarawak, Taib Mahmud, who later divested this equity to EPF, now the bank's majority shareholder.[290]
21	UEM–Renong 1997	Halim Saad took over the corporate assets owned by UMNO and situated them under the Renong group. Following the 1997 Asian financial crisis, Renong was burdened with huge debts. Subsequently, a complex share transaction occurred involving a company, UEM, within the Renong group. This UEM–Renong RM2.3 billion deal came under serious criticism.[291]
22	Offshore patrol vessels 1998	The government awarded a construction contract for twenty-seven OPVs to a private company owned by the well-connected Amin Shah. This contract failed. The government, through a listed GLC, Boustead,

---

[290] Gomez and Jomo. 1997: 110–117.

[291] For details on this complex and controversial intra-Renong group corporate deal, see: *The Edge* (31 May 2023): https://theedgemalaysia.com/node/668118

No.	Title and year	Brief description
		owned by a GLIC, LTAT, had to rescue this project.[292]
23	Konsortium Perkapalan Bhd 1998	Following the Asian Financial Crisis, KPB, a company controlled by Mahathir Mohamad's son, Mirzan, sold for cash subsidiaries laden with debt to government-controlled, Malaysian International Shipping Corp (MISC), for US$220 million. This controversial deal was reported as a 'bailout'.[293]
24	Bakun Dam 1994–1997, 2000–2004	This project, then the largest privatization at RM15 billion, was awarded without tender to Ekran Bhd, owned by Ting Pek Khiing, closely associated with Mahathir and Daim. Ekran had never built a dam.[294] After the 1997 financial crisis, the project was halted. In 2002, the contract was awarded to the Malaysian–China Hydro JV. It was completed in 2011.[295]

---

[292] See the second case study in this book, on the LCS project, for details on this issue.

[293] *Wall Street Journal* (1 May 1998): https://www.wsj.com/articles/SB893957144672200500

[294] Gomez and Jomo. 1997: 110–116.

[295] *Borneo Post* (29 March 2015): https://www.theborneopost.com/2015/03/29/bakun-dam-or-singapore/

No.	Title and year	Brief description
25	MAS renationalized 1997	The government paid RM1.8 billion for a 29 per cent interest in a now debt-ridden MAS controlled by Tajudin Ramli. Each share was valued at RM8 which was reported as twice the market price. Tajudin claimed that Daim had asked him to acquire MAS at a high price and, seven years later, following the Asian crisis, this was why the government acquired these shares at the same price.[296]
26	Selangor water industry 1994– 2002 / 2018	Since privatizing water to four companies had led to people paying a higher price for it, this led to its renationalization. Serious concerns were voiced over the sum paid by the state government for this renationalization exercise.[297]
27	Time dotCom 2001	Allegations of a bailout when KWAP was used to acquire 64 per cent of Time dotCom's unsubscribed (RM1.9 billion) IPO equity, which constituted

---

[296] *Free Malaysia Today* (2 May 2018): https://www.freemalaysiatoday.com/category/nation/2018/05/02/you-dont-say-no-to-pm-tycoon-in-tell-tale-video/

[297] *New Straits Times* (8 August 2018): https://www.nst.com.my/news/exclusive/2018/08/399182/khalid-ibrahim-why-selangor-water-deal-betrayal-people

No.	Title and year	Brief description
		6 per cent of its total funds. Time dotCom was then a subsidiary of Time Engineering, a publicly-listed company of the Renong Group controlled by Halim Saad.[298]
28	PUTRA and STAR takeover 2001	The privatized Projek Usahasama Transit Ringan Automatik (PUTRA), owned by Renong, and Sistem Transit Aliran Ringan Sdn Bhd (STAR), in which two GLICs, EPF and Tabung Haji, had an interest were deeply mired in debt, collectively amounting to RM5.7 billion by 2001.[299] Both companies had to be taken over and restructured by the government and now constitute part of the GLC, Prasarana Malaysia.
29	Scorpene 2002	See Case Study 2
30	Approved Permits 1987-2008	The AP scheme was introduced in 1970 to aid the participation of Bumiputeras in the automobile sector. In 2005, after Mahathir Mohamad

---

[298] *The New York Times* (15 March 2001): https://www.nytimes.com/2001/03/15/business/worldbusiness/IHT-time-dotbombipo-sparks-charges-of-graft.html

[299] *Malaysiakini* (25 July 2001): https://www.malaysiakini.com/news/4031

No.	Title and year	Brief description
		alleged abuse of the APs, this led to a public disclosure that 50 per cent (or 33,281) of the APs issued in just one year, 2004, went to three men. It was also reported that the award of APs to individuals and companies in 2004 and 2005 'gave them the opportunity to amass RM1.8 billion within two years'.[300]
31	Independent Power Producers 1990s	IPP licences were allegedly selectively issued to well-connected companies and GLCs. Former Tenaga Nasional Bhd (TNB) executive chairman, Ani Arope, was later quoted as stating that 'there was no negotiation. Absolutely none' and that 'it was all fixed up. They said, this is the price, this is the capacity charge and this is the number of years. They said you just take it and I refused to sign the contracts. And then, I was put out to pasture.'[301]
32	UBG Bank (1MDB) 2006–2010	In 2010, Jho Low, who was closely associated 1MDB, reportedly mounted a takeover of RHB Bank, then owned by UBG Bhd, an enterprise controlled

---

[300] *The Edge* (27 April 2009): https://theedgemalaysia.com/article/mukhriz-gets-dap-gerakan-backing-ap-issue

[301] *The Malaysian Insider* (20 December 2014): https://malaysia.news.yahoo.com/ani-arope-malaysian-stood-years-ago-094620857.html

No.	Title and year	Brief description
		by Sarawak's Taib Mahmud. This RHB takeover attempt was related to a series of business transactions that involved another government-related company, Putrajaya Perdana Bhd (PPB). In the event, after a series of complex corporate manoeuvrings, RHB Bank was acquired by EPF, a GLIC.[302]
33	Regent Star 2007	It was reported by *The Japan Times* that a cartel of nine Japanese companies had given kickbacks through a Hong Kong-based company, Regent Star, reputedly linked to then Sarawak Chief Minister Taib Mahmud and his family. Bribes amounting to RM32 million were given over a seven-year period. This money was reported to have served as a 'lubricant to facilitate their lumber trade'.[303]
34	Cowgate / National Feedlot Corp 2007	NFC, in which the government had a golden share, was incorporated to enhance beef production by nurturing the development of this industry. A public loan of about RM250 million was provided for this project. However, this project was termed the 'cows-and-condos scandal' when allegations emerged that NFC, led by

---

[302] *The Edge* (10 April 2017): https://theedgemalaysia.com/article/investigative-report-1mdb-jho-low-pocketed-rm516-million-flipping-3-companies-help-1mdb-cash?type=Corporate

[303] *Malaysiakini* (6 April 2007): https://www.malaysiakini.com/news/65572

No.	Title and year	Brief description
		the husband of an UMNO minister, had use the company's funds to invest in high-end properties in Malaysia and Singapore.[304] The minister, her husband, and their children were implicated in this controversy. It was reported that an audit by PricewaterhouseCoopers found that RM107 million had been transferred from NFC to companies owned by the minister's husband and children.[305] In the event, the court delivered a 'partial judgement' for the government. The court exonerated the family of the UMNO leader from the multiple claims of fraud, breach of trust, breach of fiduciary duties, cheating, and the misappropriation of funds. However, the court also ruled that the land owned by NFC had to be returned to the government, along with RM33.7 million of the RM250 million, as well as 'RM86.9 million seized from the defendants and currently held by the Accountant-General in escrow.'[306]

---

[304] *The Straits Times* (21 May 2019): https://www.straitstimes.com/asia/se-asia/malaysia-govt-seeks-repayment-of-824mil-from-company-in-cows-and-condos-scandal; *Reuters* (15 February 2012): https://www.reuters.com/article/idUSTRE81E041/

[305] *The Edge* (17 July 2018): https://theedgemalaysia.com/article/special-audit-nfc-flagged-public-officials-negligence

[306] *Free Malaysia Today* (13 October 2023): https://www.freemalaysiatoday.com/category/nation/2023/10/13/govt-gets-partial-nfc-award-but-sharizats-family-exonerated/

No.	Title and year	Brief description
35	Port Klang Free Zone (PKFZ) 2008	This project, originally costing RM1.9 billion ended up with a cost of RM12.5 billion. One report claimed that this controversy featured 'financial mismanagement and collusion, and ultimately taxpayers were left to shoulder billions of ringgit in debt: a complete disregard for the board of directors, government rules and regulations and a lack of checks and balances by the relevant bodies or agencies tasked with oversight.'[307] This controversy implicated two former presidents of the MCA and Tiong King Sing, now a minister in Anwar Ibrahim's cabinet.[308]
36	1MDB 2009	1MDB, a GLC, controlled by MoF Inc., though created to foster development emerged as the 'heart of one of the biggest corruption scandals in the world', serving as a tool through which 'vast sums were borrowed via government bonds and siphoned

---

[307] *The Edge* (4 February 2021): https://theedgemalaysia.com/article/special-report-pkfz-%E2%80%94-no-conviction-after-eight-years-and-six-criminal-cases; *Malay Mail* (17 March 2017): https://www.malaymail.com/news/malaysia/2017/03/17/pkfz-the-scandal-with-no-culprits/1336987

[308] For an in-depth assessment of this controversy, see: Lee Hwa Beng and Lee Siew Lian. 2012. *PKFZ: A Nation's Trust Betrayed*. Kuala Lumpur: The Malaysian Insider.

No.	Title and year	Brief description
		into bank accounts in Switzerland, Singapore and the US', while 'US$731m appeared in the personal bank account of Najib just ahead of the 2013 election.'[309]
37	SRC International 2009	Former Prime Minister Najib Razak was found guilty of misappropriating RM42 million belonging to SRC International, a subsidiary of 1MDB. This incident was seen as a 'national embarrassment' by the court.[310]
38	1BestariNet 2011	The Ministry of Education awarded the 1BestariNet project, valued at RM4 billion, to YTL Communications to provide high-speed 4G internet access and online platforms to 10,000 schools nationwide in three phases. The aim was to create a 'virtual learning environment' for these schools entailing an integrated teaching, learning, and administrative system taking place through the internet. Two years later, in 2013, a report by

---

[309] *The Guardian* (28 July 2020): https://www.theguardian.com/world/2018/oct/25/1mdb-scandal-explained-a-tale-of-malaysias-missing-billions; Tom Wright and Bradley Hope (2018). *Billion Dollar Whale: The Man Who Fooled Wall Street, Hollywood, and the World*. New York: Hachette.

[310] *The Edge* (23 December 2021): https://theedgemalaysia.com/article/najibs-src-trial-src-international-national-interest-project-became-national-embarrassment

No.	Title and year	Brief description
		the Auditor-General was critical of the implementation of this project. In 2015, the parliament's Public Accounts Committee (PAC) concluded that implementation of the first phase of the project was a failure.[311]
39	Penang Undersea Tunnel 2011–2017	Lim Guan Eng was charged with two offences: the first, using his position as Penang's chief minister to obtain bribes totalling RM3.3 million to help a contractor obtain this project, which was valued at RM6,341,383. In the second charge, Lim was charged with soliciting a bribe of 10 per cent of the future profits from the company in return for assisting the company to secure the contract.[312]
40	Sapura–Kencana Petroleum Bhd 2012	In 2018, then Prime Minister Najib Razak claimed that Mokhzani Mahathir, the son of former Prime Minister Mahathir Mohamad, had secured 'billions of ringgit worth of oil contracts' from Petronas, an allegation that Mokhzani described as 'fake news' as 'my father was no longer the PM then. It was Najib who was the PM at that time. My father was

---

[311] *New Straits Times* (9 November 2016): https://www.nst.com.my/news/2016/11/187088/ambitious-1bestarinet-flawed-start
This report was titled 'Ambitious 1BestariNet flawed from the start'.

[312] *The Star* (15 February 2023):
https://www.thestar.com.my/news/nation/2023/02/15/guan-engs-penang-undersea-tunnel-corruption-case-postponed-to-march-1

No.	Title and year	Brief description
		only the advisor to Petronas.'[313] On a similar allegation, made in 2013 by Anwar Ibrahim, Mahathir's response was that 'Petronas reports only to the prime minister and it is the prime minister who can make any instruction to Petronas. When I was the prime minister, I did not give any aid to my children,' and that 'if they are successful today, be it in business or politics, they did it on their own.'[314]
41	Taib Mahmud and Cahya Mata Sarawak 2012 / 2015	Two controversial publications have been issued by the Swiss-based Bruno Manser Fund; the first, in 2012, entitled *The Taib Timber Mafia: Facts and Figures on Politically Exposed Persons (PEPs) from Sarawak, Malaysia.*[315] In 2015, when the second report, *Corruption Management Sarawak – Cahya Mata Sarawak (CMS) and Malaysia's Taib Family*, was issued, it alleged that the company secured about US$1.4 billion in state contracts between 1993 and 2013.[316] CMS is a publicly-

---

[313] *The Edge* (8 May 2018): https://theedgemalaysia.com/article/mokhzani-says-najibs-claim-he-bagged-billionringgit-petronas-contracts-sapurakencana-fake

[314] Both quotes are from *Malaysiakini* (25 February 2013): https://www.malaysiakini.com/news/222318

[315] Bruno Manser Fund. 2012. *The Taib Timber Mafia: Facts and Figures on Politically Exposed Persons (PEPs) from Sarawak, Malaysia*. Basel: Bruno Manser Fund.

[316] Bruno Manser Fund. 2015. *Corruption Management Sarawak – Cahya Mata Sarawak (CMS) and Malaysia's Taib Family*. Basel: Bruno Manser Fund.

No.	Title and year	Brief description
		listed enterprise owned by the family of former Sarawak Chief Minister Taib Mahmud who led the state government from 1981 till 2014. He then became governor of the state, a post he held until 2024, just before his demise. However, long before the publication of this study, allegations abounded of corruption that involved Taib. In 2018, the MACC is reported to have stated that files on Taib had been opened since 2015, but 'we have to stop the investigation on Taib at this point. We have already opened 15 files on Taib. It is true he was involved in part of the allegations. But there was not even in one case where he chaired the meeting or made the decision. The law does not allow us to take action if he does not make a decision.'[317]
42	Ultra Kirana Sdn Bhd 2012	In 2012, the government awarded a contract to UKSB to serve as the sole operator of the foreign visa system (VLN), run by one-stop centres in China for people bound for Malaysia. An executive from UKSB claimed in court that he had paid more than RM70 million to eleven politicians.

---

[317] *The Edge* (3 July 2018): https://theedgemalaysia.com/article/macc-15-files-opened-against-taib-mahmud-we-cant-act-against-him

No.	Title and year	Brief description
		Among those named in court were Muhyiddin Yassin, Khairy Jamaluddin, Reezal Merican Naina Merican, Hishammuddin Hussein, Shafie Apdal, and Anifah Aman. Ahmad Zahid Hamidi, then the home minister, was also alleged to have received substantial funds from UKSB, ostensibly as political donations for election purposes.[318] In 2022, Zahid was acquitted of forty counts of accepting bribes amounting to RM42 million from UKSB because three prosecution witnesses were seen as 'unreliable and not credible'.[319]
43	Global Witness exposé (Sarawak timber deals) 2013	In an undercover investigation by Global Witness of land abuse and timber extraction in Sarawak, a series of deeply disturbing allegations were made against family members of then Chief Minister Taib Mahmud. The report alleged that Taib's family had been 'allocated land [. . .] for a tiny fraction of its real commercial value, enabling these individuals to "flip"

---

[318] *The Edge* (8 August 2022): https://theedgemalaysia.com/article/who-uksbs-hk-partner-paid-millions-malaysian-politicians

[319] *Free Malaysia Today* (23 September 2022): https://www.freemalaysiatoday.com/category/nation/2022/09/23/zahid-freed-of-all-charges/

No.	Title and year	Brief description
		these assets for multimillion dollar profits.' According to the team leader of this investigation, these people were 'willing to stash this dirty cash in jurisdictions like Singapore' and until this country as well as 'other financial service centres stop allowing corrupt politicians and criminals to shield themselves and their loot from justice back home, the likes of Taib will continue to get away with stealing from their own people.'[320]
44	Perak hydro dams 2013	In 2013, publicly-listed GCap Bhd, then controlled by politician-cum-businessman Syed Abu Hussin, acquired 51 per cent of the equity in Perak Hydro Renewable Energy Corporation Sdn Bhd (PHREC). It had the rights to build, operate, and own (BOO) thirty-one small hydroelectric dams over a period of twenty-one years, estimated to cost RM2.92 billion.[321] The other major shareholder of PHREC was the Perak state government's holding company, Menteri Besar Incorporated (Perak

---

[320] *Global Witness* (15 March 2013): https://www.globalwitness.org/en/archive/corruption-malaysia-laid-bare-investigation-catches-sarawaks-ruling-elite-camera/

[321] This is based on a statement made by Teja assemblyperson Chang Lih Kang in 2014. For the full statement, see: *Malaysiakini.com* (8 May 2014): http://lib.perdana.org.my/PLF/Malaysiakini_selection/MalaysiaKini2014/52/262212.pdf

Appendix 1

No.	Title and year	Brief description
		MBI). After Syed Hussin became an MP, in April 2021, GCap acquired 100 per cent of PHREC's equity from Perak MBI by issuing new GCap shares and redeemable convertible preference shares. With this reverse takeover, MBI Perak increased its shareholding of GCap,[322] giving it a controlling interest in this publicly-listed company.
45	MARA controversies 2013–2021	See Case Study 3(2)
46	Forest City 2014	Forest City is a mega mixed-development project on four reclaimed islands in Johor. Esplanade Danga 88 Sdn Bhd, in which the Johor Sultan had an interest, along with Johor's investment arm, Kumpulan Prasarana Rakyat Johor Sdn Bhd (KPRJ), and Daing Malek Daing Rahaman, a close business associate of the Sultan, tied-up with Country Garden, a leading Chinese property developer, to develop this US$100 billion project on a private-public-led basis with investment from China.[323]

---

[322] *The Star* (20 July 2021): https://www.thestar.com.my/business/business-news/2021/07/20/gcap-buys-remaining-stake-in-perak-hydro

[323] *Bloomberg* (21 November 2016): https://www.bloomberg.com/news/features/2016-11-21/-100-billion-chinese-made-city-near-singapore-scares-

No.	Title and year	Brief description
47	Tabung Haji (illegal dividends) 2014	In 2018, the new government in power, led by Mahathir Mohamad, tabled in Parliament a report that revealed that Tabung Haji, a GLIC deeply mired in controversies, had made 'illegal dividend distributions since 2014.' This was a shocking revelation as Tabung Haji had 'a financial hole of RM4.1 billion between total assets and liabilities, making the fund ineligible to pay dividends' to its 'nine million depositors.'[324]
48	LCS 2014	See Case Study 2
49	The Little Birds (helicopters) 2015	In 2015, a contract worth RM300 million was awarded to supply six MD530G light scout attack helicopters, dubbed 'Little Birds', to Halaman Optima Sdn Bhd, that was acquired by Destini Bhd, the same company that received the MMEA's OPV contract in 2017. In 2019, the government lodged a report with the MACC, as no helicopters were delivered, although RM112.65 million

---

the-hell-out-of-everybody; *Bloomberg News* (21 November 2016): https://casestudy.mit.edu/documents/articles-ch1.pdf

[324] *The Malaysian Reserve* (11 December 2018): https://themalaysianreserve.com/2018/12/11/tabung-haji-scandal-and-illegal-dividends/

No.	Title and year	Brief description
		had been paid. The procurement process of this contract was reportedly not done in accordance with proper approval process.[325] While deliveries of these helicopters were due in batches in 2017 and 2018, they were only delivered in early 2022.
50	Automated Enforcement System / Boustead 2015	In 2012, the AES concession was awarded to Beta Tegap Sdn Bhd and ATES Sdn Bhd, reportedly two-well-connected firms, to install 1,093 cameras to monitor federal roads and highways in Malaysia under a build, operate, and transfer (BOT) basis for a concession period of five years. In 2014, LTAT was 'invited' by the government to take over these companies for RM555 million.[326] An inquiry of this deal was done by the Public Accounts Committee (PAC), which described it as an 'indirect bailout' and that the 'RM555 million consideration was "overvalued" and "exorbitant".' However, this figure was justified by LTAT's then CEO, Lodin Wok Kamaruddin, who contended

---

[325] *The Edge* (20 May 2019): https://theedgemalaysia.com/article/report-rm300m-paid-usmade-helicopters-were-never-delivered

[326] *New Straits Times* (23 August 2018): https://www.nst.com.my/news/nation/2018/08/404323/aes-scandal-vets-association-wants-govt-pay-back-interest-too

No.	Title and year	Brief description
		that the two companies owned 'the concession [for 13 years] and other assets. So, the price was based on the return that could be generated from the concession over the 13-year period.'[327]
51	Menara FELCRA 2015	See Case Study 3(1)
52	FIC Hotel Purchase (FELDA) 2015	Isa Samad, who had served about two decades as UMNO's chief minister of Negeri Sembilan and who had served as FELDA's chairman, was charged with ten counts of CBT and corruption related to the purchase of Merdeka Palace Hotel and Suites for RM160 million by FELDA Investment Corporation Sdn Bhd (FIC) without the approval of the board of directors. Isa was reported to have received about RM3 million to secure approval of the hotel acquisition.[328] Isa was found guilty of the charge in 2021 following which he submitted an appeal against this conviction.

---

[327] *The Edge* (23 November 2021): https://theedgemalaysia.com/article/outsourcing-aes-project-implementation-inappropriate-says-pac

[328] *The Malaysian Reserve* (14 December 2018): https://themalaysianreserve.com/2018/12/14/isa-samad-charged-with-cbt-bribery-of-more-than-rm3-million-over-hotel-purchase-by-fic/

Appendix 1

No.	Title and year	Brief description
53	Melaka gateway project 2016–2023	In 2016, this RM43 billion project was awarded to property developer, KAJ Development Sdn Bhd (KAJD), which had formed a joint venture with three state-owned enterprises from China, one of which was Power China International. A controversial project involving UMNO leaders of the Melaka state government and members of the MCA, it was eventually terminated in 2020.[329] This project was revived in September 2023 to construct the Melaka International Cruise Terminal (MICT), which served as the 'only entry point for international cruise ships and ferries to Melaka'.[330] By this time, the Sultan of Johor and his business partner, Daing A Malek, had acquired a 30 per cent and 10 per cent stake respectively in KAJD.[331]

---

[329] For a comprehensive assessment of this project, see: *ISEAS* (2019): https://www.iseas.edu.sg/images/pdf/ISEAS_Perspective_2019_78.pdf

[330] *The New Straits Times* (12 September 2023): https://www.nst.com.my/business/2023/09/954162/kaj-gets-approval-revive-rm43-bln-melaka-gateway-project

[331] *Free Malaysia Today* (11 September 2023): https://www.freemalaysiatoday.com/category/highlight/2023/09/11/go-ahead-given-for-rm43-billion-melaka-gateway-says-developer/

No.	Title and year	Brief description
54	Taman Rimba Kiara land deal 2016–2023	In the Taman Rimba Kiara development project, it was alleged that the federal territories minister who controlled the ministry's Yayasan Wilayah Persekutuan (YWP) had abused his position to approve a high-rise development project. This project involved a joint venture between YWP and Memang Perkasa Sdn Bhd. After a long protest by residents in the area, the federal court quashed the development order.[332]
55	Tengku Adnan Mansor 2016	A sitting minister was charged with receiving a bribe in 2016 amounting to RM2 million. Adnan told the court that RM2 million was like 'pocket money' to him and that this money was a political donation for two by-elections held that year, though the funds were channelled to a company, Tadmansori Holdings Sdn Bhd (THSB), in which he and his family had an equity interest.[333] On appeal, Adnan was acquitted in a 2-1 decision because the issue of RM2 million being a 'donation' to UMNO was not challenged by the prosecution.[334]

---

[332] *The Star* (19 April 2023): https://www.thestar.com.my/news/nation/2023/04/19/long-fight-to-save-park-pays-off

[333] *The New Straits Times* (21 December 2020): https://www.nst.com.my/news/crime-courts/2020/12/651066/ku-nan-guilty-accepting-rm2-million-bribe-businessman-2016#:~:text=KUALA%20LUMPUR%3A%20Former%20Federal%20Territories,for%20himself%20from%20a%20businessman.

[334] *The Edge* (16 July 2021): https://theedgemalaysia.com/article/court-appeal-acquits-ku-nan-rm2-mil-graft-charge

No.	Title and year	Brief description
56	Sarawak solar hybrid project 2016	Rosmah Mansor, wife of former Prime Minister Najib Razak, received a ten-year jail sentence and a fine of RM970 million on a bribery charge. Rosmah had received bribe of RM187.5 million from the managing director of Jepak Holdings Sdn Bhd to secure the solar hybrid project that would power 369 rural schools in Sarawak. This conviction is under appeal.[335]
57	East Coast Rail Link 2016	In 2016, the government proposed the construction of a 688 km-long ECRL, a project running through four states, from Kelantan to Selangor. This project was awarded at a highly-inflated price of RM55 billion to a GLC, Malaysian Rail Link Sdn Bhd (MRL), which had gone into a joint venture with a China-based, state-owned enterprise, China Communications Construction Company (CCCC). This deal was reported as an attempt to 'bailout' the then deeply debt-ridden 1MDB and its subsidiary, SRC International.[336]

---

[335] *New Straits Times* (14 October 2022): https://www.nst.com.my/news/crime-courts/2022/10/840499/rosmah-says-she-was-wrongly-convicted-sentenced-solar-hybrid

[336] *Malay Mail* (4 September 2019): https://www.malaymail.com/news/malaysia/2019/09/04/najibs-ex-aide-says-ecrl-two-pipeline-projects-meant-to-bail-out-1mdb/1787220

No.	Title and year	Brief description
58	Pan Borneo highway project 2017	KACC Construction has a 70 per cent stake in Konsortium KPE Sdn Bhd, one of the main contractors of the 2,083 km-long Pan Borneo highway that covers Sarawak, Sabah, Brunei, and Kalimantan. KACC Construction Sdn Bhd, a company that secured a contract valued at RM1.825 million to construct a portion of the Pan Borneo highway, is linked to the family of Bustari Yusof, the brother of current Deputy Prime Minister Fadillah Yusof. Another shareholder is Jennifer Bermas Jabu, the daughter of Alfred Jabu, the longstanding former deputy chief minister of Sarawak.[337]
59	Malaysian Maritime Enforcement Agency's OPV 2017	In 2017, a RM738.9 million contract to build three offshore patrol vessels (OPVs) for the MMEA was awarded to a joint venture, THHE Destini Sdn Bhd, comprising Destini Bhd (51 per cent) and TH Heavy Engineering Bhd (THHE) (49 per cent), an enterprise that was part of the Tabung Haji group. THHE was then categorized as a PN17

---

[337] For a report on the controversial award of this portion of the Pan Borneo Highway to KACC Constructions, see: Edmund Terence Gomez. 2023. Business in Politics: Seeking Control of Malaysia's Political System. In *State of Corruption*: 127–130.

No.	Title and year	Brief description
		firm, meaning it was in financial distress. The OPVs were to be delivered in 2020, but it was then extended for eighteen months.[338] After the unity government was formed in 2022, it promised that the first and second vessels would be delivered in March and October 2023, respectively, but this did not occur. It was disclosed that the vessels were only 74.62 per cent completed, despite the numerous extensions. The MoF set up Urus Harta Jemaah Sdn Bhd, an SPV, to take over the project from THHE in January 2023 after injecting a 'rescue loan' of RM153 million.[339] Destini sold its stake in this joint venture in 2012, while THHE was delisted in 2022 and eventually sought to voluntarily wind up in 2023.[340]

---

[338] *The Edge* (8 September 2022): https://theedgemalaysia.com/article/cover-story-secrecy-and-complexity-defence-procurements-provide-perfect-cover-corruption

[339] *New Straits Times* (4 January 2023): https://www.nst.com.my/news/nation/2023/01/867123/govt-provides-rm1526m-loan-completion-mmeas-offshore-patrol-vessels

[340] *Free Malaysia Today* (13 September 2023): https://www.freemalaysiatoday.com/category/highlight/2023/09/13/end-of-the-road-for-th-heavy-engineering-opts-for-voluntary-winding-up/

No.	Title and year	Brief description
60	Musa Aman and Sabah Logging Contracts 2018	In 2018, former Sabah Chief Minister Musa Aman was charged with thirty-five counts of receiving bribes totalling US$63 million between 2004 and 2008 'via proxies in Hong Kong and Singapore, as an inducement for giving out timber concessions in Sabah' with Michael Chia mentioned in the report, a name that had been brought up in other reports alleging corruption in Sabah.[341] In 2012, Chia had allegedly tried 'to smuggle RM40 million worth of Singaporean currency from Hong Kong International Airport to Malaysia in 2008', funds which he claimed were 'meant for Musa'. After an investigation by the MACC, Musa was cleared 'of graft' because it was 'found that the RM40 million was not for his personal use, but was a "political donation" to the Sabah chapter of UMNO.'[342] As for the charges filed against Musa in 2018, they were dropped by the prosecution in 2020.[343]

---

[341] *The Straits Times* (5 November 2018): https://www.straitstimes.com/asia/se-asia/former-sabah-chief-minister-musa-aman-expected-to-be-charged-with-corruption-over

[342] Ibid.

[343] *The Malaysian Reserve* (10 June 2020): https://themalaysianreserve.com/2020/06/10/prosecution-drops-charges-musa-acquitted-of-logging-case/

No.	Title and year	Brief description
61	Pembinaan PFI Sdn Bhd 2018	Pembinaan PFI, a GLC, was created to implement a policy, private finance initiative (PFI), introduced to allow private enterprises securing public contracts to first shoulder the costs to complete these projects. However, two GLICs, the pension funds, EPF, and KWAP, were used to obtain loans totalling RM30 billion to implement PFI projects. The collateral for these loans were a huge number of government land parcels, owned by another GLC, the Federal Lands Commissioner (FLC). These tracts of land were leased to Pembinaan PFI for a mere RM10, though later increased to RM5.7 billion. These land parcels were then subleased to the government for a massive RM29 billion. Pembinaan PFI awarded these contracts to GLCs and well-connected companies. These contracts were later found to be those that were not PFI-type projects.[344]

---

[344] For a full report on the PFI scandal, see: Pushpan Murugiah and Edmund Terence Gomez. 2023. The Private Finance Initiative (PFI): Another Shocking Scam Unravelled. In *State of Corruption*: 85–120.

No.	Title and year	Brief description
62	Yayasan Akalbudi 2018	Ahmad Zahid Hamidi, the sitting UMNO president, established this foundation in 1997 to aid his endeavour to eradicate poverty. Zahid was subsequently enmeshed in what was reported as a 'multimillion-dollar corruption case [. . .] on charges he defrauded [this] foundation. Zahid had faced 47 charges involving multiple counts of criminal breach of trust, corruption and money laundering related to the misuse of \$27m of funds at Yayasan Akalbudi.'[345] In September 2023, the Attorney-General, just before he left office, instructed that all charges against Zahid be dropped. The judge, however, granted Zahid a discharge not amounting to an acquittal (DNAA) because, in his opinion, the prosecution had established a *prima facie* case against Zahid.[346]

---

[345] *Al Jazeera* (4 September 2023): https://www.aljazeera.com/news/2023/9/4/malaysia-drops-corruption-case-against-deputy-prime-minister

[346] *Free Malaysia Today* (4 September 2023):
   https://www.freemalaysiatoday.com/category/nation/2023/09/04/zahid-given-discharge-not-amounting-to-acquittal/

No.	Title and year	Brief description
63	Pharmaniaga 2018-2022	Since 2018, Pharmaniaga, part of the already long besieged LTAT–Boustead group, has been involved in a series of major controversies. In 2018, a report alleged bid-rigging of the open tender process which allowed Pharmaniaga to monopolize the procurement of medical drugs from 2013 to 2016. During this period, of government tenders totalling RM3.7 billion, about 91 per cent of them (or RM3.4 billion), were controlled by six tendering agents. The report further alleged that 'the top tendering agents are actually owned by high-ranking officials and/or politicians, or relatives of high-ranking officials and/or politicians. International pharmaceutical companies colluded with official-owned tendering agents to bid rig.'[347] In 2021, during the Muhyiddin administration, the National Audit Report revealed that Pharmaniaga Logistics Sdn Bhd, the sole Covid-19 ventilator provider for the government, had supplied equipment of which at least 79 per cent was defective. The government had, in fact, ordered 500 ventilators, but only

---

[347] *The Star* (13 June 2018): https://www.thestar.com.my/news/nation/2018/06/13/multi-billion-ringgit-expose-of-medicine-monopoly-involving-politicians-senior-officials/

No.	Title and year	Brief description
		136 were supplied of which 108 were deemed unsafe. The government could not claim back the RM13 million paid for the defective equipment, as no agreement had been signed because the procurement was done under 'emergency procurement protocols'.[348] In 2022, it was disclosed that Pharmaniaga had incurred a loss of RM664.39 million in the fourth quarter of that year, following a drop in vaccine sales. Pharmaniaga was subsequently listed as a PN17 company, as it was in huge financial distress.[349]
64	Abdul Azeez Abdul Rahim 2019	Former Tabung Haji chairman, Azeez Abdul Rahim, had to face three charges of bribery amounting to RM5.2 million and nine charges of money laundering amounting to RM139.34 million related to government projects. He was charged with accepting bribes amounting to RM5.2 million to obtain RM842.3 million worth of road upgrade projects in Kedah and Perak through direct

---

[348] *New Straits Times* (17 February 2023): https://www.nst.com.my/news/nation/2023/02/880994/mp-urges-govt-take-action-over-procurement-faulty-ventilators

[349] *Free Malaysia Today* (28 February 2023): https://www.freemalaysiatoday.com/category/highlight/2023/02/28/pharmaniaga-shares-plunge-43-after-losses-trigger-pn17/

No.	Title and year	Brief description
		negotiations.³⁵⁰ In 2022, Azeez was granted a discharge not amounting to an acquittal (DNAA) because, according to the judge, this would 'enable the prosecution to complete their investigations on "new" leads, after the accused [Azeez] submitted his representations [to the] charges. The court cannot [conclude] that the prosecution has no intention to proceed with the trial.'³⁵¹
65	Mindef land swap 2019	The well-connected Syed Mokhtar Albukhary confirmed that his company, Kelana Ventures Sdn Bhd (KVSB), was in a land swap deal with the Mindef involving land in Kinrara, in Kuala Lumpur. This piece of land had been valued by the company at RM500 million. In 2015, the Valuation and Property Services Department had valued this land at RM758 million.³⁵²

---

[350] *Free Malaysia Today* (16 January 2019): https://www.freemalaysiatoday.com/category/nation/2019/01/16/ex-tabung-haji-chief-claims-trial-to-corruption-money-laundering/

[351] *Free Malaysia Today* (23 September 22): https://www.freemalaysiatoday.com/category/nation/2022/09/23/azeez-gets-dnaa-in-graft-money-laundering-case/

[352] *The Edge* (25 February 2019): https://theedgemalaysia.com/article/syed-mokhtars-company-confirms-it-was-involved-land-swap-deal-mindef

No.	Title and year	Brief description
		Syed Mokhtar claimed that, in return for this land, KVSB was to construct three new facilities for Mindef totalling RM499.9 million.[353]
66	Public Mutual unit trust funds 2019	In 2019, Bung Moktar and his wife Zizie Izette were found to have allegedly received bribes for FELCRA to invest RM150 million in the Public Mutual unit trust funds. The bribes received amounted to RM2.8 million. See Case Study 3(1)
67	Adham Baba 2020	Adham Baba, when serving as minister of health, was indirectly linked to RM30 million public procurement contract to purchase Covid-19 test kits, personal protective equipment, and face masks. A property development company, Khazanah Jaya Sdn Bhd, had been appointed to supply reagents for Covid-19 labs,[354] though Adham denied having any ties with the shareholders of this company.[355] It was disclosed in parliament that RM650 million was spent to acquire assets and medicines to deal with Covid-19 pandemic and that Khazanah Jaya's role was to supply

---

[353] *The Star* (25 February 2019): https://www.thestar.com.my/news/nation/2019/02/25/report-syed-mokhtars-kelana-ventures-admits-it-is-involved-in-mindef-land-swap-deal

[354] *The Malaysian Insight* (28 July 2020): https://www.themalaysianinsight.com/s/263414

[355] *Mykmu*: https://mykmu.net/2020/05/11/dikaitkan-dengan-syarikat-disiasat-sprm-adham-ditohmah/

No.	Title and year	Brief description
		reagents for Covid-19 labs and 182 suppliers had been appointed.[356] The MACC initiated an investigation into the matter, calling in five contractors for questioning, but no report has been issued on this matter.
68	Jana Wibawa 2021	See Case Study 1
69	Bukit Lagong Forest quarries 2022	Of the twenty-seven quarries earmarked for operation in the Bukit Lagong Forest Reserve, some developers were linked to the Selangor state government. These state-owned GLCs included Menteri Besar Incorporated (MBI) Selangor and Permodalan Negeri Selangor Bhd (PNSB), both chaired by the chief minister.[357]
70	Batas Baru land sale 2023	Chief Minister of Terengganu Samsuri Mokhtar is alleged to have decided on the sale of state government-owned land in Batas Baru to the Khairunnisa' Association for only RM500,000, fifty-eight times cheaper than its valuation of RM29.3 million. The members of this association are the wives of current and former elected

---

[356] This was disclosed by then Deputy Health Minister II Aaron Ago Dagang in July 2020.

[357] For reports on this project, see: *Malaysiakini* (25 October 2022): https://www.malaysiakini.com/news/640922

No.	Title and year	Brief description
		representatives from Terengganu.[358] Samsuri had been serving as vice president of this association since 2019.[359]

---

[358] *Malaysiakini* (3 June 2023): https://www.malaysiakini.com/news/667429.

[359] *Center to Combat Corruption and Cronyism* (13 June 2023): https://c4center.org/batas-baru-land-sale-c4-center/

Appendix 2

Malaysia's Legal Framework: Inadequacies to Combat Corruption: Prishanth Linggaraj, Bryan Cheah, and Arief Hamizan[360]

The myriad forms of corruption in Appendix 1 and in the case studies indicate the need for reforms that entail introducing:

1. preventive measures to obstruct anyone from committing corruption in the first place;
2. monitoring mechanisms to enable the detection of offences; and
3. punitive and/or restitutionary systems to manage corruption that has been committed. In this regard, existing laws in Malaysia are not sufficiently comprehensive to appropriately address the perpetration of corruption.

When examining the criminal culpability of public officials and political leaders for corruption, the definition of a 'public officer' must first be determined, given that this expression is commonly used across the relevant criminal legislation. According to Article 132(1) of the Federal Constitution, 'public services' cover the

---

[360] The other contributors to this legal review are Nabila Syuhada Zulkeflee and Jason Lee.

armed forces, the judicial and legal service, the general public service of the federation, the police force, and joint public services mentioned in Article 133, the state public services, and the education service. Importantly, Article 132(3) goes on to state that the public service 'shall not be taken to comprise' various entities, including 'the office of any member of the administration in the Federation or a State'[361] or 'member of either House of Parliament or of the Legislative Assembly of a State'.[362] The expression 'member of the administration' is further defined under Article 160(2) as 'a person holding office as Minister, Deputy Minister, Parliamentary Secretary or Political Secretary' in relation to the federation (i.e., the federal government), and 'a person holding a corresponding office in the State or holding office as member (other than an office member) of the Executive Council' in relation to the state governments.

Therefore, the Federal Constitution does not deem the prime minister, chief ministers of the states, cabinet ministers, members of the state executive councils, and members of parliament and of the state legislative assemblies as being part of the 'public service'. Reference should also be made in this regard to the Interpretation Acts 1948 and 1967 (a statute of general application that applies to the interpretation of laws unless there exists express provision to the contrary or where its application causes inconsistency or repugnancy[363]), specifically Section 3,[364] which lists the following definitions:

---

[361] The Federal Constitution: Article 132(3)(a).

[362] The Federal Constitution: Article 132(3)(b).

[363] Interpretation Acts 1948 and 1967: Section 2(3).

[364] The definitions under Section 3 fall within Part I of the Interpretation Acts 1948 and 1967, which applies only for the interpretation of, inter alia, the Interpretation Acts themselves, all Acts of Parliament enacted after 18 May 1967, and all subsidiary legislation made under the aforementioned Acts. See Section 2(1).

1. 'federal public office' means an office in the public service mentioned in Article 132(1)(c) of the Federal Constitution, that is to say, the general public service of the federation;
2. 'federal public officer' means a person lawfully holding, acting in, or exercising the functions of a federal office;
3. 'public office' means an office in any of the public services;
4. 'public officer' means a person lawfully holding, acting in, or exercising the functions of a public office;
5. 'public services' means the public services mentioned in Article 132(1) of the Federal Constitution; and
6. 'minister' means, subject to subsection 8(2), a minister of the Government of Malaysia (including the prime minister and a deputy prime minister).

Thus, members within the cabinet generally are not subsumed under the public service—a point cogently made by the Federal Court in the case of Tony Pua Kiam Wee v. Government of Malaysia.[365] This case involved a civil tortious claim brought by Tony Pua, in his capacity as a Malaysian taxpayer, against former Prime Minister Najib Razak for misfeasance in public office in relation to 1MDB. When determining if a prime minister could be deemed a 'public officer' within the context of this claim, the Federal Court stated:

> [124] [. . .] It would appear that art. 132 of the Federal Constitution reflects the administrative structure envisaged for the governance and operation of the Federation.
>
> [125] 'Members of the administration', for example Ministers, were kept separate as apparent from art. 66 (above) for the purposes of efficient, stable, and independent administration

---

[365] Tony Pua Kiam Wee V. Government Of Malaysia: [2020] 1 CLJ 337.

of the Federation. Political impartiality was an important consideration.

[. . .]

[128] [. . .] the framers of our Federal Constitution necessarily intended to create a public service which was free from executive influence i.e., one that would work with, and not for, the Government (be it the executive, legislative, or judicial branches). That is why Ministers (or even judges for that matter), are taken as being excluded from the public service.

Comparatively, definitions included under criminal statutes such as the Malaysian Anti-Corruption Commission Act 2009[366] and the Penal Code[367] do encompass members of parliament, state legislative assemblies, and the administration. The Federal Court in Mohd Khir Toyo v Public Prosecutor[368] noted the following.

[70] There is no definition of 'officer' in the Code. But, s. 21(i) of the Code provides that 'the words 'public servant' denote [. . .] **every officer in the service or pay of Government, or remunerated by fees or commission for the performance of any public duty**' [emphasis added]. Accordingly, every officer in the service or pay of Government, which 'includes the Government of Malaysia and of the States and any person lawfully performing executive functions of Government under any written law' (see s. 17 of the Code) or remunerated by fees or commission for the performance of any public duty is a public servant (Lim Kee Butt v. PP [1953] 1 LNS 47; [1954] 1 MLJ 35, per

---

[366] Malaysian Anti-Corruption Commission Act 2009: Section 3.

[367] Penal Code: Section 21(i).

[368] Mohd Khir Toyo v Public Prosecutor: [2015] 8 CLJ 769 (FC).

Matthew CJ, delivering the judgment of the court, who cited Nazamuddin v. Queen Empress ILR 28 C 344).

[71] 'The test to determine whether a person is a public servant is (1) in the service or pay of the Government and (2) whether he is entrusted with the performance of a public duty' (Ratanlal & Dhirajlal, The Indian Penal Code 34th edn., p. 29).

As a result of this, a curious paradox arises: Political figures do not fall under the supervision or jurisdiction of any of the service commissions established under Part X of the Federal Constitution for the purposes of disciplinary control but are deemed to be public servants when it comes to criminal offences. There are generally no codes or regulations to dictate how ministers or elected representatives are supposed to conduct themselves within the scope of their official functions. This is absurd given that these are the individuals most at risk of committing acts of corruption due to the inherent influence they exert upon their subordinates by their positions. This, coupled with the limited scope of 'corruption' under Malaysia's criminal statutes, severely restricts effective control and checks on a governing politician when he exercises the roles of his office. In essence, criminal law is the sole bulwark against political corruption—a method that can only function retrospectively, after the act has already been committed and the moneys dissipated.

The Malaysian Anti-Corruption Commission (MACC) Act, 2009, is the primary anti-corruption law, and its stated principal objects are 'to promote the integrity and accountability of public and private sector administration by constituting an independent and accountable anti-corruption body' and 'to educate public authorities, public officials and members of the public about corruption and its detrimental effects.'[369] This Act establishes the MACC as an anti-corruption body tasked, inter alia, with the

---

[369] Malaysian Anti-Corruption Commission Act 2009: Section 2.

detection and investigation of 'offences under the Act', that is corruption offences. This includes 'prescribed offences', such as the various bribery-related offences under the Penal Code, offering or receiving bribes under Section 137 of the Customs Act 1967, and corrupt practices under Part III of the Election Offences Act 1954.[370] The MACC Act uses the broad term, 'gratification', in most of its offence provisions, which is defined as:

1. money, donation, gift, loan, fee, reward, valuable security, property or interest in property being property of any description whether movable or immovable, financial benefit, or any other similar advantage;
2. any office, dignity, employment, contract of employment or services, and agreement to give employment or render services in any capacity;
3. any payment, release, discharge or liquidation of any loan, obligation or other liability, whether in whole or in part;
4. any valuable consideration of any kind, any discount, commission, rebate, bonus, deduction or percentage;
5. any forbearance to demand any money or money's worth or valuable thing;
6. any other service or favour of any description, including protection from any penalty or disability incurred or apprehended or from any action or proceedings of a disciplinary, civil or criminal nature, whether or not already instituted, and including the exercise or the forbearance from the exercise of any right or any official power or duty; and
7. any offer, undertaking or promise, whether conditional or unconditional, of any gratification within the meaning of any of the preceding paragraphs (a) to (f).[371]

---

[370] Malaysian Anti-Corruption Commission Act 2009: Section 3.
[371] Ibid.

This definition is far clearer than what is stated under the Explanations to Section 161 of the Penal Code, which simply provides that gratification 'is not restricted to pecuniary gratifications, or to gratifications estimable in money.' However, all these offences (both under the MACC Act and the Penal Code) are still anchored on the base idea of giving or accepting gratifications in return for favours, i.e., bribery simpliciter. Other related concepts that are addressed in the Penal Code include dishonest misappropriation of property[372] and criminal breach of trust[373] (defined as the dishonest misappropriation, conversion, use, or disposal of property entrusted to an individual, also colloquially referred to as embezzlement).

The Anti-Money Laundering, Anti-Terrorism Financing and Proceeds of Unlawful Activities (AMLATFPUA) Act 2001—as its name suggests—specifically targets the offences of money laundering and terrorism financing. According to Section 4 of the Act, any person with the following qualities is deemed to have committed the offence of money laundering:

1. engages, directly or indirectly, in a transaction that involves proceeds of an unlawful activity or instrumentalities of an offence;
2. acquires, receives, possesses, disguises, transfers, converts, exchanges, carries, disposes of or uses proceeds of an unlawful activity or instrumentalities of an offence;
3. removes from or brings into Malaysia, proceeds of an unlawful activity or instrumentalities of an offence; or
4. conceals, disguises or impedes the establishment of the true nature, origin, location, movement, disposition, title of, rights with respect to, or ownership of, proceeds of an unlawful activity or instrumentalities of an offence.

---

[372] Penal Code: Section 403.
[373] Penal Code: Sections 405–409B.

Section 3 of the AMLATFPUA Act also elaborates on what constitutes an 'unlawful activity': any activity that constitutes any serious offence (domestic or foreign) or which is of such a nature/ occurs in such circumstances that it results in or leads to such an offence being committed. 'Serious offences' are enumerated under the Second Schedule to the Act and include offences such as trafficking in persons, smuggling of migrants, stock market manipulation, drug trafficking, corruption and bribery under the MACC Act 2009 and the Penal Code, and terrorism. Money laundering is, thus, an auxiliary offence—a method of legitimizing proceeds derived from underlying Second Schedule crimes. Section 2 of the AMLATFPUA Act also makes it clear that this law has extra-territorial application, which is important due to the growing trend of cross-border corruption and the use of foreign entities and jurisdictions to evade criminal sanctions.

Beyond the offence-creating provisions, the AMLATFPUA Act also imposes obligations on 'reporting institutions' to maintain records of any transaction exceeding specified amounts[374] and to promptly report to the competent authority any transaction exceeding specified amounts or which raises suspicions of involving proceeds of an unlawful activity or instrumentalities of an offence.[375] What qualifies as a reporting institution is set out under the First Schedule to the Act[376] and includes the following: licensed banks, insurers, and money-brokers as provided under the Financial Services Act, 2013; licensed Islamic banks and Takaful operators as provided under the Islamic Financial Services Act, 2023; prescribed institutions under the Development Financial

---

[374] Anti-Money Laundering, Anti-Terrorism Financing and Proceeds of Unlawful Activities Act 2001: Section 13.

[375] Anti-Money Laundering, Anti-Terrorism Financing and Proceeds of Unlawful Activities Act 2001: Section 14.

[376] Anti-Money Laundering, Anti-Terrorism Financing and Proceeds of Unlawful Activities Act 2001: Section 3.

Institutions Act, 2002; dealers in securities, derivatives, or fund managers under the Capital Markets and Services Act, 2007; accountants under the Accountants Act, 1967; and advocates and solicitors under the Legal Profession Act, 1976.

In essence, any intermediary who may come across suspicious transactions in the performance of their duties is obligated under the AMLATFPUA Act to report such transactions promptly, as well as to conduct customer due diligence,[377] retain records for at least six years,[378] and adopt, develop, and implement internal compliance programmes (including independent audits).[379] Non-compliance with these requirements also constitutes a criminal offence, carrying penalties in the millions of ringgit.[380] As mentioned, because money laundering is an auxiliary offence, its discovery could lead to the underlying crime that originally generated the dirty money being revealed as well.

These legal provisions are imperative because they widen the net of potential intervention points instead of focusing solely on penalties after corruption or abuse of power has already occurred. There must also be laws that create systems obstructing these offences from being performed at all. This is a pivotal consideration for lawmakers when considering avenues for legislative reform moving forward. Vitally, these laws do not cover various other manifestations of corruption and abuse of power, as illustrated in the chapters in this book. This poses a fundamental problem for investigators and prosecutors—one

---

[377] Anti-Money Laundering, Anti-Terrorism Financing and Proceeds of Unlawful Activities Act 2001: Section 16.

[378] Anti-Money Laundering, Anti-Terrorism Financing and Proceeds of Unlawful Activities Act 2001: Section 17.

[379] Anti-Money Laundering, Anti-Terrorism Financing and Proceeds of Unlawful Activities Act 2001: Section 19.

[380] Anti-Money Laundering, Anti-Terrorism Financing and Proceeds of Unlawful Activities Act 2001: Sections 17 and 86.

cannot take action against a party where no defined crime has been committed.

This, in a nutshell, is the problem with the existing Malaysian legal framework—more complex and opaque forms of corruption are simply not conceived of as being unlawful. For instance, according to the Central Bank of Malaysia's National Risk Assessment on Money Laundering and Terrorism Financing 2020 (NRA 2020), widespread systemic corrupt practices remain a concern in countering money laundering, which require intensified efforts by the MACC to pursue graft cases, as well as strong political commitment to ensure the success of national anti-corruption plans and initiatives.[381] This is indicative of the interconnected nature of these offences, which fortifies the contention that a holistic approach is required to tackle corruption at the root.

However, the solution is not as simple as merely introducing further criminal sanctions. Indeed, such an approach reveals a fallacious and reductionist view of the utility of criminal law in combatting corruption. Conflicts-of-interest such as patronage, cronyism, and nepotism, for instance, are difficult to delineate clearly under the law. For example, at what point should a restriction on appointments or the awarding of contracts end? Should the restriction only apply to immediate family members or encompass extended family members as well? In the case of the latter, where should the line be drawn?

Similarly, the abuse of objectively neutral measures, such as bailouts or dealings with land, is difficult to punish in the absence of clear regulations on when and how such measures may be employed. This emphasizes the need for proactive regulations

---

[381] Bank Negara Malaysia, 'Malaysia National Risk Assessment Report 2020: Executive Summary', p. 5, available at: https://amlcft.bnm.gov.my/documents/6312201/6322748/BNM+%5BNRA2020%5D+Assessment+Report.pdf/40fe8e13-f38c-13ef-e298-f46a8d27ef06?t=1648654707832

that govern the making of these decisions rather than retroactive punishments when a wrong has already been committed. In this regard, the government's intent to introduce a Government Procurement Act to set out binding limits on the conduct of the public procurement process is a good example of how this could be done—restricting technically lawful (but unethical) practices such as price inflation or siphoning of funds currently rife within the Malaysian bureaucracy. A Political Financing Act is also profoundly needed to monitor and control the flow of funds to political parties and politicians, which would create another intervention point for illicit transactions to be identified.

Further, existing conflicts in present laws ought to be resolved. The continued existence of the Official Secrets Act, 1972, and the wide discretion it affords to ministers and public officers to designate any material as an 'official secret' impairs the ability for whistleblowers to come forward with concrete proof to assist prosecutions. Meanwhile, Section 203A of the Penal Code (which punishes anyone who discloses any matter obtained while performing their duties or exercising their functions with a maximum fine of RM1 million and/or up to one year imprisonment) also creates a chilling effect for public servants who wish to expose wrongdoing that they come across in their departments. Such laws must be amended or repealed to facilitate exposing corruption within the public sector.

The reforms needed to combat corruption in all its forms must be crafted in a thoughtful and holistic manner. Simply introducing more punishments and expecting every issue to be solved is short-sighted. Instead, legislation and regulation must be used to create a power shift where high-ranking political elites are not allowed carte blanche to act against the public interest.